A Principled Approach to State Failure

TO LEA,
WITH GRATIDUDE
AND ADMIRATION
Chiara

Developments in International Law

VOLUME 64

A Principled Approach to State Failure

International Community Actions in Emergency Situations

By

Chiara Giorgetti

With a Foreword by

Professors Michael Reisman and Lea Brilmayer

BRILL

LEIDEN • BOSTON
2010

This book is printed on acid-free paper.

Library of Congress Cataloging-in-Publication Data

Giorgetti, Chiara.
A principled approach to state failure : international community actions in emergency situations / by Chiara Giorgetti ; foreword by Michael Reisman and Lea Brilmayer.
p. cm. — (Developments in international law, 0924-5332 : v. 64)
Includes index.
ISBN 978-90-04-18127-4 (hardback : alk. paper)
1. Failed states. I. Title. II. Series.

KZ4029.G56 2010
341.5'84—dc22

2010001516

ISSN 0924-5332
ISBN 978 90 04 18127 4

PRINTED IN THE NETHERLANDS

Volli, fortissimamente volli.

To Andre, Alex, Luisa e Giorgio,
with love and gratitude.

Contents

Acknowledgments

This study is a slightly modified version of my doctoral (J.S.D.) thesis, submitted in June 2009 to Yale Law School. It is the result of more then seven years of research pursued at the many libraries of New Haven, The Hague, Geneva and Washington D.C. The seed that set off my curiosity on the issue of State failure, however, was planted earlier, when I served as a Program Officer with the United Nations Development Program in Somalia in 1998–2000. Somalia was and remains the archetype of State failure and, I believe, an intellectual challenge for any international lawyer. I enjoyed working on this project and hope my contribution will be helpful in addressing a problem that remains as topical now as it was when I began my research.

I am glad to have the opportunity to thank the many people who helped me through this process, in so many different ways. When I applied for my J.S.D., Professor Michael Reisman warned me that writing a dissertation was a very solitary endeavor. Indeed, such an effort is only made possible with the support and confidence of the people around you.

I would first like to thank the members of my Dissertation Committee who gave me the freedom to pursue my research and the guidance to finalize it. I am especially indebted to Professor Lea Brilmayer for her constant support for so many years. Prof. Brilmayer trusted me throughout, and was generous with her comments, guidance, exceptional encouragement, and with timely and constructive criticism. She is the source of much inspiration and I am grateful for her support and friendship. I am equally grateful to Prof. Reisman. His intellectual achievements are extraordinary and our discussions remain one of the highlights of my dissertation experience. I would also like to thank Dean Harold Koh for his unconditional support and for his confidence in my work. Truly, I could not have asked for a better Dissertation Committee. It has been a pleasure, and indeed an honor, working with them.

I also wish to express my deep gratitude to my family for their continuous love and support. My husband, Dr. Andre Le Sage, is an endless source of inspiration to pursue intellectual excellence and clarity. His love and support have been invaluable. My son, Alex, brings me constant joy, and his smiles warm my days. I am also profoundly grateful to my parents, Giorgio and

Luisa, who have always loved me and supported me unconditionally in all my choices.

Finally, I would like to thank the many colleagues and friends who encouraged me to pursue my research.

Of course, the views expressed in this book are mine alone.

C.G.
June 2009

List of Abbreviations

ASEAN	Association of Southeast Asian Nations
BIT	Bilateral Investment Treaty
CEMIOR	Comprehensive Event Management for International Outbreak and Response
CCC	Core Commitments for Children in Emergencies
CDC	Center for Disease Control
DRC	Democratic Republic of Congo
EC	European Community
ECHR	European Court of Human Rights
EU	European Union
FAO	Food and Agriculture Organization
GOARN	Global Outbreak Alert and Response Network
ICAO	International Civil Aviation Organization
ICC	International Criminal Court
ICJ	International Court of Justice
ICSID	International Center for Settlement of Investment Disputes
IGAD	Inter-Governmental Authority on Development
IHR	International Health Regulations
ILC	International Law Commission
MSF	Médecins Sans Frontières
NATO	North Atlantic Treaty Organization
NID	National Polio Immunization Day
NIHR	New International Health Regulations
NGO	Non-Governmental Organization
OCHA	United Nations Office for the Coordination of Humanitarian Affairs
OHCHR	Office of the High Commissioner for Human Rights
PAHO	Pan American Health Organization
PCA	Permanent Court of Arbitration
PCIJ	Permanent Court of International Justice
RRA	Rahanwein Resistance Army
SACB	Somalia Aid Coordination Body
SARS	Severe Acute Respiratory Syndrome
SNID	National Polio Immunization Day
SC	United Nations Security Council
SG	United Nations Secretary General

TNG	Transitional National Government
UIC	Union of Islamic Courts
UN	United Nations
UNCC	United Nations Claims Commission
UNCLOS	United Nations Convention the Law of the Sea
UNECE	United Nations Economic Commission for Europe
UNEP	United Nations Environmental Program
UNDP	United Nations Development Program
UNESCO	United Nations Education Organization
UNICEF	United Nations Children's Fund
UNMIK	United Nations Interim Administration in Kosovo
UNOSOM	United Nations Operations in Somalia
UNOSOM II	United Nations Operations in Somalia II
UNTEAT	United Nations Transitional Authority in East Timor
UNITAF	United Task Force
WFP	World Food Program
WHO	World Health Organization
WFP	World Food Program

Foreword

States, organized and territorially-based political communities, are the essential building blocks of the international political system. Their governments play a major role in creating international law and are also its primary agents of implementation, both within their internal domains and in external arenas. As international law has become more ambitious in scope, the burdens on states with respect to implementation have increased. The duty to assure to their own peoples the minimum conditions of life prescribed by international law have become more onerous, as have those peoples' demands and expectations. Indeed, without effective states, the most ambitious programs of human rights, environmental protection, and the maintenance of public health will fail to be achieved. The frequently lamented failures of international law are, in fact, failures of states.

In the latter part of the twentieth century, as the responsibilities of states were increasing, the international legal system began to confront, in acute form, the phenomenon of failing and feckless states: territorial entities that could not provide the basic welfare requirements of their populations nor fulfill their basic obligations to other states. The latter dimension of the problem is of more recent prominence and is also theoretically more challenging. The term "failed states" became a new focus of concern, not simply because of the impacts on the failed state's own population, but also because of the impacts of internal failure on other states. With the rise of terrorism and international organized crime and, most recently, entrepreneurial piracy, it has become apparent that the failed state presents a clear and present danger to the international legal system.

Dealing with this widely acknowledged problem has proved difficult. At the theoretical level, the major institutions of international law are wary of authorizing interventions in the internal affairs of other states for any reason. Although there are circumstances in which such interventions appear to be required by other peremptory international policies, there is always a parallel fear that any acknowledgement of a right (let alone, as has more recently been argued, a duty) to intervene will lead to abuses. The net effect, it is feared, will be increasingly powerful limits on the autonomy of states; and autonomy is a value which is highly prized by the vast majority of state elites.

Yet the mandate to do something in the face of state failure is intuitively undeniable. When states fail, people die – innocent people, typically, and sometimes in very large numbers. It is also undeniable that international law has part of the responsibility for creating the problem. States are, to a large degree, creatures of international law. They are "recognized" as states in accordance with a body of international legal doctrine and practice, and it is this recognition that appears to entitle them to the very autonomy from outside intervention that proves to be so problematic when they fail.

"Yes, yes, I know it will work in practice," a denizen of the Ivory Tower is supposed to have lamented, "but will it work in theory?" International law often muddles through with practical solutions but failed states have presented the opposite problem. Repairing state failure in practice has proved at least as challenging as addressing it in theory; indeed, in interventions designed to remedy state failure, the cure can be considerably worse than the disease. It has proved difficult to repair failed states and, for that matter, even to provide the minimum services which the populations of such states require. Chiara Giorgetti's book is, thus, timely and important. In addition to her profound legal analysis of the theoretical legal problems presented by failed states, Dr. Giorgetti brings a unique practical perspective. She has worked as an international lawyer in a failed state on behalf of an international organization and thus, more than anyone else, is sensitive in her analyses, not only to the theoretical issues but to the gritty problems of implementing international policy for this challenging problem.

Dr. Giorgetti's insights into the conundrum of failed statehood are penetrating. One example has been alluded to above; it is that international law is responsible for recognizing or creating states in accordance with criteria that it establishes, but makes no analogous provision for taking statehood away. A simple failure to continue to satisfy the criteria for statehood (e.g. a state's loss of control over most of its territory) does not automatically deprive the state in question of its statehood. Indeed, there is no clear body of rules or practices for divesting states of recognition, once they have acquired it. This is only one of the problems that Dr. Giorgetti confronts. But it is at the center of the dispute over failed states.

As professors who supervised much of the research that went into this book and for which Dr. Giorgetti was awarded a doctoral degree from the Yale Law School, we are proud to write this introduction. The questions that she deals with are fresh, important, and theoretically challenging. That Somalia (the country of her primary area of practical expertise) has so frequently figured in the news in recent months has much to do with its status as a failed state and thus attests to the prescience of her choice of topic. Her extended discussion of topics such as air space safety, suppression of piracy, transboundary public health, business affairs and diplomatic protection give concrete meaning to the abstract concept of a "failed state" and underscore its importance both to the academy and to the people living in, or affected by conditions in, their failed neighbors. This book thus marks an important addition to the international legal discussion about failed states. This is a discussion that needs to be had, for theoretical reasons and for improvement of the human condition.

R. Lea Brilmayer
W. Michael Reisman
Yale Law School
New Haven, Connecticut
October 21, 2009

Chapter One

An Emerging Problem in International Law

In the last fifty years, the international community has undergone a transformation.

Social, economic and political dynamics have radically changed: the international power structure has shifted towards a more complex structure, new powerful international actors have emerged, security threats have mutated and economies have been largely liberalized.

These changes brought about two major consequences for Nation States. First, a new standard of governance emerged that resulted in increased responsibilities to each State's nationals. Second, States have become increasingly inter-independent and have additional (both in numbers and substance) obligations towards each other and the international community in general.

However, certain States are unable to operate in this new system of increased responsibility, in terms of obligations towards other States, the international community and their citizens. These States – often referred to as fragile, failing or failed States – become ineffective actors in the international stage. This poses multiple problems for the international community as certain necessary obligations and required acts fail to be performed, weakening the entire system.

The introductory paragraphs below briefly analyze, first, the new standards of national and international governance, and, then, explore their consequences for the international community and nation States.

1. *New Standards of Governance Bring Increased Domestic Responsibility for Each State*

The first consequence of contemporary governance is the increased overall responsibilities of each State. States must perform innumerable actions daily, directed at their own people, other States, and the international community.

Contemporary society is based on the premise that each person has multiple rights and obligations that arise from being a national of a certain State and a member of the international community. Individual rights include civil, political, economic, social and cultural rights, and range from the right to life, to the rights of free movement, ownership and vote.[1] These rights can derive from both domestic and international provisions.[2] In general, the parallel obligation that allows for the right to be enjoyed is primarily imposed upon the State as a sovereign.

Obligations to confer rights to individuals are enumerated by international binding agreements, principally concluded under the aegis of the United Nations, since its creation in 1945. Further, the United Nations Charter itself, which is almost universally ratified, provides for the fulfillment of personal rights of individuals by promoting "higher standards of living, full employment, and conditions of economic and social progress and development"[3] as well as "solutions of international economic, social, health, and related problems; and international cultural and educational cooperation"[4] and "universal respect for, and observance of, human rights and fundamental freedoms for all without distinction as to race, sex, language, or religion."[5] These obligations fall on each Member State. In fact, each member of the organization also pledged to take action to achieve these goals.[6] As such, an entire organizational structure made up of agencies and programs is created and organized by the United Nations to monitor the development and implementation of these rights by each State.[7]

---

1 These rights are principally enumerated in several international conventions that enjoy widespread ratification, including the Universal Declaration of Human Rights, 10 Dec. 1948, U.N.G.A. Res 217A(III), UN Doc. A/810 at 71 (1948), *available at*: http://un.org/Overview/rights.html, the United Nations International Covenant on Civil and Political Rights, 16 Dec. 1966, 999 U.N.T.S. 171, *available at:* http://www.hrweb.org/legal/cpr.html, and the United Nations Covenant on Economic, Social and Cultural Rights, 16 Dec. 1966, 993 U.N.T.S. 3, *available at:* http://www.unhchr.ch/html/menu3/b/a_cescr.htm.

2 In general, national constitutions include specific references to several individual rights, which are broadly similar to ones that originate from international treaties, although in certain cases more numerous and detailed. For example, these rights include, the right to self-determination, the right to life, the right to health, the right to liberty and security of the person, the right to dignity and equality, the right to fair trial, freedom of expression, freedom of religion, the right to marry and have a family, the right to participate in the political process, the right to fair wages and safe and healthy working conditions, the right to equal opportunities, the right to participate in the economic process, the right to form trade unions and organize, the right to education, the right to participate in cultural activities, and the right to the benefit of scientific progress and its applications.

3 U.N. Charter Art. 55(a).

4 U.N. Charter Art. 55(b).

5 U.N. Charter Art. 55(c).

6 U.N. Charter Art. 56.

7 U.N. Charter Arts. 57–58 (*stating* respectively that "(1) [t]he various specialized agencies, established by intergovernmental agreement and having wide international responsibilities, as defined in their basic instruments, in economic, social, cultural, educational, health, and related fields, shall be brought into relationship with the United Nations in accordance

At the same time, regional organizations – including the European Union,[8] the African Union[9] and the Organization of American States[10] – have been created in practically every region of the world. These organizations also impose additional obligations on each of their members. These include numerous individual civil and political rights, as well as economic and social rights, and rights of protection for minorities. However, some States that have only recently become independent or viable, lack political and administrative institutions that are capable of affording and organizing the enjoyment of these rights. Further, even if such institutions exist, they may not be strong enough to permit the enjoyment of a growing number of entitlements, as well as a more vocal and united population. Further, since the end of the Cold War, a new ("third") wave of human rights have surged, which includes the right to development, the right to a clean environment and the right to democratic governance. The later is particularly interesting as it provides that the running of the State must be decided through periodical, free elections that are open to the entire adult population. Moreover, it also requires the State to act upon its obligations to grant internationally recognized human rights and provide a minimum standard of living and freedom that allows all of its citizens to enjoy a productive, free and dignified life.[11]

This results in the obligation of each State to provide numerous goods and services, including protection, a functioning legal system, a working judiciary, an effective education system, healthcare, an efficient administration able to deliver goods and services, infrastructures, and the possibility to participate in the global economy.

---

with the provisions of Article 63. (2) Such agencies thus brought into relationship with the United Nations are hereinafter referred to as specialized agencies." and that "[t]he Organization shall make recommendations for the co-ordination of the policies and activities of the specialized agencies.").

[8] The European Union now has twenty-seven member states both from Western and Eastern Europe, European Union Online, http://europa.eu/abc/european_countries/index_en.htm (last visited 28 Aug. 2009).

[9] Membership to the African Union now includes fifty-three states, with Morocco as the only African State that is no longer a member after withdrawing from the organization in 1984. African Union, http://www.africa-union.org/root/au/memberstates/map.htm (last visited 28 Aug. 2009).

[10] The Organization of American States is the oldest regional organization, and includes thirty-five American States. Organization of American States, http://www.oas.org (last visited 28 Aug. 2009).

[11] *See generally* DEMOCRATIC GOVERNANCE AND INTERNATIONAL LAW (G.H. Fox and B.R. Roth eds., 2000).

Moreover, the modern economic system also requires each State to provide trade facilities, a financial market, communication systems, a road network, air-connections, port-access and security. Further, any functioning contemporary State also needs large infrastructures to provide for the health and education of its citizens, as well as for terrestrial and aerial transport of people and goods. It also needs to be able to support complicated financial and banking transactions, and also must be able to support a functioning legal system.

In sum, the burden placed on States' structures by the new economic order and democratic governance is substantial. Yet, many States are not able to fully perform their responsibilities in this system. Their institutions are not sufficiently established, and funding is often problematic. Several of these States begin to drag behind as their inability to perform their obligations enters a vicious circle that generates more failure to perform.

2. *Increased Inter-Independence Between States*

The situation is similar for a State's obligations towards other States and the international community.

The number of independent States has increased steadily since the end of World War II. Immediately following the end of the war, several colonized States gained or regained their independence. Similarly, the dissolution of the U.S.S.R. and of the Pact of Warsaw reshaped the European landscape and brought many new States into existence.

At the same time, the world has become more inter-independent. The development of communication and the ease of travel have made it possible to create a world society in which values, expectations, and political and economic views are broadly shared. Moreover, what happens in one part of the world can have immediate repercussions in other parts of the world and in a variety of domains, including financial transactions, environmental emergencies, health crises and security risks.

Further, the number of international Conventions and bilateral and multilateral treaties has increased substantially.[12]

[12] For example, the collection of the United Nations Treaty Series, a publication of the United Nations that collects treaties and international agreements registered or filed and recorded with and published by the Secretariat since 1946, pursuant to Article 102 of the Charter, currently contains over 158,000 bilateral and multilateral treaties deposited between 1946 and 2003, *available at*: http://treaties.un.org/Pages/Overview.aspx?path=overview/overview/page1_en.xml (last visited 28 Aug. 2009).

Although there is no official categorization of the obligations each State must perform, it is possible to create a significant demonstrative taxonomy by analyzing the major components and traits of those acts performed for both national and international stakeholders. A simple taxonomy based on the typical functions that a government performs[13] includes, in general, obligations concerning:

Public Health: This category includes all acts directed at the control of safety and hygiene, the containment of epidemics, health hazards, and diseases for both human and animal health. It also includes all matters related to the environment and agricultural and veterinary imports and exports.

Defense and Justice: These acts include forms of collaboration for the control of transnational criminal activities, extradition and judicial collaboration policies, and the development and implementation of policies to halt human, arms and drug trafficking. It also includes immigration policies and border patrolling and control.

Commerce: This includes banking and financial services and customs, measures related to trade and investments, collection of duties, commercial and trade permits.

Transport and Communication: These acts include all obligations to grant and provide safety in national airspace, control of coasts and maritime zones, and access to ports, roads and railways. Acts concerning communications issues include all acts that pertain to postal, radio, telephone, satellite and electronic forms of communication.

Diplomatic and Representative Functions: These include representations at international and multilateral conferences, diplomatic and consular services.

In sum, State authorities generally perform a myriad of actions daily. These actions are required to satisfy both domestic and international constituencies. Further, these actions have both internal and international components. Because of the complexity and interrelation of these acts, it is impossible, and hardly useful, to distinguish categories of acts that have only external or internal consequences. Instead, I am interested in discussing the

[13] This taxonomy is obtained from looking at the structure of governments in the U.S., France and Italy, only the functions that have relevant and necessary international components are included. *See also* Oppenheim's International Law 453–55 (Sir Arthur Watts & Sir Robert Jennings eds., 9th ed. 1992) (providing a comprehensive list of multilateral treaties in force focusing on transport and communication and on the matter of trade and finance).

consequences of the failure to perform obligations, no matter the characterization of the acts themselves.

3. *Certain States Cannot Operate in the New System*

The increased inter-independence of States and the augmenting normative structure of the international community place obligations upon each State, as it must perform numerous actions in favor of other States and the international community. This is not just a legal requirement; it is a necessity of the international community. When a State does not perform the actions that each State has come to expect, the entire system is destabilized.

However certain – failing or failed – States are unable to fully perform their obligations towards their citizens and the international community.

To be sure, failed States are only a relatively new phenomenon and are not rare occurrence. However, they have not been fully conceptualized. The lack of definition, and thus understanding, has important consequences on how other States and the international community, in general, has reacted to State failure.

State failure implies the possibility that a State cannot – rather than does not – perform its functions, even after its statehood is recognized. As such, State failure implies a gradation of sovereign capacity, while for international lawyers sovereignty either exists or it does not. If at all, international law views failed States as States with ineffective governments.[14] However, failed States are not just failed governments. Their failure is normally long-lasting and encompasses several to all of the functions of the State, not solely their governmental functions. State failure includes not only an ineffective government, but affects the basis and entire structure of the State, including its population, territory and capacity to perform international and internal obligations.

The limitation of sovereignty brought about by State failure is not sudden. State collapse is a long process. In fact, only in exceptional circumstances does sovereignty instantly cease to exist. Examples of such prompt disappearance are limited to cases of successful rapid territorial invasions, like the invasion of Kuwait by Iraq in August 1990, which only took two days to accomplish, and lasted for several months. In usual circumstances, State fail-

[14] For example, Ralph Wilde affirms that failed states denote situations in which "the governmental infrastructure in a state has broken down to a considerable degree." R. Wilde, *The Skewed Responsibility Narrative of the Failed States Concept*, 9 ILSA J. Int'l & Comp. L. 425, 426 (2003).

ure is a long and progressive process. A State may begin to lose control of parts of its peripheral territories, and, then, can only provide limited political goods or only to limited part of its populations. This phase can be very long and may or may not culminate in total State collapse. Further, State failure is better represented as a continuum. Figuratively, if we imagine that sovereignty is white and that complete State collapse is black, State failure does not come in either color, but in many shades of gray.

The fading of the exercise of sovereignty often has drastic consequences for a State's population and the international community in general.

First, rights of domestic populations are eroded. Health and other basic rights cannot be assured. As the failing of State sovereignty continues, the lack of performance of basic rights worsens. This often gives rise to humanitarian crises. Further, State structures become unable to provide most rights to their populations, particularly those situated outside the capital city. State structures are also typically unable to confront emergencies. Too often, the inability of the State to provide for its citizens is coupled with the commission of human rights abuses towards the population, by either State forces or rebel groups.

Second, State failure also has consequences on the international community.[15] Failing and failed States are unable to perform their obligations towards the international community, for example, because they are unable to guarantee protection of their borders or airspace or are unable to address health emergencies.

Further, the inability to exercise sovereignty has often been framed as a "developing country" issue, opposing the (usual) ability of developed countries to perform certain obligations to the (usual) inability of developing countries to do the same.[16] This is, however, beside the point. The issue explored in this book is not the issue of responsibility or intervention, but

---

[15] The term 'international community' is complex and not easily defined. For the purpose of this study, the term 'international community' includes States, international organizations and a supra-national community with similar interests in their relationship to State failure. On the developing concept of international community, *see* Santiago Villalpando, L'Emergence de la Communaute Internationale Dans la Responsabilite des Etas (2005); *see also* International Responsibility Today: Essays in Memory of Oscar Schachter (Maurizio Ragazzi, ed., 2005).

[16] *See* Ruth Gordon, *Saving Failed States: Sometimes a Neocolonialist Notion*, 12 Am. U. J. Int'l & Pol'y 903 (1997). Similarly, James Crawford argues "In the post-decolonization period, a number of related strands in thinking about the State have arisen. For example, there is the idea that very many of these States, and especially the new States that have emerged since 1945, are not real but are 'quasi-States' and that their statehood should in some way be discontinued. Then there is a body of literature on the so-called 'failed States'. On closer examination this is more properly a debate about intervention, security and

the issue of what norms and measures can be used to address the consequences of State collapse for both domestic populations and the international community at large so as to ensure the well-being of the population and the maintenance of the international public order. As Professor James Crawford argues "what is needed is not a more intrusive intervention *doctrine*, but more effective '*measures*'."[17] The question of failure to perform international obligations is not confined to a question of treaty violation.

In this book, I will first focus my analysis on examples in which States or the international community has acted on behalf of a sovereign when it has been incapable of performing its obligations (Chapter Two). As I will demonstrate, this is not uncommon and certain aspects of it may serve as a model to address State failure. In fact, the idea that other States or the international community can act on behalf of States is not new. However, it is not used as such in a situation of State failure. This conclusion is well demonstrated in the situation of Somalia, the paramount example of State failure, to which I will turn next (Chapter Three), to demonstrate that the toolbox developed by the international community to act on behalf of a State has proved to be insufficient. Because States failure has not been conceptualized in international law, the tools available to deal with it are limited. Thus, after defining State failure in detail (Chapter Four), in Chapters Five to Seven, I will explore alternative mechanisms available to address the phenomenon of State failure so as to draw a series of principles that could be used to confront State failure.[18]

---

development." James Crawford, The Creation of States in International Law 719 (2d ed. 2007).

17 J. Crawford, The Creation of States in International Law 723 (2d ed., 2007).

18 I should note at the outset that an agreed-upon definition of State "failure" does not exist, and some actors criticize the use of "failing" or "failed" as referred to States. The World Bank, for example, uses the term "fragile states." (*See* World Bank, *CPIA-Policies and Institutions for Environmental Sustainability, available at*: http://go.worldbank.org/7NMQ1P0W10). In this book, I use the term "failure" because it was the first term used to characterize the phenomenon studied here. The terms "failing" or "fragile" states are at times used interchangeably.

Chapter Two

The International Community has Acted on Behalf of States in the Past

The international community has developed a toolbox of instruments to deal with the problem of performing another State's obligations when, for specific reasons, the State is not capable of doing so itself. The international community should find a form to act on behalf of failed States that will ensure performance of basic obligations on the same ground.

The international community and certain States are not unfamiliar with acting on behalf of other States, either for specific obligations or for general obligations arising out of international law. Though this has not been framed as assistance to failed States, an analysis of how specific obligations have been performed by external actors may provide a useful framework and example that could be used to assist failed States.

It is interesting, first, to explore other historical examples of past comparable experiences. To assess how this issue was addressed in the past, I will study specifically precedents in which international obligations have been performed – not by the national government – but by an alternative institution. The examples studied are first, Trucial Coast States; second, Germany after WWII; third, former colonized territories; and, fourth, international territorial administrations by the United Nations.

In the first two cases, Trucial Coast States and post-WWII Germany, foreign relations were explicitly taken over by a third party, through a treaty or military occupation, but sovereignty was maintained and recognized. In the latter two cases, international obligations were performed by a third party, the United Nations or a caretake under a general mandate to administer.

Finally, I will then briefly explore U.N. development projects as examples of long-term actions to address States' weaknesses as an example of a general tool available to the international community to address specific weaknesses of the governmental structure.

1. *States Under Protection and Trucial Principalities*

An interesting example of separation between international and national obligations can be found in Protectorates, treaty arrangements by which a State puts itself under a kind of guardianship of another State.[1] Recent examples include Andorra, Morocco, both under Spanish and French protection, Tunisia, under French protection, and certain States in the Persian Gulf – collectively referred to as the Trucial Principalities, which provide the most interesting example.

In the second part of the 19th century, the United Kingdom developed a special system of protectorate, by which the British Government administered external relations of these States, but in which local rulers maintain their independence for all other matters.[2] The British Government signed treaty agreements for such a purpose with the Sultanate of Muscat and some Sheikhdoms of the Persian Gulf – including Kuwait, Bahrain, Qatar and the seven other Trucial principalities.[3] The Treaty of 1880 between Bahrain and the United Kingdom binds the former "to abstaining from entering into negotiations or making treaties of any sort with any State or Government other than the British government, and to refuse permission to any other Government than the British to establish diplomatic or Consular agencies" unless with the consent of the British Government.[4] With subsequent treaties, Bahrain also agreed to consult Britain before concluding specific commercial transactions and before conceding oil exploration permits, and in 1892, the Sheikh agreed that he would "on no account cede, sell, mortgage of otherwise give for occupation" any part of his territory save to the Government of the United Kingdom.[5] Under a similar agreement, the United

---

[1] Oppenheim's International Law 266–274 (Sir Arthur Watts & Sir Robert Jennings eds., 9th ed. 1992).

[2] *See* Elihu Lauterpacht, *The Status of Muscat and Oman, The Contemporary Practice of the United Kingdom in the Field of International Law – Survey and Comment*, V, July 1 – December 31, 1957, 7 Int'l & Comp. L. Q. 108 (1958) [hereinafter Lauterpacht, *The Status of Muscat and Oman*]; *see also* E. Lauterpacht, *Protected States. Status of Persian Gulf Sheikhdoms. Iranian Claims to Bahrain The Contemporary Practice of the United Kingdom in the Field of International Law – Survey and Comment*, VI, January 1 – June 30, 1958, 7 Int'l & Comp. L. Q. 110 (1958) [hereinafter Lauterpacht, *Protected States*].

[3] Abu Dhabi, Dubai, Sharjia, Ras al-Khaimah, Ajman, Umm al-Qaiwain and Fujairah.

[4] Lauterpacht, *Protected States* 111–112.

[5] *Id.* A similar agreement was signed by the Sultan of Muscat for the territories of Muscat and Oman on March 20, 1891, who also signed a 1923 agreement to consult the Government of India prior to granting permission for oil exploitation. *See* Lauterpacht, *The Status of Muscat and Oman* 109.

Kingdom also represented the Sultan of Muscat in a dispute with France at the Permanent Court of Arbitration.[6]

Protectorate agreements were not unusual in the colonial and pre-colonial period,[7] however, the agreements of the Trucial Principalities stand out because of the degree of power in external obligations given to the British Government, which never claimed any authority in internal affairs of these States. The Trucial States were recognized by the UK as separate sovereign entities in special relation with to the UK, which was responsible for their international relations and defense.[8] Maintaining a recognized separate sovereignty distinguishes States under protection from dependent, or colonized, territories.

2. *Occupied Territories*

Foreign control of the international obligations of a State can also be the result of a lawful war and the resulting occupation of the territory of the aggressor.[9] For example, at the end of World War II in 1945, the Allied powers occupied Germany and assumed supreme authority over the country, without annexing it or succeeding to it, but by replacing *ad interim* the German Government. The Allied powers also assumed the role of conducting German foreign relations on its behalf.[10] Control Council Proclamation No. 2 of 20 of September 1945 authorized the Allied Representatives to "regulate all matters affecting Germany's relations with other countries. No foreign obligations, undertakings or commitments of any kind will be assumed or entered into by or on behalf of German authorities or nationals without the sanction of the Allied Representatives."[11] For existing treaties, the Proclamation provided that

> The Allied Representatives will give directions concerning the abrogation, bringing into force, revival or application of any treaty, convention or anther

[6] *See* Lauterpacht, *The Status of Muscat and Oman* 108–109 (stating that this kind of agreement was irrelevant for the independence of Muscat).

[7] *See* J. Crawford, The Creation of States in International Law 288–294 (2d ed., 2007).

[8] Oppenheim's International Law 266–274 (Sir Arthur Watts & Sir Robert Jennings eds., 9th ed. 1992).

[9] Ian Brownlie, Principles of Public International Law 69–83 (6th ed. 2003).

[10] Robert Y. Jennings, *Government in Commission*, 23 Brit. Y.B. Int'l L. 126 (1946).

[11] *Official Gazette*, 8–19, *reprinted in* Robert Y. Jennings, *Government in Commission*, 23 Brit. Y.B. Int'l L. 126 (1946).

> international agreements, or any part of provision thereof, to which Germany is or had been a party.[12]

This example epitomizes, probably for the first time in modern history, a situation in which winning countries provisionally administer another, whose aggressive and unacceptable government they had defeated, with the objective of national reconstruction through the preventive implementation of specific policies. A similar arrangement was imposed at the end of the war on Japan.[13] In both of these cases, the existence of a distinct sovereignty State of Germany or Japan was not questioned.

3. *Mandate, Trusteeships Arrangements and other Mechanisms from the Colonial Heritage*

One way the League of Nations and then the United Nations dealt with non-self-governing territories and former colonies was to create a mandate or trusteeship mechanism, in which the member States were to administer trust territories until their independence, and under the supervision of the Trusteeship Council.[14]

A similar option is set out in Article 73 of the U.N. Charter for non-self-governing territories.[15]

---

12 *Id.* at 127.

13 Michael J. Kelly, Restoring and Maintaining Order in Complex Peace Operations: The Search for a Legal Framework 128, 249 (1999).

14 Chapter XII of the U.N. Charter regulates the International Trusteeship System. Art. 77 of the Charter limits the scope the Trusteeship system to "a. territories now held under mandate; b. territories which may be detached from enemy states as a result of the Second World War; and c. territories voluntarily placed under the system by states responsible for their administration." Similarly, Art. 76 defines the objectives of the Trusteeship system, which are "a. to further international peace and security; b. to promote the political, economic, social, and educational advancement of the inhabitants of the trust territories, and their progressive development towards self-government or independence as may be appropriate to the particular circumstances of each territory and its peoples and the freely expressed wishes of the peoples concerned, and as may be provided by the terms of each trusteeship agreement; c. to encourage respect for human rights and for fundamental freedoms for all without distinction as to race, sex, language, or religion, and to encourage recognition of the interdependence of the peoples of the world; and d. to ensure equal treatment in social, economic, and commercial matters for all Members of the United Nations and their nationals, and also equal treatment for the latter in the administration of justice, without prejudice to the attainment of the foregoing objectives and subject to the provisions of Article 80."

15 Article 73 of the U.N. Charter states that "Members of the United Nations which have or assume responsibilities for the administration of territories whose peoples have not yet

The mandate system was established under the League of Nations after WWI, while trusteeship agreements are characteristic of the post WWII system. Both arrangements are temporary and emphasize the priority of the natives' interests and the obligations of the administrating States[16] to guarantee and respect their well-being, with the objective to develop self-government or independence.[17]

In this instance, international obligations are temporarily taken care of by the trustee country. There is no explicit mandate for international obligations, but only a general obligation to promote the interests of the inhabitants to the utmost and to promote their political, economic, social, and educational advancement. This general guideline is also used to pursue international obligations. Therefore, the general mandate to administer the affairs of a State could include all international obligations identified above.

---

attained a full measure of self-government recognize the principle that the interests of the inhabitants of these territories are paramount, and accept as a sacred trust the obligation to promote to the utmost, within the system of international peace and security established by the present Charter, the well-being of the inhabitants of these territories, and, to this end: a. to ensure, with due respect for the culture of the peoples concerned, their political, economic, social, and educational advancement, their just treatment, and their protection against abuses; b. to develop self-government, to take due account of the political aspirations of the peoples, and to assist them in the progressive development of their free political institutions, according to the particular circumstances of each territory and its peoples and their varying stages of advancement; c. to further international peace and security; d. to promote constructive measures of development, to encourage research, and to co-operate with one another and, when and where appropriate, with specialized international bodies with a view to the practical achievement of the social, economic, and scientific purposes set forth in this Article; and e. to transmit regularly to the Secretary-General for information purposes, subject to such limitation as security and constitutional considerations may require, statistical and other information of a technical nature relating to economic, social, and educational conditions in the territories for which they are respectively responsible other than those territories to which Chapters XII and XIII apply."

16 Usually the administration of territories and trusteeships was taken up by the former colonial powers. In very few cases, the United Nations directly took the role of trustee. For example, in 1962–1963, during the transition period from Dutch to Indonesian rule, the Netherlands and Indonesia requested the Trusteeship Council to administer New Jaya. Namibia is another important example. In this case, after a prolonged refusal of South Africa to expedite the independence process of Namibia, the United Nations took over the administration of Namibia without the consent of the trustee state of South Africa and created the Council for Namibia.

17 The objective of independence is only mentioned in relation to the Trusteeship arrangement, while U.N. members that assumed responsibility for the administration of Non-Self Governing Territories should encourage the development of self-government only. For a discussion on the differences and implications, *see* THE CHARTER OF THE UNITED NATIONS, A COMMENTARY 923–930 (Art. 73), 939–948 (Art. 76) (Bruno Simma et al. eds., 1994).

4. *International Territories Administered by the United Nations*

Another method in which the international community has discharged external obligations in the absence of national ability to do so is by taking control in various degrees of several (and all) national functions. In a continuum, one side is exemplified by development and cooperation projects; and the opposite side by nation rebuilding exercises that the United Nations implemented in East Timor and Kosovo.

Since their inception, both the United Nation and its predecessor the League of Nations have been entrusted by their members with some form of temporary administration powers for international territories in special circumstances.[18] The League administered the Free City of Danzig from 1920 to 1939. The United Nations was to do the same for the planned Free Territory of Trieste in 1947, but the Territory was never released for reasons unrelated to the United Nations.

The involvement of the United Nations in the administration of special territories has constantly grown, especially during peacekeeping missions like Cyprus, Lebanon or Palestine.[19]

Two recent United Nations interventions pushed the nation-building role further, and created international authorities to administer territories in Kosovo and East Timor. Both efforts were directed at the creation of new States, and their mandates encompassed most traditional governance functions.[20] Their mandates did not include specific provisions for the fulfillment of international obligations, but in the running of their current affairs, both *interim* administrations regulated issues that have international implications.

In both of these examples, the United Nations was involved in nation-building efforts and had complete power over the administration of territories in Kosovo and East Timor, which included the fulfillment of international obligations. Both missions were temporary and directed at the reconstruction of an efficient administration for the creation of a politically viable autonomous entity.

---

[18] *Id.*

[19] *See* T.D. Grant, *Internationally Guaranteed Constitutive Order: Cyprus and Bosnia as Predicates for a New Traditional Actor in the Society of States*, 8 J. Transnat'l L. & Pol'y 1 (1998).

[20] Wilde, for example, suggests an interesting differentiation between governance and sovereignty functions as a pillar of different actions carried out by the United Nations in its international administration of territories. R. Wilde, *The Skewed Responsibility Narrative of the Failed States Concept*, 9 ILSA J. Int'l & Comp. L. 425, 426 (2003).

4.1. *The United Nations Interim Administration of Kosovo*

In Kosovo, the General Assembly gave the power to the Secretary-General "to establish in the war-ravaged province of Kosovo an interim civilian administration led by the United Nations under which its people could progressively enjoy substantial autonomy."[21] In particular, Security Council Resolution 1244 (1999) authorized the United Nations Interim Administration in Kosovo (UNMIK) to:

> Perform basic civilian administrative functions;
> Promote the establishment of substantial autonomy and self-government in Kosovo;
> Facilitate a political process to determine Kosovo's future status;
> Coordinate humanitarian and disaster relief of all international agencies;
> Support the reconstruction of key infrastructure;
> Maintain civil law and order;
> Promote human rights; and
> Ensure the safe and unimpeded return of all refugees and displaced persons to their homes in Kosovo.[22]

The same resolution, approved under Chapter VII of the U.N. Charter, authorized the deployment of KFOR, a peacekeeping force led by the North Atlantic Treaty Organization ("NATO").

The mandate of UNMIK in Kosovo included as its Head a Special Representative of the Secretary-General for Kosovo who presided over the work of the administration and facilitated the political process designed to determine Kosovo's future status.[23] The Special Representative was appointed by the Secretary-General under the advice of U.N. member States.

To implement its mandate, UNMIK initially brought together four "pillars" under its leadership. These are: Pillar I: Police and Justice, Pillar II: Civil Administration, both under the direct leadership of the United Nations, Pillar III: Democratization and Institution Building, led by the Organization for Security and Cooperation in Europe, and Pillar IV: Reconstruction and Economic Development, led by the European Union.[24]

---

[21] United Nations Interim Administration in Kosovo, http://www.un.org/peace/kosovo/pages/kosovo12.htm (last visited 28 Aug. 2009).

[22] S.C. Res. 1244, U.N. Doc. S/RES/1244 (10 June 1999).

[23] A copy of the mandate is available at United Nations Interim Administration in Kosovo, http://www.un.org/peace/kosovo/pages/kosovo12.htm (last visited 28 Aug. 2009).

[24] For a critical assessment of UNMIK, *see*, International Crisis Group, *UNMIK's Kosovo Albatross: Tackling Division in Mitrovica*, Europe Report 131 (3 June 2002), http://www.crisisgroup.org/home/index.cfm?id=1603&l=1.

The responsibility for enforcing Pillars I and II has been transferred to the institutions of provisional self-government in Kosovo. The United Nations, however, still monitors their enforcement.

Following a major internal restructuring of its activities, the 'Pillars structure' underwent a change. Pillar I was dissolved and, as a consequence, the Police Commissioner and the Director of the Department of Justice reported directly to the Special Representative of the Secretary General ("SRSG") instead of reporting to a Deputy Special Representative of the Secretary Genera ("DSRSG") as had been the case earlier. Pillar II was scaled down to a Department of Civil Administration and its Director also reported directly to the SRSG.

In June 1999, UNMIK set up the Joint Interim Administrative Structure to re-establish and deliver central and municipal administrative services. In most municipalities, Municipal Assemblies with Presidents, Deputies, Chief Executive Officers and mandatory committees on Policy and Finance, Communities, and Mediation were elected by the end of 2000.[25]

In the implementation of its mandate, under the authority of Security Council Resolution 1244 (1999), UNMIK regulated several internal matters that included international obligations. For example, the Special Representative adopted several regulations establishing customs and taxes.[26] Regulation No. 12/1999 established an international postal service. Regulation no. 1999/20 created the Banking and Payments Authority of Kosovo which also included specific provisions for international technical cooperation.[27] Regulation No. 2000/25 established the administrative department of transport and infrastructure, which included special provisions for air transport, directed at supervising and regulating "air transport carriers, air transport system operations, including air traffic and air transport facility construction and maintenance"[28]

---

[25] *See* U.N., What is UNMIK?, http://www.un.org/peace/kosovo/pages/unmik12.html (last visited 28 Aug. 2009).

[26] These regulations include 2000/2; 2000/26; 2000/31; 2000/35; 2000/56, http://www.unmikonline.org/regulations/index_reg_2000.htm.

[27] In Chapter 8, Technical Cooperation, the regulation provided that "(8.1) The BPK may participate in meetings of international councils and organizations concerning technical aspects of payments systems, bank supervision and the other matters that are within its fields of competence; (8.2) The BPK may provide banking and payments services for the benefit of foreign governments, foreign banks and foreign monetary authorities and for public international organizations and other international institutions."

[28] Regulation 2000/25 states at 2.3 that "[i]n the area of Air Transport, the Department shall: (a) Administer matters and services concerning the operation, use, construction and maintenance of air transport systems and facilities; (b) Supervise and regulate air transport

Under the SC Resolution mandate, UNMIK approved a Constitutional Framework which established Provisional Institutions of Self-Government for Kosovo including an Assembly and a Government headed by a Prime Minister. The creation of these institutions went in tandem with the transfer of administrative powers to them from UNMIK.

Inevitably, on 7 February 2008, the Assembly of Kosovo declared the independence of Kosovo,[29] which is still under the scrutiny of the international community.[30]

4.2. *The United Nations Transitional Authority in East Timor*

The United Nations mission in East Timor was based on a framework that is similar to the one developed in UNMIK. Resolution 1272 of the Security Council provides that the United Nations Transitional Authority in East Timor ("UNTAET") "has overall responsibility for the administration of East Timor and is empowered to exercise all legislative and executive authority, including the administration of justice."[31] This 1999 Resolution mandates UNTAET "to provide security and maintain law and order throughout the territory of East Timor; to establish an effective administration; to assist in the development of civil and social services; to ensure the coordination and delivery of humanitarian assistance, rehabilitation and development assistance; to support capacity-building for self-government; to assist in the establishment of conditions for sustainable development."[32]

---

carriers, air transport system operations, including air traffic and air transport facility construction and maintenance; (c) Co-ordinate non-commercial air transport services and facilities; (d) Produce and disseminate general information, technical documentation and statistics on air transport system operations and on air transport facility construction; and (e) Seek grants, loans or subsidies to support the operation, construction, maintenance or upgrading of air transport systems and facilities" (21 Apr. 2000), http://www.unmikonline.org/regulations/index_reg_2000.htm.

[29] Declaration of Independence (7 Feb. 2009), http://www.assembly-kosova.org/?krye=news&newsid=1635&lang=en.

[30] The General Assembly of the United Nations has recently filed a request for an Advisory Opinion in front of the International Court of Justice on the validity under international law of the unilateral declaration of independence of Kosovo. Press Release, International Court of Justice, Accordance with International Law of the Unilateral Declaration of Independence by the Provisional Institutions of Self-Government of Kosovo, No. 2009/27, http://www.icj-cij.org/homepage/index.php?lang=en.

[31] *See* U.N., *East Timor – UNTAET Mandate* (25 Oct. 1999), http://www.un.org/peace/etimor/UntaetM.htm.

[32] S.C. Res. 1272, U.N. Doc. S/RES/1272 (25 Oct. 1999).

UNTAET's mandate included the provision of security and maintenance of law and order throughout the territory of East Timor; the establishment of an effective administration; the assistance in the development of civil and social services; insurance of the coordination and delivery of humanitarian assistance, rehabilitation and development assistance; support to the capacity-building for self-government; and assistance in the establishment of conditions for sustainable development.[33] The regulations adopted in 1999–2001 period included Regulation 2000/12, Provisional Tax and Custom Regimes, and Regulation 2001/30 Banking and Payment Authority, which include specific provisions for international technical cooperation.[34] In the case of East Timor, the Administrative Authority chose not to be involved in regulating international obligations to UNMIK's extent.

UNTEAT was much more short-lived than UNMIK, and East Timor became an independent country on 20 May 2002. On the same day, the United Nations Mission of Support in East Timor ("UNMISET") succeeded UNTAET. UNMISET was established under UN Security Council Resolution 1410 (2002) with the aim to provide assistance to administrative structures of the now independent East Timor.[35]

5. *Development Programs and Humanitarian Assistance*

In situations where a State cannot entirely provide for specific needs and rights of its people, many donor countries have established cooperation programs and agencies to provide economic and technical development assistance. In these situations, international organizations and foreign States often provide substantial budgetary and technical support to essential governmental activities. Indeed, in some cases, international experts manage several key internal functions of a government. Development projects, for example, can range from the delivery of healthcare services to the restructuring of the legal and judicial systems. These types of interventions have generally been pursued with the consent of the government where

[33] U.N., *East Timor – UNTAET Mandate* (25 Oct. 1999), http://www.un.org/peace/etimor/UntaetM.htm.

[34] All regulations promulgated by UNTAET in 1999, 2000, 2001 are available on the United Nations' website. East Timor – UNTAET, *News and Developments*, http://www.un.org/peace/etimor/UntaetN.htm (last visited 28 Aug. 2009).

[35] *See* United Nations Transitional Administration in East Timor, http://www.un.org/peace/etimor/etimor.htm (last visited 28 Aug. 2009).

the interventions took place,[36] although some critics have at times found it to be neo-colonial behavior.[37]

The World Bank and the United Nations were the first international organizations to study and expand the model of good governance as a development policy. The World Bank mostly implemented governance programs centered on economic governance, while the United Nations focused on legal issues.

Within the United Nations, two agencies have been tasked specifically with the implementation of 'good governance' projects: the United Nations Development Program ("UNDP") and the Office of the High Commissioner for Human Rights ("OHCHR"). Of the two, the UNDP has a general and overarching role in 'good governance' while the effort of the OHCHR is mostly directed at the protection of human rights through the strengthening of the rule of law.

The work of UNDP is directed at strengthening 'democratic governance.' UNDP is active in parliamentary development, electoral systems and processes, access to justice and human rights, access to information, decentralization and local governance and public administration and civil service reform.[38]

In the area of governing institutions, the UNDP focuses on the legislature, the judiciary and electoral bodies.[39] Projects in this area include assistance in setting up effective parliamentary "structures, systems, processes and procedures,"[40] as well as providing training to Parliamentarians; providing assistance for electoral processes and for the establishment of systems of justice and laws, including legal and judicial reforms like "improving the structure, organization and administration of court systems; training judges, magistrate, lawyers and support personnel."[41]

---

[36] Typically the government of a state signs a general agreement allowing an international organization or a state mission to be present in its territory. Every project is then specifically discussed with the government and cosigned by the government and the executing agency.

[37] R. Gordon, *Saving Failed States: Sometimes a Neocolonialist Notion*, 12 AM. U. J. INT'L & POL'Y 903 (1997).

[38] *See* United Nations Development Programme, *Democratic Governance*, http://www.undp.org/governance/index.htm (last visited 28 Aug. 2009); *see also* J. Faudez, *Legal technical assistance*, GOOD GOVERNMENT AND LAW: LEGAL AND INSTITUTIONAL REFORM IN DEVELOPING COUNTRIES (J. Faudez ed., 1997) (addressing legal technical assistance).

[39] UNDP, *Governance for Sustainable Human Development – A UNDP policy document, Reconceptualizing Governance* 16–17 (Jan. 1997), http://mirror.undp.org/magnet/policy/.

[40] *Id.*

[41] *Id.*

In the initial phase of governance programming, between 1992 and 1996, the UNDP allocated approximately USD 1.3 billion to governance projects. Of these, about USD 650 million were given to Latin America and the Caribbean, approximately USD 260 million to Asia and the Pacific, and some USD 390 million to Africa and the Middle East. Governing institutions received approximately USD 200 million directed mostly at projects in Africa, Latin America and the Caribbean.[42] This effort has increased substantially. In 2008 alone, the UNDP provided USD 1.4 billion to programs fostering democratic governance.[43]

Nowadays, UNDP works on governance issues in 129 countries, at both national and local levels. For example, in 2008, UNDP provided technical and financial support to strengthen the multi-party system to institutions in Tanzania, including the parliament, electoral management bodies, political parties and civil society.[44] UNDP also directly supported electoral processes. For example, it supported electoral reform efforts in Lebanon through national awareness campaigns and the publication and dissemination of draft law booklets in several languages to libraries, universities and the public.[45]

Development and humanitarian assistance include delivery of food, mainly by two U.N. programs: the World Food Program ("WFP") and the Food and Agriculture Organization ("FAO");[46] and well as water, sanitation and health products, mainly by the World Health Organization ("WHO") and the UN Children's Program ("UNICEF").[47] Together with these principle organizations, other UN agencies, national aid agencies and non-governmental organizations participate in the implementation and delivery of development and humanitarian programs.

In failed States, where a national government cannot control large parts of the country that they represent or in situations where a government is absent, the international community has tried to replicate this behavior and looked for consent of the local authorities in control of the territories. In these cases, the conduct by international organizations of several areas of

---

[42] UNDP, Governance for Sustainable human development – A UNDP policy document, Reconceptualizing Governance, Ch. 2 (Jan. 1997), *available at*: http://mirror.undp.org/magnet/policy/.

[43] UNDP, Annual Report 2009 7 (2009), *available at*: http://www.undp.org/publications/annualreport2009/pdf/EN_FINAL.pdf.

[44] *Id.* at 14–15.

[45] *Id.* at 15.

[46] *See generally* World Food Programme, http://www.wfp.org (last visited 28 Aug. 2009); Food and Agriculture Organization of the United Nations, http://www.fao.org (last visited 28 Aug. 2009).

[47] *See generally* World Health Organization, http://www.who.int (last visited 28 Aug. 2009); United Nations Children's Fund, http://www.unicef.org (last visited 28 Aug. 2009).

internal affairs has been even more extensive. Undoubtedly, in such situations, international organizations extensively impact the conduct of several areas of internal affairs. Thus, the extent of their influence is particular relevant in cases of very weak governments.[48]

6. *Conclusion*

This chapter analyzes the – limited – toolbox available to the international community to address the problem of the inability of certain members of the community to fulfill the entirety of their international obligations.

These examples demonstrate that the international community – or certain actors within it – have temporarily exercised certain or all sovereign functions on behalf of a State. Historically, the international community has, often through the United Nations and its predecessor the League of Nations, developed a framework to deal with certain international obligations that could not be performed by a specific State because of turmoil or other crises. However, this framework often focused on a complete replacement of national authority, like in the case of protectorates, occupied territories, mandates and to a certain extent the international administration of territories. It has not focused on enabling an actor to exercise only specific sovereign functions, which would be the correct approach in a situation of State failure.

Alternatively, interventions have been limited to the implementation of humanitarian and development programs, which are too weak to have a concrete impact on sovereign functions.

While these examples show that certain instruments exist to deal with the problem posed by the inability of certain States to perform their international obligations. They also show that the tools are limited. The example of Somalia, which will be explored in depth in the next chapter, underscores the limits of the existing tools and the need to explore new venues to effectively address the problem of State failure.

[48] In Somalia, for example, most of the projects implemented by the UNDP include 'good governance' elements. The Somalia Civil Protection Project (SCPP) is one the most important and log-running projects of the UNDP in Somalia. It provides assistance to two regional administrations in strengthening the role and skills of local parliaments, it trains police and judges in criminal procedure and criminal law, and it assists the reintegration of ex-combatants in post-conflict society. Somalia Civil Protection Project (an abstract of the project document is *available at*: www.un-somalia.org).

Chapter Three

The Failed State *Par Excellence*: The Role of the International Community in Somalia Demonstrates the Inadequacy of the System to Deal with State Failure

Somalia has been without a functioning government for the past 17 years and it is often referred to as the main example of State failure.[1] In the absence of a viable government, Somalia has become the center of a civil war as well as source of regional and international instability. Somalia is the center of arms, drugs and human smuggling, it is the host of active al-Quaeda cells and its training camps; Somali pirates attack international shipping off its coasts, and Muslim radicals control significant part of the territory. Somalia is also one of the poorest countries in the world. Famine struck its population, the great majority of which has been internally displaced for many years or has left the country all together.

The following paragraphs will first give a simple historical background, and will then analyze the activities of the international community and the United Nations in Somalia.

Since gaining independence in 1960, Somalia has never performed as a self-sufficient State, and has relied heavily on external assistance for its existence. Presently, Somalia is in the unique position of being recognized in the international community as an independent State, but with no central government able to exercise control since the fall of the Barre regime in 1991.

The Republic of Somalia gained its independence in July 1960 from the unification of the Italian-administered Trusteeship Territory of Somalia and the protectorate of British Somaliland. Somalia is characterized by a rather uniform population in terms of language and religion: all Somalis speak one

---

1 Ken Menkhous calls Somalia "a failure among failed States," K. Menkhous, *Somalia: State Collapse and the Threat of Terrorism*, 364 Adelphi Paper – I.I.S.S. 17 (2004). *See also*, Abduqawi A. Yusuf, *Government Collapse and State Continuity in Somalia*, 13 Ital. Y.B. Int'l L. 112003; and Riikka Koskenmaki, *Legal Implications Resulting from State Failure in Light of the Case of Somalia*, 73 Nordic J. Int'l L. 1–36 (2004).

language, Somali, and respect one religion, Sunni Islam. The identity of Somalis, an estimated population of about 6 million people, is given in substantial part by their clan affiliations. There are four main clans and numerous sub and sub-sub clans. Economically, Somalia is one of the poorest countries in the world.[2] The majority of Somalis are pastoralists and earn their living through cattle rising. The South of the country has some rich agricultural land in the Shebelle region, which can produce bananas and sugar for export markets. Somalia also has one the longest coast lines in Africa. However, the fishing industry for export is nowadays economically irrelevant. Its strategic position in the Horn of Africa gives it easy access to both the Arab peninsula and East Africa and in the past awarded Somalia many international friends.[3]

General Mohammmed Siad Barre became Head of State and President of the Somali Supreme Revolutionary Council in 1969, after a military coup and the assassination of Abdirashid Sharma'arke, the elected President. His military regime was repressive and corrupt and successfully played on clans' rivalries. He was also able to obtain substantial foreign assistance, first by the Soviet Union and then by the United States.

Opposition to his regime and the deer economic situation grew in the late mid eighties, mostly following clan lines. The central power became increasingly unable to control the territory and, in 1991, Siad Barre fled Mogadishu. Civil war broke out throughout the entire country and the country was taken over by several rebel movements. As a consequence of the fighting, Somalis faced a growing humanitarian crisis.[4]

In January 1992, the U.N. Security Council[5] urged all parties involved in the fighting to cease hostilities and imposed an arms embargo under Chapter

---

[2] UNDP, National Human Development Report: Somalia 1998 (1998), available at: http://mirror.undp.org/somalia.hdr98.htm.

[3] For example, Berbera, in the Northwest region on Somaliland, has one of the few international landing sites for the Space Shuttle.

[4] *See* The United Nations in Somalia 1992–1995, The United Nations Blue Book Series (1996); F.K. Abiew, The Evolution of the Doctrine and Practice of Humanitarian Intervention 159–174 (1999); J. Clark, *Debacle in Somalia: Failure of the Collective Response*, ENFORCING RESTRAINT: COLLECTIVE INTERVENTION IN INTERNAL CONFLICTS 205–240 (L.F. Damrosch ed., 1993); W. Clarke and Jeffrey Herbst, *Somalia and the Future of Humanitarian Intervention*, 75 Foreign Aff. 70 (1996).

[5] S.C. Res. 733, U.N. Doc. S/RES/733 (23 Jan. 1992) (strongly urging all parties to the conflict to immediately cease hostilities and agree to case-fire; and deciding, under Chapter VII of the UN Charter, that all States shall, for the purpose of establishing peace and stability in Somalia, immediately implement a general and complete embargo on all deliveries of weapons and military equipment to Somalia". The Council also raises concerns over the rapid deterioration of the situation in Somalia and the heavy loss of human life.).

VII of the U.N. Charter.[6] In April 1992, the United Nations Operation in Somalia was launched.[7]

The United Nations decided to intervene in Somalia on humanitarian grounds, as the Security Council was "deeply disturbed by the magnitude of the human suffering cased by the conflict and concerned that the continuation of the situation in Somalia constitutes a threat to international peace and security"[8] and thus decided to deploy a security force to "provide urgent humanitarian assistance."[9]

The operation was also a test ground for the possible effectiveness of the newly active United Nations, as it provided the opportunity to assess its authority for the first time after the end of the Cold War. The U.N. intervention took place without the consent of the government of Somalia, as there was no government that could give such consent, and under Chapter VII of the U.N. Charter as a measure to ensure international peace and security.

In August of the same year, the size of the mission increased[10] and in December it was authorized to "use all necessary means to establish as soon as possible a secure environment for humanitarian relief operations in Somalia."[11] This development marked the beginning of the second upgraded stage of the mission, which was initiated by the United States and called by them Operation Restore Hope – known internationally as United Task Force ("UNITAF").

[6] Chapter VII refers to situations that threaten international peace and security. Art. 39 states that "the security council shall determine the existence of any threat to the peace, breach of the peace, or act of aggression and shall make recommendations, or decide what measures shall be taken in accordance with Articles 41 and 42, to maintain or restore international peace and security." Art. 41 confers upon the Security Council the power to decide what measures not involving the use of armed force can be employed to give effect to its decision, and empowers the Council to call upon the Members of the United Nations to apply such measures. Measures can include complete or partial interruption of economic relations and of rail, sea, air, telegraphic, radio, and other means of communication, and the severance of diplomatic relations. Art. 42 states that "[s]hould the Security Council consider that measures provided for in Article 41 would be inadequate or have proved to be inadequate, it may take such action by air, sea, or land forces as may be necessary to maintain or restore international peace and security. Such action may include demonstrations, blockade, and other operations by air, sea or land forces of members of the United Nations."

[7] S.C. Res. 751, U.N. Doc. S/RES/751 (24 Apr. 1992). The operation was established under the authority of the Security Council to facilitate an immediate and effective cessation of hostilities and monitor a cease-fire "in order to promote the process of reconciliation and political settlement in Somalia and to provide urgent humanitarian assistance." *Id.* ¶ 7.

[8] *Id.* at Introductory part of Resolution.

[9] *Id.* ¶ 7. *See infra* Chapter Seven, Section 2.

[10] S.C. Res. 775, U.N. Doc. S/RES/775 (28 Aug. 1992).

[11] S.C. Res. 794, U.N. Doc. S/RES/794 (3 Dec. 1992).

In a subsequent permutation, the intervention undertook another expansion, was named UNOSOM II,[12] and was given a broader mandate that included disarmament and enforcement powers, and the creation of a civilian police.[13] As opposition to the mission by local militias intensified and insuring peace and stability became more problematic, the mission was scaled back in January 1994[14] and ended in 1995.[15]

The operation achieved mixed results and was considered a failure on many aspects, especially because of its failure to restore peace and stability. However, it is estimated to have saved approximately 100,000 people. The United Nations, as an organization, seriously suffered from lack of coordination and was accused of biases and inefficiencies. The U.N. peacekeepers suffered more than one hundred casualties, while the intervention became a manhunt against one warlord, General Mohamed Farah Aideed. Importantly, the mission failed to achieve its goal of reestablishing peace and security, leaving the country without a central government and with diffused local power structures.

In evaluating the intervention in Somalia, then Secretary General of the United Nations, Boutros Boutros-Ghali, noted that

> At the present time, the international community does not seem to have the will or the resources to intervene effectively in support of a failed State [...] the Charter of the United Nations provides for the admission to the international community of a country which gains the attributes of a sovereign State, for instance, through independence or decolonization. It does not, however, provide for any mechanisms through which the international community can respond when a sovereign State loses one of the attributed of statehood, such as its Government. [...] The situation in Somalia will continue to deteriorate until the political will exist among the parties to reach a peaceful solution to their dispute, or until the international community gives itself new instruments to address the phenomenon of failed states.[16]

---

[12] S.C. Res. 814, U.N. Doc. S/RES/814 (26 Mar. 1993).

[13] *Id.* at Sec. B, ¶¶ 5–7. *See also* The Secretary-General, *Report of the Secretary General on Situation in Somalia*, U.N. Doc. S/25354, ¶¶ 56–69 (3 Mar. 1993),

[14] Security Council Resolution 897 reduced the size of UNOSOM II and revised the mandate of the mission excluding enforcement powers, S.C. Res. 897, U.N. Doc. S/RES/897 (4 Feb. 1994).

[15] A final mandate extending UNSOM II for a final period until 31 March 1995 was authorized in S.C. Res. 954, U.N. Doc. S/RES/954 (4 Nov. 1994). *See also*, for a summary description, Dept. of Public Information, U.N., *Somalia – UNOSOM II* (21 Mar. 1997) (*available at:* http://www.un.org/Depts/DPKO/Missions/unosom2b.htm), or for a more comprehensive report, The United Nations in Somalia 1992–1995, The United Nations Blue Book Series (1996).

[16] The United Nations in Somalia 1992–1995 87 (1996).

Eighteen years after the beginning of the civil war, the situation in Somalia has scarcely improved and it is still characterized by the absence of a central authority. In the Northwest of the country, the secessionist province of Somaliland declared its independence in 1991 and established a rather stable central government in the capital town of Hargeisa together with a working system of district administrations. However, in the last few years an insurgent radical Islamic movement has been shaken the stability of Somaliland. Its claims of international recognition, based on its status of successor State to the former British Somaliland, have gone mostly unnoticed, as the international community still only recognizes one central State of Somalia. In the Northeast of the country, the Puntland regional administration was created in 1998. Puntland does not claim independence but awaits the creation of a central State in Mogadishu, which it plans to rejoin.[17] These local administrations are based on clan alliances.

Numerous reconciliation efforts sponsored by the United Nations and other international and national actors have focused on Somalia in the attempt to recreate a functional government. In August 2000, the Government of Djibouti hosted and sponsored a reconciliation conference to which more than one hundred delegates from the whole of Somalia participated. The Harta process (from the name of the location in Djibouti where the conference took place) concluded with the formation of a Transitional National Government ("TNG") and the election of Abdiquasim Salad Hasan as the new President on August 26, 2000. Shortly after the election, the TNG moved to Mogadishu. It never controlled more that few square blocks of the capital city and little territory beyond the city limits.[18]

More recently, in 2002–2004, the Somalia National Reconciliation Conference was held in Eldoret and Mbagathi in Kenya, and was also backed by the regionally-based Inter-Governmental Authority on Development ("IGAD"), the European Union ("EU") and the United Nations. This effort resulted in the formation of the Transitional Federal Government ("TFG"), which has been the most successful effort at rebuilding a functioning State since the

[17] In the late 1990's, in the central part of Somalia, the Rahanwein Resistence Army ("RRA") – a militia faction – created another separate regional authority. Both Puntland and the RRA formed weak and unstable administrations, and the RRA has lost control. In fact, the RRA ceased to exist in 2000. Until 2005, RRA was split into RRA1 and RRA 2. Since then, they have both lost relevance.

[18] For a good analysis of who is who in Somali politics, see the BBC introductory article on Somalia: *Analysis: Somalia's Powerbrokers*, BBC News, 8 Jan. 2002, http://news.bbc.co.uk/hi/english/world/africa/newsid_1747000/1747697.stm (last visited 28 August 2009).

collapse in 1991. A Transitional Assembly was nominated and a President elected in 2004. The TFG moved to Mogadishu in 2007. However, at the same time the Union of Islamic Courts ("UIC") emerged to challenge the TFG for control of Somalia. The two factions fought each other, and Ethiopian troops entered the Somali territory to protect the TFG in 2007. At present, regional armies are fighting proxy wars in Somalia and the situation is still unstable.[19] Islamic fundamentalists are gaining grounds and the TFG remains unable to assert its authority beyond certain limited areas.[20]

Somalis are largely dependent on the efforts of the international community, which provides most of the basic services. Economically, most Somalis also rely on foreign remittances from the Somali Diaspora. This source of income, however, was severely reduced in the aftermath of the terrorist attacks of September 11, 2001 in New York and Washington, DC. In 2001, because of suspected links to the international terrorist network, U.S. President George W. Bush froze the assets of "al-Barakaat," an informal banking system.

Most international organizations and NGOs are presently working in Somalia and deliver basic humanitarian and development assistance, including health services, education projects, micro and macro finance projects and "good governance" programs. U.N. agencies working in Somalia include the U.N. Children Fund, the U.N. Development Program, the U.N. Education Organization, the World Health Organization, and several branches of the U.N. Secretariat. Most of the major humanitarian NGOs also have a Somalia office,[21] as well as most donor countries.[22]

The mandate of the U.N. intervention in Somalia was wide. Security Council Resolution 814 of 26 March 1993 contained language recognizing a specific, limited mandate of State reconstruction to the U.N. mission for the first time, these included assistance:

---

[19] International Crisis Group, *Ethiopia/Eritrea* (2009), http://www.crisisgroup.org/home/index.cfm?id=1229&l=1 (last visited 3 Feb. 2010).

[20] In its last meeting on Somalia, IGAD expressed "profound concern regarding the political paralysis in Somalia, contributing to the continuing deterioration of the security situation in the country as well as the near hopelessness of the existing situation, with respect to achieving the objectives of the transitional period as evidenced in the complete failure to establish institutions of governance only nine months before the end of the transition period." IGAD directed the TFG to implement detailed directives, including appointing a cabinet and finalizing the new Constitution within a tight timeframe. *Declaration On Somalia*, 29 Oct. 2008, done at the 13th extraordinary session of the Inter-Governmental Authority on Development Assembly of Heads of State and Government.

[21] Including OXFAM, Care and Médicins Sans Frontières (MSF).

[22] Including the EC and ECHO, USAID, Italy, Sweden, Denmark.

in the provision of relief and in the economic rehabilitations of Somalia;
in the repatriation of refugees and displaced persons;
to promote and advance political reconciliation, through all sectors of Somali society, and the re-establishment of national and regional institutions and civil administration in the entire country;
in the re-establishment of Somali police, as appropriate at the local, regional or national level, to assist in the restoration and maintenance of peace, stability and law and order, including in the investigation and facilitating the prosecution of serious violation of international humanitarian law;
in the creation of conditions under which Somali civil society may have a role, at every level, in the process of political reconciliation and in the formulation and realization of rehabilitation and reconstruction programs.[23]

With the end of the peacekeeping mission, the mandate was also revised but still retained extensive influence. With Resolution 954 of November 1994, the Security Council mandated U.N. agencies to "provide rehabilitation and reconstruction assistance, including assistance to police and judiciary to the extent that the situation in Somalia develops in such a way as to make that practible."[24] The international community is presently involved in, among others, ports and roads rehabilitation, judicial and legal restructuring, health service delivery and vaccination, and education – including choice of curriculum and of the language of instruction.[25]

A special body, the Somalia Aid Coordination Body ("SACB"),[26] was formed in December 1993 to coordinate and organize funding and projects to provide assistance to the people of Somalia by the organizations working on and in Somalia. It comprises donor countries, UN agencies and programs, and NGOs. The framework for the SACB actions in Somalia is outlined in the Addis Ababa Declaration[27] and the Code of Conduct for International Rehabilitation and Development Assistance.[28] In practice, the SACB coordinates and controls most of the aid given to Somalia. It develops and implements policies and guidelines for interventions, and in many cases it is a veritable partial substitute for government action. As for its relations with existing local authorities, a 1996 document produced by the SACB states that

[23] S.C. Res. 814, U.N. Doc. S/RES/814 (26 Mar. 1993).

[24] S.C. Res. 954, U.N. Doc. S/RES/954 (4 Nov. 1994) (extending the mission for a final period to 31 March 1995).

[25] In the absence of the required authority able to sign the project documents, the UNDP developed a special framework by which authority to implement a development project is given on a case by case level by the UNDP Administrator.

[26] *See* Somalia Aid Coordination Body, Handbook (2001).

[27] *Id.* at 2.

[28] *Id.* at 10.

> the international aid community is ready to maintain close contact with the competent regional, local, traditional or any other kind of effective authorities in the country throughout the duration of their project activities [...] however, international aid agencies must be free to act in accordance with their mandate when determining the modalities for the delivery of any assistance.[29]

The structure of the SACB includes an Executive Committee, which deals with current operational and policy issues, a Consultative Committee, which provides a forum to exchange information on the political, security and humanitarian situation in Somalia, and a Sectoral Steering Committee composed of the chairs of the Sectoral Committees. So far, five Sectoral Committees have been established, with a mandate to address and deal with the following specific operational issues: Health and Nutrition, Education, Food Security and Rural Development, Governance and Water, Sanitation and Infrastructure. The Committees decide and implement development policies.[30]

The following paragraphs will analyze specifically how the United Nations and other international actors working in Somalia approach issues linked to air and sea safety, health emergencies, trade barriers and diplomatic representation in Somalia.

1. *Transport and Safety in Air Space: The United Nations as Caretaker for Obligations of Somalia Benefiting the International Community in General*

The management of the airspace of Somalia by the UNDP and the International Civil Aviation Organization ("ICAO") is the most interesting example of an international obligation performed by the international community for and on behalf of the Somali government.

States have a mutual responsibility to guarantee the safety of their airspace. This obligation is contained in the 1944 Chicago Convention on the International Civil Aviation and is fundamental for the safety and reliability of civilian air traffic.[31]

---

[29] Working Arrangements between the international aid community and responsible Somali authorities, Nairobi June 1996. SACB HANDBOOK, (2001).

[30] The United Nations in Somalia appealed for more than USD 83 million to the international community. For a description of humanitarian and development needs and planned projects, *see* OCHA, *Consolidated Inter-Agency Appeal for Somalia Appeal* (2002), *available at:* http://www.reliefweb.int/appeals/2002/files/som02.pdf, (last visited 28 Aug. 2009).

[31] Convention on Int'l Civil Aviation, U.S. Dep't of State, Publ'n No. 2816, Treaties and Other International Acts Series 1591, *available at:* http://avalon.law.yale.edu/20th_century/decad048.asp.

During the peacekeeping intervention in Somalia, UNOSOM interpreted its mandate to include the control of the airspace of Somalia.[32] The Force Commander found such authority in Resolutions 814 and 837 (1993). The mandate that required UNOSOM to secure all ports and airports for the delivery of humanitarian assistance was interpreted as an authority to control temporarily the airspace of Somalia. In March 1993, UNOSOM therefore stipulated an agreement with ICAO, which provided civil aviation functions from Mogadishu.

The mandate for this operation expired in 1995, at the end of the peacekeeping mission. However, the situation in Somalia had not improved and there was no central authority that could take over the running of the Aviation Authority at that time. Therefore, the United Nations authorized UNDP and ICAO to maintain essential safety services for international air transportation. Since March 1996, the resulting "Civil Aviation Caretaker Authority for Somalia" (CACAS) has operated from facilities in Nairobi, Kenya.[33]

The mission of the program is

> To provide, under the supervision of the Director of the Technical Cooperation Bureau of ICAO, for the operation and maintenance of essential facilities, equipment and services for international air transport operations, including humanitarian and relief flights and local flight operations within the Mogadishu Flight Information Region (FIR – Airspace and ground facilities in Somalia), on a self-financing basis, in order to meet immediate requirements for safety, and to assist in the rehabilitation and development of the aviation infrastructure where feasible provided that these latter related activities are financed from sources other than air navigation charges.[34]

Interestingly, the authorization for the project was given by the U.N. to UNDP and ICAO. As of today, the project is still being executed in the same format and implemented on behalf of the Government of Somalia and, pending its restoration, within the framework of the authority given to the UNDP Administrator by the Governing Council of the United Nations.[35]

The project is still run from Nairobi and, as the situation of Somalia is not ameliorating, its end is not envisaged. In fact, the creation of a similar

[32] The Trust Fund Agreement, which encapsulate the essential elements, reads "the force commander UNOSOM II is the airspace authority for Somalia airspace."

[33] UN Somalia, *Civil Aviation Caretaker Authority for Somalia*, http://www.un-somalia.org/Country_Team/cacas.asp (last visited 28 August 2009).

[34] *Id.*

[35] *Id.*

U.N. caretaker role was recently suggested by the U.N. Secretary General to protect offshore natural resources.[36]

The United Nations in this case has assumed the role of caretaker of a specific internal matter of a State, substituting the government of Somalia. The absence of such mechanism would have severe consequences for safety in air space and would significantly disrupt air traffic. The Secretary General found the authority to approve such a mechanism in the mandate given by the Security Council to ensure safety in airports. This is a unique approach. Despite some criticisms, this arrangement has worked well and served its purpose. It is in fact a good example of actions that could generally be taken on behalf a failed State by an international organization more regularly.

2. *The Safety of Territorial Borders and the Fight Against Piracy in Somali Waters*

The safety of territorial and maritime borders is paramount for maintaining order and stability in the international community.

Somali borders are porous and undefended. However, only limited actions can be taken by one State alone to defend the safety of its borders. The difference between the actions taken by the international community in relation to territorial and maritime borders is striking and worth analyzing.

So far, only limited actions have been taken to protect territorial borders. On 28 July 2001, President Arap Moi of Kenya declared a ban on cross-border trade between Kenya and Somalia due to a rise in small arms influx into Kenya.[37] This meant that all relations between the two countries were severed and airports closed. A similar trade ban lasting about six months was imposed in August 1999 for similar reasons. The ban was imposed to tackle the smuggling of *khat* produced in Kenya into Somalia.[38] Other related

[36] The Secretary-General, *Report of the Secretary-General on the Situation in Somalia*, U.N. Doc. S/1999/882, ¶ 71 (16 Aug. 1999) (where the Secretary General considers "whether, in advance of political agreements on the formation of a national government, actions could be taken by the international community to assist Somalia to recover its sovereignty in certain limited fields, for example the protection of offshore natural resources").

[37] *KENYA-SOMALIA: Moi bans cross-border trade*, IRIN NEWS, 30 July 2001, http://www.reliefweb.int/rw/rwb.nsf/AllDocsByUNID/16e1c85b128c7a4085256a990007c602d (last visited 3 Sept. 2009); KENYA-SOMALIA, *Kenya trade ban has serious repercussions*, IRIN NEWS, 31 July 2001, http://www.irinnews.org/Report.aspx?Reportid=24088 (last visited 3 Sept. 2009).

[38] Kenya is a main producer of *khat*, a mildly narcotic drug that is consumed fresh by a vast number of Somali men. The estimate revenue for Kenya for *khat* trade and production is of about USD 250 million a year. Unsurprisingly, exporters quickly found alternative

concerns include arms smuggling, heavy drugs smuggling, the creation of terrorists' safe-havens[39] and identity recognition. Further, extremely porous borders have also resulted in the increased presence of international terrorists in Somalia: Al Qaeda and several other extremist Islamic groups are known to be present and several terrorist acts have been planned in Somalia.[40] By itself, Kenya or regional powers can do very little to stop illegal trafficking and restore normality.

Alternatively, the interest and relevance of Somali maritime borders has resulted in unique actions by the United Nations. As such, the fight against piracy in Somali waters is a particularly relevant example of possible actions the international community has recently been ready to take to address this problem.

Piracy in the territorial waters of Somalia and in the high seas off the Somali coast has been a problem for many years.[41] Several ships have been hijacked for ransom while attempting to deliver food aid to Somalia. Commercial shipping, including from the United States and Egypt, has also been targeted.[42]

In 2005, the increasing number of piracy episodes was brought to the attention of the U.N. Security Council through Resolution A.979(24) of the Assembly of the International Maritime Organization ("IMO"). In 2006, the President of the UN Security Council issued a Statement, urging States with ships operating in international waters in the region to be vigilant and to take appropriate actions to protect commercial shipping, especially ships used for the delivery of humanitarian assistance. However, the situation provided only temporary respite. In July 2007, at a meeting at the headquarters of the IMO, Secretary General of the IMO Mitropoulous met the

---

shipping routes, mostly through other countries. *See SOMALIA-KENYA: Pilots arrested for evading trade ban*, IRIN NEWS, 4 Sept. 2001, http://www.irinnews.org/PrintReport.aspx?Reportid=25862 (last visited 3 Sept. 2009).

39 For example, there are some reports indicating that Somalia may be part of the drug routes from Asia to Europe. The U.S. administration has also raised concerns that Somalia may have become a safe heaven for Islamic terrorists and a training ground for al-Qaeda recruits, and has indicated Somalia may be a possible target in its war on terrorism. For example, *see Somalia's role in terror*, BBC NEWS, 21 Dec. 2001, http://news.bbc.co.uk/hi/english/world/africa/newsid_1723000/1723586.stm (last visited 3 Sept. 2009).

40 *See* Andre Le Sage, *Prospects For Al Itihad and Islamist Radicalism In Somalia*, 27 REV. OF AFR. POL. ECO. (2, Sept. 2001); J. Prendergast and C. Thomas-Jensen, *Blowing the Horn*, 86 FOREIGN AFF. 59–70 (Mar./Apr. 2007).

41 *See*, for example, BBC's article *Somalia's Dangerous Waters*, BBC NEWS, 26 Sept. 2005, http://news.bbc.co.uk/2/hi/africa/4283396.stm.

42 *See Contemporary Practice of the United States Relating to International Law, Continued U.S. Navy Operations Against Piracy in Somalia* (John R. Crook ed.) 102 AM. J. INT'L L. 169 (2008).

UN Secretary General Ban Ki-Moon, briefed him on the impact of piracy acts in Somali and adjacent waters, and requested the support of the United Nations. In November 2008, the IMO Assembly adopted a new Resolution – A.1002(25) On Piracy and Armed Robbery Against Ships in Waters Off the Coast of Somalia – requesting the TFG to take necessary actions to prevent and suppress acts of piracy and armed robbery that originated from its coasts. The Resolution specifically requests the TFG give its consent to the U.N. Security Council to allow foreign military ships to enter its territorial waters to engage in operations against pirates.[43]

On June 2, 2008, after extensive deliberation, the U.N. Security Council issued a groundbreaking Resolution – 1816 (2008) – in which it decided to allow foreign military ships to enter Somali waters to repress piracy under specific conditions.

Security Council Resolution 1816 (2008) is extraordinary for several reasons. First, it allows States that collaborate with the TFG to enter Somali territorial waters for the purpose of repressing acts of piracy and armed robbery at sea. Second, it allows the use of force to repress acts of piracy and armed robbery in Somalia. Third, it explicitly recognizes the situation of crisis in Somalia and its lack of capacity to fulfill its obligations, specifically to interdict pirates or patrol and secure international sea lanes and territorial waters.[44] This is exceptional as it is the Security Council, acting under Chapter VII of the Charter, which allows Member States to enter territorial sovereign waters of one of its members. In fact, although the Resolution specifically acknowledged that it is premised on the letter from the Permanent Representative of Somalia to the United Nations conveying the consent of the TFG,[45] it is nonetheless the Security Council that calls for action, not the TFG.

The application of the Resolution is also limited in several ways. First, it is only valid for six months,[46] with a renewal of the mandate possible if requested by the TFG.[47] Further, only situations for which advanced notice was provided by the TFG can trigger the intervention of foreign forces.[48] Further, the Resolution specifically reaffirmed the sovereignty and territorial

---

[43] *See* IMO Briefing 24, *IMO welcomes Security Council moves on Somali Piracy* (3 June 2008), http://www.imo.org/Newsroom/mainframe.asp?topic_id=1709&doc_id=9212 (last visited 3 Sept. 2009).

[44] S.C. Res. 1816, U.N. Doc. S/Res/1816, ¶ 7(a)–(b) (2 June 2008).

[45] *Id.* ¶ 9.

[46] *Id.* ¶ 7.

[47] *Id.* ¶ 15.

[48] *Id.* ¶ 7.

integrity of Somalia,[49] and states that the Resolution cannot be considered as precedent or as establishing customary international law.[50]

A second Resolution was approved by the Security Council on 7 October 2008 that further extended the mandate of foreign forces.[51] The Security Council, specifically referring to several requests for assistance made by the President of Somalia as well as its previous resolutions, and acting under Chapter VII of the Chapter of the United Nations, called upon States

> whose naval vessels and military aircraft operate on the high seas and airspace off the coast of Somalia to use on the high seas and airspace off the coast of Somalia the necessary means, in conformity with international law, as reflected in the Convention, for the repression of acts of piracy.[52]

The Resolution also called upon States interested in the security of maritime activities "to take part actively in the fight against piracy on the high seas off the coast of Somalia," in particular, by "deploying naval vessels and military aircrafts."[53]

The Resolution directly urges forces in the region to use all necessary means, including force, to repress acts of piracy in the high sea. It does not reiterate permission to enter Somalia waters as the six-month time limit has not expired and the relevant section of the Resolution continues to be applicable.

Several naval vessels and military aircrafts are now present in the Gulf of Aden, including vessels from NATO, the U.S., the EU, Russia, as well as a combined international force (CTS-150).[54] Moreover, the United Kingdom is said to be negotiating an agreement with Somalia to let its Royal Naval Forces launch attacks against pirates from within Somali territorial waters.[55]

It remains to be seen how the resolution will be applied by Member States in the future. It is certainly an interesting development in the way States and

---

49 *Id.* at Introduction.

50 *Id.* ¶ 12.

51 S.C. Res. 1838, U.N. Doc. S/Res/1838 (7 Oct. 2008).

52 *Id.* ¶ 3.

53 *Id.* ¶ 2.

54 *See* Tony Barber, *Somali pirates push the EU into uncharted naval waters*, FIN. TIMES, 11 Nov. 2008, http://blogs.ft.com/brusselsblog/2008/11/somali-pirates-push-the-eu-into-uncharted-naval-waters/ (last visited 3 Sept. 2009); *see also* U.S. Naval Forces Central Command, *Combined Task Force 150*, http://www.cusnc.navy.mil/command/ctf150.html (last visited 3 Sept. 2009).

55 *See* UPI.COM *Britain, Somalia in anti-pirate talks*, (15 Oct. 2008) http://www.upi.com/Top_News/2008/10/15/Britain_Somalia_in_anti-pirate_talks/UPI-58731224086246/ (last visited 3 Sept. 2009) (stating that "Britain is holding talks with Somalia aimed at allowing Royal Navy warships to enter Somali territorial waters to fight Gulf of Aden pirates").

international organizations approach relations to States that are incapable of performing certain international acts. It also shows that the international community is willing to take action in important matters of international security, though through a very carefully crafted approach.

The Security Council has shown that it is willing to act in certain circumstances, specifically those that have an immediate impact on international public order (and namely air space and piracy). However, so far, its actions have been limited. International actors can do little without the explicit mandate of the Security Council, and even then, the extent to what can be achieved remains to be assessed.

3. *Transboundary Issues of Public Health: The UN as a Guarantor of National Standards for the Continuation of Bilateral Commercial Relations*

In general, States must control human and animal health to avoid the spread of diseases outside its boundaries. The importance of these obligations is grasped by analyzing the ban on livestock exports imposed by certain Arab nations because of a Rift Valley Fever outbreak in Somalia.[56]

In September 2000, Saudi Arabia and other Gulf States imposed a crippling ban on livestock from Somalia because of reports of an outbreak of Rift Valley Fever ("RVF"), a virulent hemorrhagic disease which can be transmitted to humans, and can, in rare cases, lead to death.[57] The ban affected a large percentage of the population as livestock generates substantial employment and export income.[58] In general, the normal procedure to address a ban imposed for health reasons is to request the national health authority to perform certain controls and adopt specific measures, if possible,

[56] *See* UN Office for the Coordination of Humanitarian Affairs, *Consolidated Inter-Agency Appeal for Somalia Appeal 2002* (26 Nov. 2001) *http://www.reliefweb.int/w/rwb.nsf/* 9ca65951ee22658ec125663300408599/57189af43585c894c1256b0e00547926 (last visited 3 Sept. 2009).

[57] *See* Gulf livestock ban hits Africa, BBC News, 25 Sept. 2000, *available at*: http://news.bbc.co.uk/2/hi/africa/941725.stm (last visited 9 Nov. 2009).

[58] UNDP, *Support to the Somali Meat Export Sector Project (2007–2008)*, http://www.so.undp.org/index.php/Support-to-the-Somali-meat-export-sector-project.html (last visited 3 Sept. 2009) (stating that the livestock sector provides employment and livelihoods employment for about 55% of the Somali population and would normally account for 80% of the export income).

including vaccinations, and ultimately, having satisfied all the required criteria, to officially certify that the product is safe for export.[59] In Somalia, however, there was no such national certification authority and none could be created.

This issue was addressed specifically by the United Nations and NGOs within the Somalia Aid Coordination Body.[60] Despite little evidence of the presence of the virus in Somalia, in the absence of a central veterinary authority who could officially certify the absence of pathogens in the livestock, the only possible action was limited to negotiations and gathering alternative scientific evidence. The UNDP and the Food and Agriculture Organization ("FAO") sponsored exhaustive and extensive research, which concluded that there was no presence of RVF in the Somali stock. FAO published a report by an expert stating that "given the fact that there had been no reported cases of RVF outbreak anywhere in the Horn of Africa recently, the chance of an animal infected with RVF virus entering the human food chain in the abattoirs in Somalia must be practically insignificant at present."[61] Similarly, a report of the USAID-sponsored Famine Early Warning System program concluded that "after tests on thousands of animals were analyzed by the best laboratories, the investigation showed persuasively that Somali livestock was free of life-threatening diseases, including RVF."[62] Regardless of the scientific evidence, however, there was not much the international community could do. All official venues, including WHO and WTO, were closed; and the only possible reaction of the SACB and other concerned parties was to hold and facilitate informal negotiations with the Arab governments.

Saudi Arabia, the most significant importer of Somali meat, lifted the ban only recently, after nine years.[63]

This case poignantly demonstrates the limitations that an external entity encounters in dealing with specific health related issues without a specific mandate. In this case, the inability to perform obligations related to public

---

[59] *See*, for the example, the United Kingdom and the EU in the recent outbreak of foot-and-mouth disease.

[60] The issue was discussed at the levels of the Sectoral Steering Committee and Sectoral Committee and in the Consultative Committee, Somalia Aid Coordination Body Handbook (2001).

[61] *Mission Report on Rift Valley Fever,* IRIN News, 7 Mar. 2001, *available at:* http://www.irinnews.org/Report.aspx?Reportid=18989 (last visited 3 Sept. 2009).

[62] *See* UNDP, *Support to the Somali Meat Export Sector Project*, http://www.so.undp.org/index.php/Support-to-the-Somali-meat-export (last visited 3 Sept. 2009) (UNDP confirming the continued existence of the ban).

[63] *Saudi lifts Somali livestock ban*, BBC News, 5 Nov. 2009, *available at*: http://news.bbc.co.uk/2/hi/africa/8345370.stm (last visited 9 Nov. 2009). Other countries had lifted the ban earlier, *see SOMALIA: Ban on chilled meat officially lifted*, IRIN News, 9 Apr. 2001, http://www.irinnews.org/Report.aspx?Reportid=19976 (last visited 3 Sept. 2009).

health has important trade repercussions. The SACB has very limited space to maneuver and is limited to simple diplomatic and negotiating tools. This is not an example of a stalled international reaction, but a demonstration of the limitations imposed by the absence of clear guidelines on State failure. In public health matters, the performance of international obligations imposed by one country can scarcely be substituted by an alternative actor.

Interestingly, as a result of the ban and in effort to minimize its future impact on Somalis' livelihoods, UNDP initiated, in 2007–2008, a development program that will result in the development of a 'Quality Assurance' system consistent with international standards and the requirements of importing countries.[64]

4. *Economic and Business Relations*

With the collapse of the central government, the entire banking and financial systems stopped working. These encompass all international investments and commercial transactions, bank guarantees and circulation of currency outside Somalia. Most Somalis rely heavily on the income of relatives abroad. The closure of all international financial institutions significantly impacted Somalis' available assets and potential sources of revenues.

Similarly to the sensitive defense domain, the equally delicate field of commercial transactions left little space for clear international interventions to maneuver. However, it left space for private actors to operate. The Somali Diaspora, a significant percentage of the population, bypassed this impediment and relied on a traditional system of wire transfer services, *al-Barakaat*, – a money remitter – to send around 30% of their income to relatives back home.[65] The *al-Baraakat* system is also used to guarantee other commercial transactions, like imports of goods, between Somalia and other Arab States. However, in 2001, after the terrorist attacks of 11 September in the U.S., the U.S. froze the assets of *al-Barakaat* and closed all of its offices in the U.S. The U.S. accused it of money laundering on behalf of al-Qaeda, a charge

[64] *Id.* (stating the expected outputs of the project include a "Quality Assurance (QA) system, consistent with importing country requirements and international standards, designed and implemented, including the minimum legal, regulatory institutional requirements necessary to make it operational and institutionalized.")

[65] Hassan Barise, *Somali company 'not terrorist'*, BBC News, 8 Nov. 2001, *available at* http://news.bbc.co.uk/hi/english/world/africa/newsid_1645000/1645073.stm (last visited 3 Sept. 2009).

al-Barakaat officials have denied.[66] This meant a sharp decline in *al-Barakaat* business.[67] The ban was also then implemented by the EU. Appeals to these measures are still running through the Courts.[68]

In many aspects the *al-Baraakat* system bypassed international regulations and requirements and provided Somalis with a necessary service. Of course, this was not a flawless system, but it showed the elasticity and volatility of some international obligations. While the international community stalled, Somalis' entrepreneurship took control, circumventing international obligations and using financial institutions to their benefit. This also stresses the need to address the lacuna found in international law on the matter of international obligations.

5. *Diplomatic and Representative Functions*

Predictably, most Somali embassies were closed at the beginning of the civil war and ambassadors were recalled.[69] The seat of the State of Somalia has remained empty in most of the meetings of international and multilateral organizations for many years, as there was no authority that could issue the credentials necessary to be admitted to these meetings.[70]

However, Somalia has remained a member of the United Nations[71] and other international organizations, albeit without paying its dues.[72]

Interestingly, since 2004, moreover, the seat in the General Assembly has been occupied by a representative of the Transitional Government, and

---

[66] National Commission on Terrorist Attacks Upon the United States, Monograph on Terrorist Financing 67–86 (2004), *available at:* http://govinfo.library.unt.edu/911/staff_statements/index.htm.

[67] Ishbel Matheson, *Somalia Pushed to brink of disaster*, BBC News, 28 Dec. 2001, *available at:* http://news.bbc.co.uk/2/hi/africa/1732101.stm (last visited 12 Sept. 2009).

[68] For background, including a brief overview of litigation, *see* http://www.statewatch.org/terrorlists/listslatest.html.

[69] Some Embassies, for example in Egypt, are still open, but they have no official recognition in the country.

[70] However, when the TNG was formed in August 2001, the newly appointed Somali President participated to the U.N. Millennium Summit. This was possible because credentials of President of States and Prime Ministers are not checked by the U.N. Credential Committee.

[71] The list of members of the United Nations indicates that Somalia has been a member since 1960. United Nations, Member States, http://www.un.org/en/members/index.shtml (last visited 3 Sept. 2009).

[72] No payments were received by the United Nations from Somalia between 2000–2006. Office of the Spokesman for the Secretary-General, U.N., Payments to the U.N. Regular Budget for 2006, http://www.un.org/News/ossg/honroll.html (last visited 3 Sept. 2009).

Somalia has been elected as one of members of the U.N. Economic and Social Council ("ECOSOC").[73] Further, Somalia now maintains a mission to the United Nations in New York.[74]

However, in terms of standing in international organizations, it is clear that Somalia has no representation. Moreover, there are no embassies or consulates that can assist Somalis citizens abroad, renew passports, or issue visas and identity and other consular documents. This situation also has repercussions for Somalis wishing to emigrates or relocate through United Nations relocation programs.[75]

In the late 1990s, during the height of the collapse, in some instances, specific Agencies of the United Nations acted on behalf of government officials and sponsored participation to UN conferences and meetings, together with Somalia representatives of civil society. For example, a group of Somali women participated to the 1995 World Conference on Women organized by the UN in Beijing. Similarly, UNESCO represented Somalia in the 2001 Dakar + 5 meeting "Education for All."

Thus, in the matter of international and diplomatic representation, the State of Somalia is still considered a member. However, the exercise of that membership is limited.

* * *

In sum, the example of Somalia shows that, although some actions can be taken on behalf of a government that is too weak to perform its own obligations towards the international community, these actions are limited and insufficient.

In matters that directly impact the safety of international public order, the international community has been capable of united action. This has been demonstrated through the management of Somalia airspace. Further, the unique decision of the Security Council to allow for the use of force to fight piracy in territorial waters of Somalia shows the willingness to act to ensure

[73] The list of members is available on the UN website. Press Release, United Nations, U.N. Doc. ORG/1479 (17 Jan. 2007), *available at*: http://www.un.org/News/Press/docs//2007/org1479.doc.htm.

[74] *See* the website of the Somali Permanent Mission in New York, http://www.un.int/wcm/content/site/somalia/ (last visited 3 Sept. 2009).

[75] The lack of recognized authority in Somalia means that no administration can legitimately issue travel documents for Somali citizens. This situation implies that Somalis cannot have valid travel documents, apply for visas, or certify identity. This situation entails obvious consequences for foreign immigration authorities that need to identify Somali nationals. On the issue of travel documents, UNDP held a workshop in Fall 2000 with immigration officials from several countries, but very little can be done in the absence of a central authority empowered to certify identities.

maritime safety. A delicate balance between the general interest of the international community and of the State is at issue.

However, in most instances, the international community and its members have been unable to tackle the problems arising from the inability of the Somali State to act. For example, no policy exists to comprehensively deal with health and environmental emergencies. Somalis are likewise cut off from any official trade, banking or postal services.

Moreover, Somalia is still one of the poorest, most unstable and most violent countries in the world. Life expectancy is low, infant mortality high, and entire generations have received no education or healthcare at all.

The incapacity of the international community to properly confront the problems that arise from state failure originates from its inability to properly conceptualize it. International law has, in fact, been oblivious to the existence of failing and failed States. In the next chapter, I will define and assess State failure in international law. This will lead to a proper appraisal of the instruments available to the international community to efficiently confront State failure.

Chapter Four

What is State Failure? The Inadequacy of Existing Legal Techniques to Deal with Failed States

In the previous chapters, I demonstrated that the international community is ill-prepared to deal with the incapability of a State to perform the obligations owed to it and to other subjects. Though some tools exist, they are mostly *ad hoc* and cannot properly address the dilemmas of State failure. This is because State failure is a complex phenomenon, yet a phenomenon that is not recognized by international law.

As discussed in this study, State failure is best defined as the incapacity of a State to perform its obligations towards its citizens and towards the international community in general. Failed States are characterized by an implosion of States' structures, which results in the incapability of governmental authorities to perform their functions, including providing security, respecting the rule of law, exercising control, supplying education and health services, and maintaining economic and structural infrastructures. In fact, State failure can be seen as a *condition* in which the State is unable to provide political goods to its citizens and to the international community. These goods include security, border control, political structure, physical infrastructures, a judicial system, education and healthcare, and commercial and banking systems.

State failure is multifaceted and can be depicted as a continuum, as the State becomes progressively less capable of performing its functions and becomes more and more 'failed.' Complete State collapse is the ultimate, and rare, result, while different stages of State failure can be encountered along the continuum. State failure is not uncommon and examples exist in today's world. As discussed in the previous chapter, these include Somalia, which has been without a government for more than a decade, the Democratic Republic of Congo, which was shattered by internal rivalries and the presence of regional troops fighting for its mineral resources, and Sudan and Afghanistan, whose governments only control parts of their territory.

Curiously, however, a rigorous analysis of the legal implications, significance and consequences of State failure is missing. In fact, because definitions of what constitute a 'failed State' are, in general, informed by the analysts' definition of the State and of their own view over the functions and role of the State, international law has not recognized and named the phenomenon of State failure. This is because international law focuses on the creation and dissolution of a State, but has not focused on the evolution, changes or temporary failures that may occur after a State is created.

State failure implies the possibility that a State cannot – rather than does not want to – perform its functions, even after its statehood is recognized. Moreover, State failure implies a gradation of sovereign capacity, while for international lawyers sovereignty either exists or it does not. If at all, international law views failed States as States with ineffective governments.[1] However, failed States are not just failed governments. Their failure is normally long-lasting and encompasses several to all the functions of the State, not solely their governmental functions. State failure includes not only an ineffective government, but affects the bases and entire structure of the State, including its population, territory and capacity to perform international and internal obligations.

Historically, State collapse is the product of several key events. Although it is not possible to single out one cause of State failure, several interlinked causes exist, both endogenous and exogenous to the State. Endogenous causes include corruption, structural weaknesses, and misadministration. Exogenous causes include macroeconomic and political policies, foreign interventions, either in support of those in power or opposition groups, the decline of foreign financial and political support, and generally the processes of modernization "which encourage[s] social and geographical mobility but [is] not counterbalanced by nation-building processes capable of placing the State on a firm foundation."[2]

Three conditions are also generally associated with State failure: the end of the Cold War, ethnic unbalances and the heritage of the colonial regimes.[3]

[1] For example, Ralph Wilde affirms that failed States denote situations in which "the governmental infrastructure in a State has broken down to a considerable degree." R. Wilde, *The Skewed Responsibility Narrative of the Failed States Concept*, 9 ILSA J. Int'l & Comp. L. 425, 426 (2003).

[2] D. Thürer, *The "Failed State" and International Law*, Int'l Comm. of the Red Cross (31 Dec. 1999), *available at*: http://www.globalpolicy.org/component/content/article/173/30464.html.

[3] *See, inter alia,* William Reno, *Shadow States and the Political Economy of Civil Wars*, Greed and Grievance, Economic Agendas in Civil Wars 43 (M. Berdal and D.M. Malone eds., 2000); W. Reno, Warlord Politics and African States (1998); Making States Work: State Failure and the Crisis of Governance (S. Chesterman, M. Ignatieff, and R. Thakur eds., 2005); R. Joseph, J. Herbst, *Correspondence: Responding to State failure in Africa*, 22 Int'l Security 175, 175–184 (1997); C. Tilly, *Where Do Rights Come From?*, Democracy, Revolution and History 55–72 (Theda Skocpol ed., 1995);

First, State failure may be considered a typical post-Cold War phenomenon. In fact, the end of the cold war brought about a major change in the dynamics of international relations, which resulted in a shift of political alliances among States and regions. As a result of the end of the Cold War, super powers became less inclined to support weak regimes and declined their economical and military support to former allies in Africa and Asia. As financial assistance and political support given to politicians dried up, governments became too weak to maintain power. Historically, a wave of failed States coincided with the end of the Cold War. Somalia and the Congo, the main examples of State failure, were heavily supported both financially and politically by both super powers at different stages. Their regimes collapsed in the early 1990s, shortly after the end of the cold war.

However, although State failure is undoubtedly connected to the end of the Cold War, the seed that grew into State failure was planted before, when State's rulers began to personalize and pray on State's resources, while disenfranchising and isolating the majority of the population. Hence, the end of the Cold War exposed a flawed governance system that already existed. The end of the Cold War, therefore, only took away the economic and political resources that sustained a system that was already pathogenic.

The issue of ethnic differences is also often considered an important source of State weakness and, hence, failure. Ethnic tension is an important structural reason for internal conflict that weakens the institutions of governance and uses up valuable human and financial resources. However, empirical research shows that although the failure of States in the beginning of the 1990s coincided with an increase in the frequency of civil war, there is no direct link between civil war and ethnic tensions, and thus between ethnic differences and State collapse.[4]

J. Herbst, States and Power in Africa, Comparative Lessons in Authority and Control (2000); Christopher Clapham, *Failed States and Non States in the International Order* (paper presented at the Conference on Failed States, 7 April 2000, Florence, Purdue University); I. William Zartman, *Introduction: Posing the Problem of State Collapse*, Collapsed States, The Disintegration and Restoration of Legitimate Authority (I.W. Zartman ed., 1995).

[4] To reach this conclusion, Fearson and Laitin implement a three-step approach. They first showed that there was no direct connection between the end of the Cold War and the increase in civil wars. They analyzed 127 post-WWII internal conflicts and concluded that, contrary to common opinion, "the prevalence of civil war in the 1990s was *not* due to the end of the Cold War and associated changes in the international system. The current level of about one in six countries had already been reached prior to the breakup of the Soviet Union and resulted from a steady, gradual accumulation of civil conflicts that began immediately after World War II." They then demonstrated that it was not true that a greater degree of ethnic or religious diversity could, by itself, make a country more prone to civil

Colonialism is another historical element considered a root cause of State failure, as often State failure occurs in former colonized territories, mostly in Africa. Two main reasons are often given to explain this position: first, colonization often resulted in the imposition of governmental structures that were alien to the political systems that existed prior to colonization. Empirical evidence, however, provides limited support to this argument, as there are no common governmental characters in failed States.[5] A second negative legacy of colonization was the creation of artificial inter-state boundaries, which was based upon colonial boundaries that did not respect ethnic alliances or geographical characters.[6] Problematic boundaries have been a recurrent source of conflict in post colonial countries, and several failed States have unsettled borders, including Somalia and the DRC.

The narrative of State failure as colonial heritage has also been used in legal discourse. Ruth Gordon defines State failure as a 'neo-colonial' notion.[7] Ralph Wilde affirms that the way the term is used "suggests exclusive responsibility on the part of the State and its people for the breakdown of gover-

war. Third, they demonstrated that the degree of grievances by ethnic minorities had no causal link to civil war. *See* James D. Fearon and David D. Laitin, *Ethnicity, Insurgency, and Civil War*, 97 Am. Pol. Sci. Rev. 75, 75–90 (2003).

[5] Zartman suggests that State collapse in independent Africa is not a postcolonial phenomenon, as "no common theme or characteristic runs through the cases of collapse that would indicate that collapse was the result either of the same 'Western-style' malfunction in the state or of particularly badly adapted Western institutions. While parliaments, parties, and bureaucracies in Africa seem to have difficulties in living up to Montesquieu's, Madison's, or Weber's standards, these shortcomings do not seem to be the key to collapse; nor do these institutions function any better in noncollapsing states in Africa. Nonetheless, it can be said that the poor performances of their functions – representation, interest articulation, output efficiency – are broad causes of state collapse, whether performed by the 'proper' institution (in Western terms) or by a surrogate more suited to African conditions." I. William Zartman, *Introduction: Posing the Problem of State Collapse*, Collapsed States, The Disintegration and Restoration of Legitimate Authority 6 (1. William Zartman ed., 1995). Post colonialism was an enabling factor because it recognized elites that dismissed western style democracy. Moreover, the colonial legacy created and empowered phony elites and destroyed the traditional forms of social structure of control, which existed before colonization, without creating new viable ones. Their governments are often deficient in the political will, institutional authority, and organized power to protect human rights or provide socioeconomic welfare. *See*, *inter alia*, William Reno, Warlord Politics and African States (1998), David Campbell, National Deconstruction, Violence, Identity, and Justice in Bosnia (1998), and Robert H. Jackson, Quasi-states: Sovereignty, International Relations and the Third World (1990).

[6] J. Herbst, *Responding to State Failure,* 21 Int'l Sec. 120, 120–144 (1996–1997).

[7] Ruth Gordon, *Saving Failed States: Sometimes A Neocolonialist Notion*, 12 Am. U. J. Int'l L. & Pol'y 903, 914 (1997).

nance."[8] Helman and Ratner talk about "saving failed States."[9] However, I argue that these descriptions are flawed because they confine themselves to describing how failed States are regarded (by the viewers themselves), rather than searching for the legal consequences of State failure and the role that the international legal community can play in making them viable again. It is incorrect to apply value judgments to State failure. It is much more useful to understand the phenomenon politically and legally and seek solutions.

In the following sections, I will assess this situation and will argue that failed States are characterized by their incapacity to fulfill their social contract and by their inability to be recognized as having a specific character in international law.

1. *State Failure as Unfulfilled Social Contract*

State failure has been defined in political theory as a State that is unable to fulfill its social contract.[10] As briefly discussed above, in the introduction of this chapter, this is a most fitting definition.

In essence, the theory suggests that the existence of States is founded on a tacit, mutually beneficial 'contract' between the rulers and the ruled, based on rights and obligations that each party to the contract agreed to perform. Thus, while the ruled parties agreed to be ruled, pay taxes and obey the law, the rulers provide in exchange several political goods, including security, education and health care systems, and physical infrastructures.[11]

---

[8] R. Wilde, The Skewed Responsibility Narrative of the Failed States Concept, 9 ILSA J. Int'l & Comp. L. 425, 426 (2003).

[9] Gerald B. Helman and Steven R. Ratner, *Saving Failed States*, 89 Foreign Pol'y 1, 3 (1992).

[10] For the main proponents of the theory of the state as social contract *see* Thomas Hobbes, Leviathan (1851), John Locke, Two Treatises of Government and A Letter Concerning Toleration (1690), Jean-Jacques Rousseau, Le Contrat Social (1762).

[11] An alternative view describes the State as the legitimate holder of the monopoly of violence in a given territory. This view, however, is too limiting and cannot encompass the complexities highlighted by State failure. *See* Max Weber: The Theory of Social and Economic Organization (Talcott Parsons ed., 1947). Weber's characterization of the State as the holder of the monopoly of violence has informed a specific understanding of failed states. In particular, Weber's views are reflected in Ignatieff's approach to State failure. Ignatieff affirms that failing States are characterized by "an inability to maintain a monopoly of the internal means of violence." In application of this approach, Ignatieff states that State failure is first and foremost the result of the colonial legacy and of the mismanagements of the governments that took control in the post colonial era. Other enabling elements for state failure include outside interference, poverty, corruption, planning choices and ideological doctrines. The consequences of a State's inability to secure and maintain order are not

Transposed to State failure, this theory suggests that State collapse means that the State cannot perform its side of the contract and thus State's functions are no longer performed.[12] In particular, in failed States:

> As the decision-making center of the government, the State is paralyzed and inoperative: laws are not made, order is not preserved, and societal cohesion is not enhanced. As a symbol of identity, it has lost its power of conferring a name on its people and a meaning to their social action. As a territory, it no longer

limited to the failing State, but become serious for the entire surrounding region. In fact, failing States can 'metastasize' and spread their problems to their neighbors. Therefore, in his article, Ignatieff identifies specific regional spots around failed States. He singles out nine 'bad neighborhoods' which include twenty-two failing and failed States (These are: 1. Latin America: Colombia, Ecuador, Peru; 2. South Balkans: Macedonia, Montenegro, Kosovo; 3. South Caucasus: Georgia, Ossentian, Azerbaijan, Nagorno, Karabakh; 4. West Africa: Liberia, Sierra Leone; 5. Central Africa: Congo; 6. Southern Africa: Angola; 7. East Africa: Sudan, Somalia; 8. South Asia: Sri Lanka; 9. Central Asia: Pakistan, Afghanistan, Uzbekistan, Tajikistan.) These regional clusters witness grave human rights violations, including forced population displacement, ethnic and religious violence, banditry, enslavement and forced recruitment of child soldiers. *See* M. Ignatieff, *Intervention and State failure*, DISSENT 115–119 (2002); MAKING STATES WORK: STATE FAILURE AND THE CRISES OF GOVERNANCE (M. Chestemann, M. Ignatieff, R. Thakur eds., 2005) The loss of the monopoly of violence by the State is a key characteristic of failed States. However, the application of the definition includes states that have not failed, but are in midst of serious civil unrest, like Sri Lanka and Colombia. Moreover, a definition based on Weber's theory might not be sufficiently focused. Explanations of State failure are only relevant in so far as they help identify and clarify the phenomenon in its uniqueness. A definition based on the concept of monopoly of violence does not encapsulate the unique elements of the phenomenon of State failure. The limitations of the view of State failure entranced on the monopoly-of-power theory are evident in the work of the State Failure Task Force, created by Vice-President Al Gore in 1994, which embraced Ignatieff's view of State failure. The Task Force was mandated to identify measurable characteristics of countries that went through failure, with the goal of extrapolating statistically significant data to forecast State failure. The Task Force tried to identify the underlying or structural conditions associated with State failure and considered a broad definition of State failure that included a wider range of civil conflicts, political crises, and massive human-rights violations, typically associated with state breakdown. This resulted in the inclusion 114 state-failure events between 1995 and 1998. *See* STATE FAILURE TASK FORCE REPORT: PHASE III FINDINGS (30 Sept. 2000). A definition of State failure founded on the loss of monopoly of violence by a national government, however, is not sufficiently precise and provides limited understanding of the unique features of State failure. It includes too many events that do not result in State failure but remain limited to political unrest. Moreover, such a definition is also not targeted enough. The distinguishing characteristic of State failure lays in the implosion of government institutions and the inability of any group to effectively replace the government, not merely its inability to hold on the use of power.

[12] I. William Zartman, *Introduction: Posing the Problem of State Collapse*, COLLAPSED STATES, THE DISINTEGRATION AND RESTORATION OF LEGITIMATE AUTHORITY 1 (I.W. Zartman ed., 1995).

> assures security and provisionment by a central sovereign organization. As the authoritative political institution, it has lost its legitimacy, which is therefore up for grabs, and so has lost its right to command and conduct public affairs. As a system of socioeconomic organization, its functional balance of inputs and outputs is destroyed; it no longer receives supports from, nor exercise controls over its people, and it no longer is even the target of demands, because its people know that it is incapable of providing supplies. No longer functioning, with neither traditional nor charismatic nor institutional sources of legitimacy, it has lost the right to rule.[13]

As such, in failed States it is not only governmental functions that are at bay, societal infrastructures also break down, and the very foundations of society have collapsed.[14] In fact, the State becomes utterly unable to deliver any political goods to its people.[15]

State failure, therefore, is not univocal. Rather, it is a long and multi-shaped process, in which States may go through different stages of 'failure' and which can encompass diverse public functions, can take more or less time, and may cover parts or the entirety of a State territory.

State failure is not a static phenomenon, but a continuum from strong to weak States in which it is possible to identify weak or fragile States, failing States, failed States, and finally the extreme version: collapsed States. Collapsed States present a total vacuum of authority.[16] Thus, although nation States exist to deliver political goods to their citizens – including security, education, health services, environmental protection infrastructures and administration systems – failed States are "no longer able or willing to perform the job of a nation-State in the modern world."[17]

State failure occurs "when violence cascades into all-out internal war, when standards of living massively deteriorate, when the infrastructure of ordinary life decays, and when the greed of rulers overwhelms their responsibilities to better their people and their surroundings."[18]

---

[13] I. William Zartman, *Introduction: Posing the Problem of State Collapse*, Collapsed States, The Disintegration and Restoration of Legitimate Authority 1, 5 (I.W. Zartman ed., 1995) (internal citation omitted).

[14] *Id.* at 1–9. Zartman argues that State collapse is also characterized by a loss of control over both political and economic systems. Hence, the informal economy grows at the expense of the formal economic system, while the peripheral regions of the State strengthen their economic links to neighboring countries. Similarly, the political space is also taken over by neighboring states, which become more and more involved in the state's affairs.

[15] Robert I. Rotberg, *The New Nature of Nation-State Failure*, 25 The Wash. Q. 85 (Summer 2002).

[16] *Id.* at 90.

[17] *Id.* at 87.

[18] *Id.* at 86.

The inability of the State to provide goods to its citizenry may be translated into a specific hierarchy of political goods that a failed State cannot deliver. The failure to provide specific goods can also be used to assess a modern State as being strong, weak or failed. The principle function of a State is to provide the good of internal security, and to eliminate external and domestic threats, to prevent crime and ensure stability. Other specific political goods that failed States cannot deliver include: a functioning justice and dispute resolution system; access to a free and open political process; a system of healthcare and education; physical infrastructure; and functioning commercial, financial and banking systems.[19]

As a consequence of the inability to provide political goods, failed and collapsed States are distinguished by a series of unique elements, including frictions between communities, incapability of controlling borders and territory, ethnic and other inter-communal hostilities, predatory behavior by the elites, growth of criminal violence, flawed institution, absence of democratic debate, deterioration of infrastructures, privatization of health and education systems, rise in corruption and decline in income levels. Another important distinguishing feature of State failure is the enduring character of violence that is peculiar to them.[20]

Based on the criteria identified above, the more poorly States perform in each of the criterion, the closer they get to failure.

By most accounts, it is possible to identify seven failed States in the last twenty years alone: Afghanistan, Angola, Burundi, the DRC, Liberia, Sierra Leone and the Sudan. These States are still mostly all weak or failed, with the possible exceptions of Angola, Burundi and Liberia, which are on their way to recovery.[21]

---

[19] Robert I. Rotberg, *Failed States, Collapsed States, Weak-States: Causes and Indicators,* State Failure and State Weakness in a Time of Terror 3–4 (Robert I. Rotberg ed., 2003).

[20] Robert I. Rotberg, *The New Nature of Nation-State Failure,* The Wash. Q. 85–87 (Summer 2002). *See,* also Robert I. Rotberg, Failed States, Collapsed States, Weak-States: causes and indicators 5–10 (Robert I. Rotberg ed., 2003).

[21] Robert I. Rotberg, *Failed States, Collapsed States, Weak-States: Causes and Indicators,* State Failure and State Weakness in a Time of Terror 9–10 (Robert I. Rotberg ed., 2003). Zartman also espouses a definition of failed States based on the collapse of the social contract. However, he does not distinguish between different kinds of State failure. He only identifies collapsed States as a general category, without further divisions based on the degree of failure. However, he identifies a useful pattern of State failure based on political changes that occurred around the time of failure. His work is concentrated in Africa, where he distinguishes two past waves of State failure and one current one. Leaving aside the particular case of Congo, which became independent as an already weak and failing State, the first wave of State failure began about twenty years after these States achieved

State collapse is an extreme case of State failure and occurs when

> a regime – which is often ruled by the independence generation of civilians – after being in power for a long time wears out its ability to satisfy the demands of the various groups in society. Resources dry up, either for exogenous reasons or through internal waste and corruption (selective misallocation). Social and ethnic groups feel neglected and alienated, causing an atmosphere of dissatisfaction and opposition which in turn draws increased repression and use of the police and military to keep order.[22]

In today's world, only one State is completely collapsed, and political goods are only available at the private or *ad hoc* level: Somalia.

To conclude, failed States are characterized by their inability to fulfill their social contract with their citizens and the international community. As the social contract forms the basis of their legitimacy to rule, the impossibility to fulfill the contract undermines their power and authority.

Failing States can be more or less failed: they can be incapable of providing all political goods or only some of them. Similarly, there is a continuum between failed and collapsed States: States that cannot provide any of the political goods for a long period of time become collapsed. The definition of State failure also includes a temporal connotation. State failure can be a temporary or a prolonged situation. Further, the theory of State failure as a consequence of the disintegration of the social contract must include the failure to provide international political goods as well. The classification of political goods as goods that must be delivered to different constituencies is particularly relevant and will be used throughout the remaining chapters of

independence, and when they the original nationalist generation. Chad, Uganda and Ghana at the end of the 1970's and beginning of 1980s all belong to this first wave. In Chad, the guerrilla had succeeded in destroying the center of the State and had destroyed the State's bureaucracy, together with executive, legislative and judicial powers before dividing into factions and turning against each other in civil war. In Uganda, the opposition could not fill the vacuum left by the departure of the delegitimized power of Idi Amin. The second wave occurred approximately ten years after the first one. Similar to the first wave, "the authoritarian successors of the nationalist generation were overthrown by a new successor regime that can destroy but not replace, and government, and government functioning and legitimacy have receded." Liberia and Somalia are the key examples of this second wave. In Somalia, the archetypical example of failed State, the end of the dictatorship of Siad Barre was followed by a situation of confusion where no faction was capable of acquiring full power. Finally, the current wave includes: Sudan, Rwanda, Burundi, Zaire, and those countries still collapsed from previous waves. *See* I. William Zartman, *Introduction: Posing the Problem of State Collapse*, Collapsed States, The Disintegration and Restoration of Legitimate Authority 3 (I.W. Zartman ed., 1995).

[22] I. William Zartman, *Introduction: Posing the Problem of State Collapse*, Collapsed States, The Disintegration and Restoration of Legitimate Authority 8 (I.W. Zartman ed., 1995).

this book to identify alternative ways to provide the missing goods, particularly health and environmental safety.

2. *The Problem of Statehood (Easy to Give, not to Take Away)*

Legally, State failure epitomizes a fallacy in international law, as failed and failing States continue to be considered fully fledged sovereign and are required to fulfill their many obligations towards other States and the international community in general. In fact, while international law carefully considers the creation and dissolution of States, it has not recognized their evolution while in existence. In the paragraphs below, I will discuss the legal absurdity found in the notion that States can easily gain statehood, whereas there is no method to assess changes in the constitutive elements of a State, and thus adjust the standing and responsibilities of States when they start to fail. Failed States are not dissolved because of their failure, and their status in international law is not altered. In fact "once in the club [of States], the rules by which admission was tested – and that always with a degree of flexibility – become less important."[23]

2.1. *State Failure does not Dissolve States*

It is beyond doubt that State failure does not extinguish statehood, once it is given, and, in fact, failed States do not become extinct because of their inability to 'behave like States.' Under classic international law, there are only a finite number of ways in which statehood can become extinct.[24] These include State incorporation into another State, State annexation into another State or fusion of the State into one or more other States. States can also become extinct because of the dismemberment of the State into smaller units.[25] For example, at the end of the Cold War, several States ceased to exist and others were created. These include the German Democratic Republic, which ceased to exist in 1990, when it merged into the Federal Republic of Germany. Czechoslovakia also ceased to exist in 1993, when it dissolved

---

[23] Higgins, Problems and Process, International Law and How We Use It 41 (1999). In fact, as Henkin concludes "the system knows a State when it sees one." L. Henkin, *International Law: Politics, Values and Functions, General Course on Public International Law*, 216 Recueil des Cours 29 (1989).

[24] Oppenheim's International Law 206–208 (Sir Arthur Watts & Sir Robert Jennings eds., 9th ed. 1992).

[25] *See* U. Fastenrath, *State, Extinction*, in Encyclopedia of Public International Law (Rudolph Bernhardt ed. 2000).

and was divided into two new States, the Czech Republic and the Republic of Slovakia.[26] Similarly, when the Union of the Soviet Socialist Republics collapsed, the Russian Federation was created as the successor State, along with several other new States. By contrast, the process that brought to the extinction of Yugoslavia and the creation of its successor States was much more complex.[27]

State failure – as defined above – does not describe any of these processes of State extinction. A failed State does not merge with another State, or it is not annexed or incorporated into another State. Similarly, failed States do not dismember into several smaller States. Failed and failing States just become unable to behave like States.

2.2. *Statehood is not Altered by Changes to the Constitutive Elements of a State*

State failure does not seem to alter the identity of a State, once it has been recognized by the international community. In fact, under contemporary international law, State failure does not modify the tenets of statehood.

The 1933 Montevideo Convention on the Rights and Duties of States highlight the commonly agreed definition of what is a State. Article 1 of the Convention provides that

> The State as a person in international law should possess the following qualifications: A permanent population; A defined territory; A Government; and Capacity to enter into relations with other States.[28]

President Higgins confirms that, in a rapidly changing world "the definition of 'a State' has remained virtually unchanged and continues to be well described by the traditional provisions of the Montevideo Convention on the Rights and Duties of States."[29] Similarly, Professor Shaw also concludes that this definition is the "most widely accepted formulation of the criteria of statehood."[30]

---

[26] Malcom N. Shaw, International Law 186–187 (5th ed. 2003).

[27] Conference on Yugoslavia Arbitration Commission, *Opinions on Questions Arising From the Dissolution of Yugolavia*, 31 I.L.M. 1488 (1992) (with an Introductory Note by Maurizio Ragazzi).

[28] Montevideo Convention on the Rights and Duties of States of 26 Dec. 1933, 165 League of Nations Treaty Series 19 (1933).

[29] Rosalyn Higgins, Problems and Process, International Law and How We Use It 39 (1994).

[30] Malcom N. Shaw, International Law 178 (5th ed., 2003). Moreover, the validity of the Montevideo criteria have been confirmed and restated most recently by the Conference on Yugoslavia, Arbitration Committee, which concluded in its First Opinion that "the State is commonly defined as a community which consists of a territory and a population subject

This agreed-upon definition of statehood is analyzed below to assess the impact of State failure on States.

2.2.1. *Permanent Population*
The first requirement for the existence of a State is that it possesses a permanent population, i.e. a community of people living in a given area. However, the details of how and what defines a population are unclear. In fact, an analysis of the definition demonstrates that the elements of a 'permanent population' are general. No detailed requirements exist: there is no minimum requirement for the number of people in the territory needed to inhabit a certain territory or their permanency in that territory for that territory to qualify as a State.

An analysis of the process of admission to the United Nations of new members provides the best guidance to study the requirement of a permanent population. In fact, although the criterion of permanent population has not been specifically analyzed as a requirement for State recognition, the issue was addressed when the requirements for membership to the United Nations was examined.[31]

Article 4 of the U.N. Charter[32] states that membership to the organization is open to States only, without specifying the size of their population.[33] The minimum standard to fulfill the requirement of having a 'permanent population' was assessed during the debate over the membership to the organization of microstates in the 1970's. On that occasion, several permanent members of the Security Council expressed their concern that admitting microstates to the United Nations will be equal to a practical revision of the Charter, in

---

to an organized political authority" and that "such a State is characterized by sovereignty". *See* Conference on Yugoslavia Arbitration Commission: Opinions on Questions Arising From the Dissolution of Yugolavia, 31 I.L.M. 1488, 1495 (1992).

[31] R. Higgins, The Development of International Law Through the Political Organs of the United Nations 17 (1963); *see also generally id.* at 17–42.

[32] Article 4 states: "1. Membership in the United Nations is open to all other peace-loving states which accept the obligations contained in the present Charter and, in the judgment of the Organization, are able and willing to carry out these obligations. 2. The admission of any such state to membership in the United Nations will be effected by a decision of the General Assembly upon the recommendation of the Security Council."

[33] Shaw affirms: "The existence of a permanent population is naturally required and there is no specification of a minimum number of inhabitants, as examples such as Nauru and Tuvalu demonstrate. However, one of the issues raised by the Falkland Islands conflict does relate to the question of an acceptable minimum with regards to self-determination issues, and it may be that the matter needs further clarification as there exists a number of small islands awaiting decolonisation." Malcom N. Shaw, International Law 178–179 (5th ed. 2003) (internal citation omitted).

terms of the balance of power provided by the Charter. The question was referred to a Committee of Experts. The Committee examined the situation and put forth two proposals: one by the United States supporting the proposal for an associate membership and one by the United Kingdom suggesting the voluntary renunciation of certain rights and obligations, including voting rights and financial obligations, upon admission to full membership. However, the U.N. Legal Counsel found that such arrangement would be contrary to the principle of sovereign equality and equal membership, and that an amendment of the Charter would be required. Equally, an alternative suggestion by the Legal Counsel to guarantee microstates an observer status was not retained. Eventually, the impasse was resolved and all microstates became equal members of the United Nations.[34]

As a consequence and in application of the U.N. conclusion, there are no specific requirements for a minimum population living in a State to be considered a State for U.N. membership.

Thus, population as a criterion to define a State is lenient and not well defined, and the number of people residing in a State may vary greatly. Further, changes in the number of people living in a State and their relation with the central authority, which often characterizes failed States, are not in principally capable of affecting the element of permanent population as a criterion that defines statehood.

Failed and failing States often witness major shifts in population dynamics. Often, large portions of the population migrate outside the State border, as it happened in Sudan and Somalia. Moreover, people also shift their allegiance from the central to the local level, as shown in Afghanistan and the Democratic Republic of Congo. However, neither of these changes alters the condition of 'State' when it has already been acquired.

Thus, the requirement for a permanent population as a definition of a State provides only limited assistance in appraising the status of a State that undergoes population shifts. Once recognized, States continue to exist and be part of the international community even if their population changes. As such, changes in one of the fundamental requirements of statehood do not alter the identity of the State once recognized.

Failed and failing States, therefore, continue to be considered fully-fledged States despite changes in their population, with all the obligations that follow.

---

[34] *See* Michael N. Gunter, *What Happened to The United Nations Ministate Problem?*, 71 AM. J. INT'L L. 110, 110–124 (Jan. 1977). *See also* Ginther, *Commentary to Article 4 of the UN Charter* 180–182, THE CHARTER OF THE UNITED NATIONS, A COMMENTARY (B. Simma ed., 2d ed. 2002).

2.2.2. *A Defined Territory*

The second element that defines a State is the possession of a defined territory in which a community is settled. This is a fundamental criterion as "the relevant framework [of statehood] revolves essentially around territorial effectiveness."[35] This requirement is interlinked with the requirement for a permanent population. As Brownlie observes, the criterion of permanent population "is intended to be used in association with that of territory, and connotes a stable community."[36] However, an analysis of this requirement proves that changes in territorial composition hardly alter the personality of a State.[37]

The requisite of a defined territory is particularly interesting in the analysis of State failure because failed States are characterized by porous borders and the inability of a government to exercise territorial sovereignty. In fact, the territory of failing and failed States is often controlled by several opposition groups and militias. Typically, the recognized government is only capable of controlling circumscribed areas around the capital. Examples include the DRC, whose government controled little territory outside the capital; Afghanistan where the Taliban, and not the recognized government, controlled most of the country; as well as Somalia, Sudan, Liberia and Ivory Coast.

In the context of State failure, the issue to be examined is the consequence of a modification of the element of territory on statehood. Several interesting issues regarding territorial sovereignty need to be addressed, including the loss of all or parts of the territory, the issue of undetermined borders and the occupation of territory by rebel forces.

Similarly to the criterion of a permanent population examined earlier, the requisite for a determined territory is not fully defined and is limited to requiring "a certain coherent territory effectively governed."[38] This is a formula, as Professor Crawford points out, "which demonstrates that the

---

[35] Malcolm N. Shaw, International Law 178 (5th ed. 2003).

[36] Ian Brownlie, Principles of Public International law 70 (6th ed. Dec. 2003).

[37] The State's requirement for defined territory is well defined by international practice. Famously, the Sole Arbitrator Max Huber in the *Island of Palmas Case*, stated that "sovereignty in relation to a portion of the surface of the globe is the legal condition necessary for the inclusion of such portion in the territory of any particular State." *See Island of Palmas Case* (*Netherlands/U.S.A*), 1928, 1 R.I.A.A. 829, 838. The Sole Arbitrator further stated that "the principle that continuous and peaceful display of the functions of State within a given region is a constituent element of territorial sovereignty is not only based on the conditions of the formation of independent States and their boundaries (as shown by the experience of political history) as well as on an international jurisprudence and doctrine widely accepted." *Id.* at 840.

[38] J. Crawford, The Creation of States in International Law 40 (1st ed. 1979).

requirement of territory is rather a constituent of government and independence that a separate criterion of its own."[39]

The requisite of a defined territory was examined by the United Nations in the context of the application for membership to the organization by Israel. At the time, several States contested the application on the grounds that Israel's undefined borders meant that it could not be considered a State. However, other members considered it sufficient that some territory was conferred to Israel by the General Assembly, even if certain details remained undefined. Eventually, Israel was admitted to the United Nations in 1949, although its borders were still unsettled.[40] Thus, settled borders are not a requisite of the element of 'territory' for statehood.

Moreover, there is no requirement of a minimum area for a territorial community to claim statehood. The Security Council of the United Nations considered this issue when it examined the question of admission of micro-states to the Organization (in conjunction, as we have seen *supra*-, to the question of population). No specific requirement was found, and nowadays, small island States, including Singapore, Monaco and San Marino are all recognized States and members of the United Nations.

Indeed, there is even no requirement of territorial continuity, as split territories are accepted as constitutive of statehood. For example, prior to the creation of Bangladesh in 1971, Pakistan's territory was divided on either side of India. Nowadays, the Musadam Peninsula belongs to Oman but shares territorial borders only with the United Arab Emirates and is reachable from Oman only by sea.

Hence, the requisite of a determined territory is not strict and is fulfilled even when territorial disputes exist. Moreover, even the control over a territory needs not be undisputed. Competing claims over a territory do not alter the status of a State, and a State continues to exist even if another entity has a claim over parts or the totality of its territory.[41] Likewise, a new State can come into existence even if competing claims exist over its territory.[42] As Brownlie concludes "it is clear from past practice that the existence of fully defined frontiers is not required and that what matter is the effective establishment of a political community."[43] This is a well-settled principle in international

[39] *Id.*

[40] As reported by R. Higgins, The Development of International Law Through the Political Organs of the United Nations 17–18 (1963).

[41] J. Crawford, The Creation of States in International Law 37 (1st ed. 1979); *see also id.* 38 (stating that statehood is not challenged even if the entirety of a territory is claimed by other entities, including Israel, Kuwait and Mauritania).

[42] J. Crawford, The Creation of States in International Law 37 (1st ed. 1979).

[43] Ian Brownlie, Principles of Public International law 71 (6th ed. 2003).

law. Prior to WWI, for example, Albania was recognized as a State by many countries, despite disputes over its borders. As Shaw concludes, "there is no necessity in international law for defined and settled boundaries,"[44] the central element is the existence of a particular territorial base which is the center of activities of a group of people.[45] Moreover, "although continuous in principle, sovereignty cannot be exercised in fact at every moment in every point of a territory."[46] In fact, international tribunals have accepted modest indication of *effectivité* as evidence of territorial sovereignty.[47]

In sum, the requisite for a definite territory is minimal and it only requires that a certain territorial base exists for the State to operate, no details usefully define the requirement further.

Failed and failing States are characterized by porous borders. For example, Somalia witnesses continuous incursions into its territory by Ethiopian troops. The Democratic Republic of Congo became the center of the first pan-African war with troops from Uganda, Rwanda, Zimbabwe, Angola, Namibia, Chad, and Sudan fighting for its mineral resources.[48] Moreover, competing claims often exist over parts or all of failed States' territory. For example, in Sudan, domestic rebel groups claim independence of parts of the Southern territory. However, the territorial requirement is nonetheless fulfilled, and failed and failing States continue to qualify as States as far as the criterion of a defined territory is concerned.

---

[44] Malcolm N. Shaw, International Law 179 (5th ed. 2003).

[45] Relevant case law exists. One of the most famous cases, decided in 1929, concerned a dispute between a German company and Poland. The Tribunal in the in *Deutsche Continental Gas – Gesellschaft v. Polish State* concluded that "[w]hatever may be the importance of the delimitation of boundaries, one cannot go so far as to maintain as long as this delimitation has not been legally effected the State in question cannot be considered as having any territory whatever... In order to say that a State exists... it is enough that this territory has a sufficient consistency, even tough its boundaries have not yet been accurately delimited, and that the State actually exercises independent public authority over that territory." *See Deutsche Continental Gas – Gesellschaft v. Polish State*, IX UNRIAA 36. More recently, the International Court of Justice similarly concluded in the *North Sea Continental Shelf Case*, there is "no rule that the land frontiers of a State must be fully determined and defined." *See Northsea Continental Shelf*, 1969 I.C.J. 3, 33 (20 Feb.) (citing the example of Albania and the *Monastery of St. Naoum Case* (1924), PCIJ, Series B, No. 9, 10).

[46] *Island of Palmas Case* (Netherlands/U.S.A), 1928, 1 R.I.A.A. 829, 840.

[47] In the *Legal Status of Eastern Greenland Case*, the Permanent Court of International Justice concluded that "it is impossible to read the records of the decisions in cases as to territorial sovereignty without observing that in many cases the tribunal has been satisfied with very little in the way of actual exercise of sovereign rights, provided that the other state could not make a superior claim." *Legal Status of Eastern Greenland*, 1929, 2 R.I.I.A. 829.

[48] *Armed Activities on the Territory of the Congo* (Democratic Republic of the Congo v. Uganda), 2005 I.C.J., Judgment (19 Dec. 2005).

To conclude, the scrutiny of the requisite of a determined territory as a necessary element of Statehood shows that its definition is fluid. There is no requirement for defined borders, strict control over the territory or even for the territory to be uncontested. Failed States are characterized by ill-defined, porous borders and slim evidence of territorial control. However, these situations do not seem to affect the status or the existence of a State. The territory criterion is satisfied even in situations of State failure, so that failed States continue to be considered fully fledged and fully responsible States even if their territories are altered.

2.2.3. *A Government*

The third – and most scrutinized – Montevideo criterion is the requirement for an effective government.

One of the main characteristics of failed and failing States is a weak and ineffective government, which does not and cannot provide for its people. Government should be capable of exerting exclusive control over a determinate territory and a given population. However, "the requirement of stable and effective government was always problematic for countries newly independent from colonial rule."[49]

During decolonization, several States gained independence even if there were no existing powers capable of exercising governmental functions. The Congo, for example, obtained its independence from Belgium on 30 June, 1960 in the midst of internal fighting. Few days after independence, the Congolese Public Force mutinied, Belgian troops intervened, and one of the provinces, Katanga, announced secession from the main territory. However,

---

[49] Higgins, Problems and Process, International Law and How We Use It 40 (1994). Prior to post-war decolonization, the requirement for effective government was more strictly defined. For example, in the A*aland Islands* case, the International Committee of Jurists concluded that the independence of Finland from Russia "did not take place until a stable political organization had been created, and until the public authorities had become strong enough to assert themselves throughout the territories of the State without the assistance of the foreign troops." (*Aaland Islands* Case, L.N.O.J., Sp. Supp. No. 4 (1920) 8–9). However, the definition of an effective government has since evolved and become less strict. In fact, in the post-colonialism period the criterion of an effective government has undertaken important transformations. Shaw identifies a historical evolution in the relationship between the principle of self-determination and the requirement of an effective government structure. The evolution is shown in the growing importance given to the right of self determination for non-independent people, to the detriment of the requirement of a centralized and well functioning administration. *See* Malcom N. Shaw, International Law 180 (5th ed. 2003). In fact, self-determination for non–independent people gained priority over administrative conditions in the decolonization period. Statehood was granted even when an effective government was not entirely fulfilled.

the Congo was admitted to the United Nations in September 1960,[50] as two different factions of government sought to be accepted at the UN as legitimate representatives.[51]

The independence of Guinea-Bissau from Portugal is another similar example. Although still under Portuguese rule, the African Party for the Independence of Guinea and Cape Verde declared independence unilaterally in 1973. A UN General Assembly vote in the same year denounced illegal Portuguese aggression and occupation, and discussed the issue of "illegal occupation by Portuguese forces" of the territory of Guinea-Bissau. Western States denied the existence of the necessary criteria for statehood, but GA Resolution 3061(XXVIII) accepted the "recent accession to independence of Guinea-Bissau", though its government controlled neither a majority of the population nor its main towns.[52] Similar examples exist.

Thus, as President Higgins concludes, citing *inter alia* the examples of Rwanda and Burundi, "statehood for purposes of UN admission, was attributed even when the new governments clearly lacked effective control."[53]

In sum, the criterion of effective government is loosely defined, and several States have acceded to statehood without enjoying effective control over their territory. The contradictory nature of the definition of State is particularly poignant here, as an effective government is very much viewed as the core of statehood.

Moreover, it is generally accepted that once statehood is recognized, momentary disruption of governmental effectiveness does not terminate it. Thus, Oppenheim concludes that

> once a State is established, temporary interruption of the effectiveness of its government, as in civil war or as a result of belligerent occupation is not inconsistent with the continued existence of the State.[54]

Similarly, Brownlie holds that

> once a State has been established, extensive civil strive or the breakdown of order through foreign invasion or natural disasters are not considered to affect personality.[55]

---

[50] Statehood is a requisite for admission to the United Nations. U.N. Charter Art. 4.

[51] In the end, credentials were given to the delegation authorized by the Head of State.

[52] *See* 1973 U.N. Yearbook 143–147.

[53] Higgins, Problems and Process, International Law and How We Use It 40 (1994).

[54] Oppenheim's International Law 122 (Sir Robert Jennings and Sir Arthur Watts eds., 9th ed. 1992).

[55] I. Brownlie, Principles of International Public Law 71 (6th ed. 2003). In fact, already in 1903, the Italian-Venezuela Commission in *Sambiaggio* rejected the proposition that Venezuela was a *sui generis* form of a State to which the normal rules of international

One of the principle characteristics of a failed State is the absence of a government capable of exercising governmental functions. The government is either altogether inexistent, as in the case of Somalia, or is incapable of effectively exercising its governmental prerogatives, like in the Democratic Republic of Congo, Sudan, Guinea Bissau and many other African States. However, international law presently does not attribute any fundamental consequence to the temporary disappearance of an effective government. Therefore, it seems that failed States, and generally all States, will continue to be States even when the element of effective government is lacking or altered.[56] In fact, "civil wars and international disturbances, while often rendering the domestic legal order of State totally ineffective, are not treated by State practice or legal theory as situations that annul the legal personalities of States."[57] For example, continuation of statehood has also been recognized in the case of Somalia, which has been without a functioning government since 1991. Accordingly, for example, in Security Council Resolution 1558, of 17 August

law should not apply because of its instability and because it had been the subject to frequent revolutions. *Sambiaggio*, R.I.A.A. 10, 499, at 523–524.

56 In addition, a State does not cease to exist even if it is occupied, either lawfully or unlawfully, by another State. For example, when the four Allied powers assumed supreme power in Germany after the defeat of Nazi Germany, "there can be no doubt that the German State continued to exist as a person in international law and it was this person of international law for which the Allied government was acting and answering," R. Y. Jennings, General Course of International Law, 121 *Recueil des Cours* 351 (1967–II), and "indeed, the legal basis of the occupation depended on its [Germany] continued existence," I. Brownlie, Principles of International Public Law 107 (6th ed. 2003). Also, statehood continues even in cases of unlawful occupation. In fact, "a State may continue to exist under international law even if it is occupied by foreign powers, lacks an autonomous constitution, and is represented during that phase only by a government-in-exile." U. Fastenrath, *State* in Encyclopedia of Public International Law (Rudolph Bernhardt ed. 2000). In the case of foreign occupation, although government is unable to exercise its authority, a State does not cease to exist. Brownlie states that "illegal usurpation of power as a result of foreign invasion will not cause the demise of a State…it will compromise its enjoyment of the incidents of statehood within a part or the whole of its own territory." For example, the invasion of Kuwait by Iraq in 1990 did not extinguish the State of Kuwait. Security Council Resolution 662 of 9 August 1990, stated that it was "determined to bring the occupation of Kuwait by Iraq to an end and to restore the sovereignty, independence and territorial integrity of Kuwait," and called "upon all States, international organizations and specialized agencies not to recognize that annexation, and to refrain from any action or dealing that might be interpreted as an indirect recognition of the annexation." It continued to exist through the occupation and its exiled government was restored in 1991.

57 Alexandros Yannis, State Collapse and the International System, Implosion of Government and the International Legal Order from the French Revolution to the Disintegration of Somalia 174 (2000) (unpublished Doctoral Thesis, University of Geneva, on file with the Library of the Graduate Institute of International and Development Studies, Geneva).

2004, in support of the Somali National Reconciliation Process, the Council reaffirmed "the importance of the sovereignty, territorial integrity, political independence and unity of Somalia."[58]

Hence, although weak and inexistent governments generally characterize failed States, this does not undermine or change their standing as States in international law. Even a serious lack of government effectiveness does not extinguish statehood. Statehood seems to be resilient to powerless governments, anarchy and foreign occupation. Consequently, as Jennings concludes:

> The existence of a stable or effective government is generally reckoned to be one of the essential elements – indeed the most important element – in the make-up of a State. Yet although a new State can hardly come into existence until it is provided with a stable and effective government, it would seem that an established State can continue to exist in law even whilst rival government contend for power, or even whilst the government of the State is vested elsewhere.[59]

Further, as Higgins summarizes "what is absolutely clear is that a loss of 'stable and effective government' does not remove the attribute of statehood, once statehood has been acknowledged."[60]

In sum, international law may be geared for the analysis of the creation of States, but does not provide effective guidance when the elements required for the establishment of statehood are missing. Thus, even protracted ineffective governments qualify as governments, and statehood continues to be afforded to them. In fact, analyzing government as a defining element of statehood provides limited help to the understanding of statehood and State fragility. Thus, as States with ineffective governments continue to be States in international law, failed and failing States must continue to be considered States with all the international obligations and responsibilities that that entails.

2.2.4. *Capacity to Enter into Relations with other States*

The fourth, and final, requirement that defines a State is its capacity to perform international obligations.

However, in looking at the existence of the constitutive elements of States, a legal analysis of this element is missing. The capacity to enter into relations with other States has, in fact, been found problematic for its lack of substantive contribution to the definition of State. The ability and will to fulfill inter-

---

58 S.C. Res. 1558, U.N. Doc. S/RES/1558 (7 Aug. 2004).

59 R. Y. Jennings, *General Course of International Law*, 121 Recueil des Cours 351 (1967–II).

60 Higgins, Problems and Process, International Law and How We Use It 40 (1994).

national obligations is identified as a consequence of statehood, rather than a criterion to define statehood.[61] Hence, this requirement has been variously interpreted as a 'will' rather than a capacity, and as a test to ensure compliance with international law (and especially of exiting treaties).[62] Most scholars only briefly examine this criterion as such in their legal considerations, while others argue that the principle of State continuity makes it redundant.[63]

Conversely, other scholars have equated it to independence, which then becomes the "decisive criterion for statehood."[64] Shaw, for example, affirms that

> it is essential for a sovereign State to be able to create such legal relations with other units as it sees fit. Where this is not present, the entity cannot be an independent State.[65]

In so far as it has been retained, therefore, the focus of the international obligations requirement has been on the capacity of a State to independently undertake international obligations, not in its capacity of discharging them. The issue has been interpreted as whether States would lose or maintain their independence in situations where other entities undertake international obligations on their behalf.

---

[61] *See* T. Grant, *Defining Statehood: the Montevideo Convention and its Discontents*, 37 COLUM. J. TRANSNAT'L L. 403, 434–435 (1999). He also underlines that the capacity of entering into treaties is not exclusive to States and that this "casts doubts on its inclusion in the definition of statehood."

[62] M.J. Peterson, Recognition of Governments, Legal Doctrine and State Practice (1815–1995) 69–70 (1997).

[63] *Id.* at 71.

[64] IAN BROWNLIE, PRINCIPLES OF INTERNATIONAL PUBLIC LAW 70–77 (1998). Brownlie defines the term 'dependent' as pertaining to "one or more of the following distinct situations: 1. the absence of statehood, where the entity concerned is subordinated to a state so completely as to be within its control and the origin of the subordination does not establish agency or representation; 2. a state which has made concession to another state in matters of jurisdiction and administration to such an extent that it has in some sense ceased to be sovereign; 3. a state which has legally conferred wide powers of agency and representation in foreign affairs on another state; 4. a state, which in fact suffers interference from another state and may be a 'client' state politically, but which quantitatively is not under the complete and permanent control of the 'patron'; 5. a legal person of a special type, appearing on the international place for certain purposes only, as in the case of mandates and trust territories and some protectorates; 6. a state which fails to qualify as an 'independent' state for the purpose of a particular instrument." *Id.* at 73

[65] MALCOLM N. SHAW, INTERNATIONAL LAW 181 (5th ed. 2003).

However, independence and ability to perform international obligations cannot be completely equated. The independence/dependence binomial implies that external relations are performed by an actor. This definition shifts the focus from the ability to perform the action to how the action is performed, i.e. independently or not. Moreover, States often delegate the performance of their external obligations to another State or international organizations – by treaty or otherwise – without altering their condition of State. The relevant element of the criterion is whether international obligations are performed or not.[66]

The consequences of the temporary incapability of performing international obligations are not clear. However, it is clear that a State continues to exist irrespectively of its capacity to fully perform its international obligations. A State may incur international responsibility or liability for its failure to perform a certain obligation, but it does not, because of its incapability to perform a certain obligation, alter or lose its qualification of State.

The question of whether the same conclusion is applicable to a protracted inability to fulfill international obligations begs analysis. Failed and failing States only have limited capability of engaging into international relations, and often undergo long periods of time in which no authority is capable of discharging their international obligations. In fact, this is the main international characteristic of failed and failing States. A concrete analysis, however, shows that the inability of a State to fulfill its international obligations does not alter its qualification of State. Countries like Somalia, the Democratic Republic of Congo, Afghanistan and Liberia, for example, have been incapable of

[66] Another interpretation of the requirement is given by Crawford, who affirmed that the "capacity to enter into relations with other States, in the sense in which it might be a useful criterion, is a conflation of the requirements of government and independence." James Crawford, *The Criteria for Statehood in International Law,* 48 Brit. Y.B. Int'l L. 93, 119 (1976–1977). In this view, States pre-eminently are capable of entering into relations with other States and that this characteristic is a consequence, and not a requisite, of statehood. Therefore "[i]t might still be said that *capacity* to enter into the full range of international relations is a useful criterion. But capacity or competence in this sense depends partly on the power of internal government of a territory, without which international obligations may not be carried into effect, and partly on the entity concerned being separated for the purpose of such relations so that no other entity both carries out and accepts responsibility for them." *Id.* This view is useful in so far as it identifies the link between effective government and the capacity to enter into international relations. However, in this connotation, the requirement is similar to the requirement of an effective government. Moreover, it is not considered a criterion for statehood, but a consequence of it, so that its existence or not is irrelevant for the qualification of a 'State.' Thus, it becomes useless to assess the definition of a State.

fulfilling all or parts of their international obligations for nearly a decade, but they are still recognized as States by the international community and their status in the international community has not changed.

Thus, the element of the capability of entering into international relations, identified by the Montevideo Convention as a requirement for statehood, is – similarly to what was concluded for the previous three elements – useful to determine whether a new State can be recognized as such. However, it is not useful to assess the status or continuation of the existence of a failed or failing State.

It seems that changes in the constitutive elements of statehood do not affect States' standings in international law. This is because when analyzed, the definitions of the four elements concentrate solely on the initial existence of certain requirements and not on their continuation throughout the existence of the State. Further, the elements do not provide a clear indication of the consequences of changes in the elements that define the State.

To conclude, failed and failing States continue to be considered States even when they are incapable, for long periods of times, to fulfill their international obligations.

3. *Conclusion*

Failed States are characterized by the dispersion of State powers and the alteration and diffusion of the elements that constitute a State. However, the paragraphs above show that the loss of any or all of the elements that define a State does not result in the alteration or disappearance of statehood, or in the extinction of a State in international law. The instances of State extinction are well defined and do not include State failure. Moreover, definitions of the constitutive elements of statehood have developed so limitedly that they provide little help in understanding statehood.

Disguised under the premise of rigorousness, the definition of State in the Montevideo Convention is in fact lax and imprecise. It is limited to an indication of the elements necessary for a State to be created, but it is not helpful in assessing changes in the standing and responsibilities of the States once they are created.

Hence, although all States must posses the four Montevideo requirements when they are created, it is difficult in practice to transpose the analysis of the constitutive elements to verify any modification in a recognized State. In fact, although these requirements must exist for the creation of States, the consequences of the change of one of the elements in practice are not clear, and in fact do not extinguish or alter the position of States within the international system.[67]

[67] In addition to the Montevideo criteria, two further requirements are often considered essential elements of Statehood: recognition of the existence of the State by the international community, and the requirement of democratic governance. These requirements are briefly assessed here. This analysis aims at providing further appraisal of the characteristics of statehood, and whether they alter the definition of failed States as States in international law. Recognition of the State by fellow States is considered as a requisite for statehood, "effectively forming an additional category to those stipulated in the Montevideo Convention." HIGGINS, PROBLEMS AND PROCESS, INTERNATIONAL LAW AND HOW WE USE IT 42 (1994). However, an analysis of this additional element does not seem to provide any further assistance in the definition of State. Two main theories on the nature of recognition exist: the constitutive theory and the declaratory theory. First, the constitutive theory maintains that only states that are recognized by other States can effectively participate in the international community. This theory implies that only recognized States have legal capacity to act and thus have international obligations. This, however, is not manifestly the case. Second, the declaratory theory maintains that recognition is only a declaration by a State and does not have general legal consequences. An interpretation of recognition as a declaratory act, which merely acknowledges an existing situation, seems to be more appropriate. MALCOLM N SHAW, INTERNATIONAL LAW 367–408 (5th ed. 2003). *See also* J. CRAWFORD, THE CREATION OF STATES IN INTERNATIONAL LAW 24 (1st ed. 1979) (stating that "the tentative conclusion is that the international status of a State 'subject to international law' is, in principle, independent of recognition, although the qualifications already suggest that the differences between declaratory and constitutive school are less in practice than might have been expected.") In fact, State recognition is mostly due to political consideration. The Institute de Droit International expressly acknowledged that recognition has a declaratory effect and stated that "the existence of the new State with all the legal effects attached to that existence are not affected by the refusal of recognition by one or more States." Resolution on Recognition of New States, adopted at the Brussels Session of the Institute de Droit International on 23 April 1936, Art. 1 (*available at:* http://www.idi-iil.org/idiF/resolutionsF/1936_brux_01_fr.pdf (translation from French by the author)). Moreover, although contemporary States' policy is to recognize States and not governments, several scholars agree that it is the recognition of governments rather than the recognition of States that yield legal consequences. *See* S. TALMON, RECOGNITION OF GOVERNMENTS IN INTERNATIONAL LAW 3–17 (1998); HIGGINS, THE DEVELOPMENT OF INTERNATIONAL LAW THROUGH THE POLITICAL ORGANS OF THE UNITED NATIONS 131–166 (1963). In fact "although it is the State which is the person in international law, it is nevertheless the recognition of a government of the State which is the prerequisite for the actual flow of practical legal consequences from recognition. The recognition of a State without the recognition of some government of that State is purely an academic exercise; but the recognition of a *de facto* government without the recognition of any corresponding State has immediate legal consequences on an important order." R. Y. JENNINGS, GENERAL COURSE OF INTERNATIONAL LAW, 121 *Recueil des Cours* 351 (1967–II). Recognition, thus, does not provide any useful assistance to the definition of Statehood, nor, as it stands, helps to better understand State failure. A second requirement of Statehood is that of democratic governance. Some scholars claim that recent developments in the practice of State recognition are contributing to the creation of a 'democratic entitlement'. *See generally* DEMO-

In fact, even when one – or more than one – of the Montevideo's elements of statehood is weakened, the standing of a State in the international legal system has not been questioned. Professor Crawford concludes that

> a State is not necessarily extinguished by substantial changes in territory, population, or government, or even, in some cases, by a combination of all three.[68]

Once statehood has been recognized, changes in the elements upon which such recognition was granted do not alter the status of the State.

Thus, based upon the overview of the constitutive elements of the State, failed States continue to be considered unaltered States in international law. In practice, this means that the status of failed States cannot be properly addressed.

This conclusion is both unsatisfactory and problematic.

It is unsatisfactory because it demonstrates that the defining elements of statehood, the pillar of international law, provide only a very limited elucidation of what constitutes a State. The definitions of a 'permanent population' and of a 'determined territory' are limited to the existence of a community living in a territory, even if the borders are not defined and population not fixed. Similarly, the requirement of a 'government' continues to exist even when the effectiveness of such government is disrupted by civil war. Finally,

---

CRATIC GOVERNANCE AND INTERNATIONAL LAW (G.H. Fox and B.R. Roth eds., 2000). This view is supported by the practice of states vis-à-vis the recognition of new states formally part of the Soviet Union. In 1991, when the Soviet Union began to dissolve, the European Council issued a declaration containing 'Guidelines on the recognition of New States in Eastern Europe and in the Soviet Union' requiring respect for democracy and human rights as a criteria for recognition. Danilo Türk, *Annex I: Declaration on the 'Guidelines on the Recognition of New States in Eastern European and in the Soviet Union* 4 EU, J. INT'L. L. 72 (1993). A similar requirement was imposed on the former members of the Yugoslav Federal State by the Badinter Arbitration Commission, although the practice in this case is more complex. S.D. Murphy, *Democratic legitimacy and the recognition of States and governments*, DEMOCRATIC GOVERNANCE AND INTERNATIONAL LAW 123–154 (G.H. Fox and B.R. Roth eds., 2000). However, there is no evidence that States refuse to recognize the existence of another State only because it is not democratic, in fact, "notions of democratic legitimacy are certainly present in contemporary practice concerning recognition of States. However, the evidence of these notions is not uniform, and it derives exclusively from practice of States that are themselves democratic." *Id.* at 139. Besides, respect of democracy may be a requirement for recognition of the State, but it is not a requisite for the existence of the State. These two additional criteria, therefore, do not provide any additional clarification to the definition of State in international law. It follows that they are also not relevant to assess whether these criteria need to be found in failed and failing States.

[68] J. CRAWFORD, THE CREATION OF STATES IN INTERNATIONAL LAW 417 (1st ed. 1979). Similarly Professor Crawford also states that the "presumption – in a practice a strong one – is in favour of the continuance, and against the extinction, of an established State. Extinction is, thus, within broad limits, not affected by more or less anarchy with the State." *Id.*

the requisite of 'capability of engaging in international obligations' has been useful only as a definition of independence. This conclusion is all the more surprising as the 'State' is the fundamental keystone over which international law is built. This anomaly derives from the fact that the Montevideo definition of State looks at the elements needed to create a State, rather than at the elements needed for the maintenance of statehood. Therefore, it does not provide effective guidance when the elements required for the establishment of statehood are changed or lost after statehood is recognized.

This conclusion is also problematic. At present, State failure is not acknowledged in the framework of international law. Failed States continue to be considered fully equal and capable States under international law, as international law does not react to the weakness and failure of the State as an organic structure. State failure often implies severe migration and population displacements. It infringes on the certitude of a State territory, as borders become porous, rebel groups control important sections of the territory and neighboring countries often secure their borders by patrolling foreign territory. Additionally, governments are not effective and the capacity to enter into relations with other States is lacking.

International law does not contemplate the case of a State that ceases to be able to deliver political goods, and has created no mechanisms for the recreation or substitution of State power when the State is no longer capable of performing its duties. There is no space for an even temporary power vacuum. In the most serious case of State failure, States continue to exist on the map – like in the case of Somalia – and maintain their former borders and population, but there is little more beyond that.

The phenomenon of failed States is broad and complex, as failed States are "the product of a collapse of the power structures providing political support for law and order."[69] However, "the international community has not previously faced the total breakdown of a State unaccompanied by some other centralized entity claiming statehood"[70] and has been slow to appraise State failure.

Oddly, although States are the building blocks of international law, the definition of their constitutive elements remains general, and failed States continue to be required to behave like States and fulfill the many obligations

[69] D. Thürer, *The "Failed State" and International Law*, INT'L COMM. OF THE RED CROSS (31 Dec. 1999), *available at:* http://www.globalpolicy.org/nations/sovereign/failed/2003/0725law.htm.

[70] Ruth E. Gordon, *Some Legal Problems with Trusteeship*, 28 CORNELL INT'L L. J. 301, 338 (1995).

incumbent upon them. Obligations continue to exist, although no power can actually perform them.[71]

To remain significant, however, any juridical definition of State must confront reality and must be elaborated so as to respond to changes in international law and politics. It needs to evolve and take into consideration the reality of statehood, and namely fragile, failed and failing States.

Failed and failing States vary a great deal, and there is a lot of gradation in how capable they are of fulfilling their obligations and whether their incapacity is transitory or protracted. In any case, I propose that introducing a concept by which international obligations are – temporarily and for limited areas – performed by other actors in the international community would take this reality into consideration. This will ensure that the necessary obligations are indeed performed, while at the same time preserving failed States' sovereignty. Failed States remain independent, equal to other States and the sole sovereign of their territory. Once their ability to perform their obligations is restored, they will again be required to perform all obligations owed to other States or other subjects of the international community.

Failed and failing States must be assessed in light of the political and legal changes that resulted in State failure. Failed States have factually lost the ability to deliver the goods that they agreed to deliver. Thus, while it is necessary to recognize that a State does not cease to exist because certain characteristics that made its existence possible are no longer present,[72] it is also important to acknowledge that these transformations have altered the ability of the State to perform its obligations.[73]

---

[71] Weiss and Chopra remark that while under international law, there is no degree of sovereignty, in the sense that it either exists of it does not, "[i]n contrast, political scientists and international relations theorists have formulated a concept of sovereignty, which they perceive in terms of degrees...For these scholars it is possible to be *more* sovereign or *less* sovereign. *Sovereignty* becomes an elastic term that refers to a category of social and political organization that is linked geographically to delimited territory." T. Weiss and J. Chopra, *Sovereignty under Siege: from Intervention to Humanitarian Space*, BEYOND WESTPHALIA? STATE SOVEREIGNTY AND INTERNATIONAL INTERVENTIONS 99–100 (G. Lyons and M. Mastanduno eds., 1995) (emphasis in original).

[72] As Oppenheim concludes "once it is appreciated that it is not so much the possession of sovereignty which determined the possession of international personality but rather the possession of rights, duties and powers in international law, it is apparent that a State which possesses some, but not all, of those rights, duties and powers is nevertheless an international person." OPPENHEIM'S INTERNATIONAL LAW 123 (Sir Robert Jennings and Sir Arthur Watts eds., 9th ed. 1992).

[73] State inability or failure is not an accepted circumstance that precludes wrongfulness in international law. However, if there are no institutions that are authorized to act on behalf of the State, the State cannot be held responsible. Recently, however, the international community has more frequently intervened to restore the protection of fundamental

In the next three chapters, I will assess if and how particular obligations are performed in crises situations similar to State failure, and who has the authority to perform them. In particular, I will assess the performance of acts directed at addressing health emergencies, environmental crises and gross human rights violations that have international impacts. In fact, performance of these obligations is not only important for the failed State, but has become necessary to ensure the safety and survival of the entire international community.

human rights when a State has been unable or unwilling to do. Examples include Somalia and Kosovo. This has not been without controversy. *See* J. CRAWFORD, COMMENTARY TO THE DRAFT ARTICLES ON RESPONSIBILITY OF STATES FOR INTERNATIONALLY WRONGFUL ACTS ADOPTED BY THE INTERNATIONAL LAW COMMISSION AT ITS FIFTY-THIRD SESSION (Nov. 2001); D. Thürer, *The "Failed State" and International Law*, INT'L COMM. OF THE RED CROSS (31 Dec. 1999) (*available at:* http://www.globalpolicy.org/nations/sovereign/failed/2003/0725law.htm).

Chapter Five

Responding to Public Health Emergencies in Failed States

The correlation between State failure and global health is an international issue of paramount importance. In fact, when a State is unable to control and prevent the spreading of communicable diseases in parts or in the entirety of its territory, the threat of disease may become global.

Based on the definition of State failure elaborated in the previous chapters, this chapter focuses on the mechanisms that the international community may adopt to address to the threat of an uncontrolled spreading of disease developing into an international risk.

1. *Health Emergencies as Global Security Issues*

Health has become a central tenant of international law. Its importance is recognized in several international agreements, including in international and regional human rights treaties.[1] Similarly, global health[2] has developed into a centerpiece of international law and international relations. The U.N.

---

[1] *See*, for example, Article 25 of the Universal Declaration on Human Rights, Article 12 of the International Covenant on Economic, Social and Cultural Rights, Article 24 of the UN Convention on the Rights of the Child; and Article 16 of the African Charter on Human and Peoples' Rights. *See* David P. Fidler, International Law and Public Health: Materials On and Analysis Of Global health Jurisprudence 277–331 (2000).

[2] The term 'global health' is preferred in this section to 'international health' because, as Støre et al. explains "'global health' is rapidly overtaking the paradigm of 'international health' as the organizing principle for health cooperation. While the latter term focuses on relations among sovereign nations, the concept of global health encompasses health affairs within and among nations-states, as well as transnational challenges not defined by political borders. Global health thus recognizes multiple actor groups in the production of health, including but not limited to national government." J.G. Støre, J. Welch and L. Chen, *Health and Security for a Global Century*, in L. Chen, J. Leaning and V. Narasimhan, Global Health Challenges for Human Security 67–68 (2003).

Charter references the need to collaborate on health issues in several articles,[3] and several international organizations have been created with mandates related to health.[4]

Moreover, in the last twenty years, the importance of global health has increased for several reasons.

First, the development of faster, easier and cheaper transportation methods has brought about a phenomenal increase in the movement of people and goods. At the same time, new technologies for the conservation of perishable goods have increased their international trade. Notably, however, both improvements have also made it easier for diseases to spread faster and to more distant locations. In fact, easier movement of people and goods facilitated the spreading, emergence and reemergence of infectious diseases in both human and animals.

Second, 'globalization' has, to a certain extent, undermined the ability of one State to alone protect its people from the spreading of infectious diseases. As a result, only collective efforts can efficiently address public health emergencies. As Fidler concludes, "most public health experts agree that the distinction between national and international public health is no longer relevant because globalization has enabled pathogenic microbes to spread illness and death globally."[5] Diseases like tuberculosis, malaria and cholera are still widespread in many regions. Further, some of their pathogens are becoming drug-resistant, and some of these diseases are again spreading in previously disease-free regions. For example, cases of West Nile fever were recently diagnosed in New York City. Additionally, a new wave of tuberculosis – which is resistant to usual medications – has been found in

---

[3] Article 13 states "The General Assembly shall initiate studies and make recommendations for the purpose of (b) promoting international co-operation in the [...] health fields". Article 55 affirms "With a view to the creation of conditions of stability and well-being which are necessary for peaceful and friendly relations among nations based on respect for the principle of equal rights and self-determination of peoples, the United Nations shall promote: (b) solutions of international economics, social, health." Article 57 further states: "The various specialized agencies, established by intergovernmental agreement and having wide international responsibilities, as defined in their basic instruments, in [...] health, and related fields, shall be brought into relationship with the United Nations in accordance with the provision of Article 63." Finally, Article 62 states "The Economic and Social Council may made or initiate studies and reports with respect to [...] health and related matters and may make recommendations with respect to any such matters to the General Assembly, to the Members of the United Nations, and to the specialized agencies concerned."

[4] For example the World Health Organization (WHO), the United Nations Children's Fund (UNICEF), UNAIDS.

[5] D.D. Fidler, International Law And Public Health, Materials on and Analysis of Global Health Jurisprudence 16 (2000) (internal citations omitted).

Europe and the North America. Denghi Hemorrhagic Fever is now considered endemic in fifty countries, a significant rise from the only nine countries where it was considered endemic before 1970.[6] Moreover, new infectious diseases, such as Severe Acute Respiratory Syndrome ("SARS") and Ebola hemorrhagic fever, have emerged and can only be handled properly by the coordinated efforts of multiple national and international actors.

Third, the connection between national security and health has also become more apparent.[7] For the first time, some States have recently identified certain diseases as national security threats and have developed measures to halt and control their spread as part of foreign policy considerations. A primary example is HIV/AIDS. In 2002, President Clinton designated the worldwide spread of AIDS as a threat to the national security of the United States.[8] He therefore mandated the U.S. National Security Council develop an appropriate response. Following the same path, in his 2003 State of the Union Address, President Bush announced the Emergency Plan for AIDS Relief, a five-year, USD 15 billion initiative.[9] A similar approach is used by

---

[6] *See* Gro Harlem Brundtland, *Failed States and Global Security: How Health Can Contribute to a Safer World* (address to the Brookings Institute of 26 Sept. 2002) (*available at*: http://www.brook.edu/comm/events/20020926.pdf).

[7] There is a new growing literature on this phenomenon. For example, *see generally* L. Chen et al., Global Health Challenges for Human Security (2003) (specifically J.G. Støre, J. Welch and L. Chen, *Health and Security for a Global Century*, 67–84; D.L. Heymann, *Evolving Infectious Disease Threats to National and Global Security*, 105–123); J.C. Chow, *Health and International Security*, 19 Wash Q. 63–77 (1996); J.B. Tucker, R.P. Kadlec, *Infectious Disease and National Security*, 29 Strategic Review 12–20 (2001). Heymann affirms: "This principle [of global public health security] has evolved in response of three concurrent trends. First, the highly publicized resurgence of the infectious disease threat illustrated the vulnerability of all nations to outbreaks and epidemics, often of new or unusual diseases. Second, the impact of AIDS on sub-Saharan Africa demonstrated the capacity of an emerging disease to destabilize a large geographical region in ways that undermine the very infrastructures needed for governance. Third, a reconsideration of the determinants of national security broadened the perception of what constitutes a security threat in the post-Cold War era, making space to accommodate infectious diseases – at least in their most internationally disruptive forms." D.L. Heymann, *Evolving Infectious Disease Threats to National and Global Security*, in L. Chen et al., Global Health Challenges for Human Security 106 (2003). *See also* J. Siddiqui, World Health and World Politics, The WHO and the UN System (1995).

[8] *See* BBC News, *US: AIDS is Security Threat*, 1 May 2000, *available at*: http://news.bbc.co.uk/1/hi/world/americas/731706.stm (last visited 4 Sept. 2009); *see also* Barton Gellman, *AIDS is Declared Threat to US National Security*, Wash. Post. 30 Apr. 2000, *available at*: http://www.commondreams.org/headlines/043000-02.htm.

[9] *See In Global Battle on AIDS, Bush Creates Legacy*, N.Y. Times 5 Jan. 2008, *available at*: http://www.whitehouse.gov/infocus/hivaids. Also, the U.S. Government created the role of United States Global AIDS Coordinator, presently occupied by Ambassador Randall L. Tobias.

the United Nations Joint Programme on HIV/AIDS ("UNAIDS"), the joined U.N. program on HIV/AIDS, which states in its website that "HIV/AIDS is a security issue, whether one is looking at the more traditional meaning of security (threats to defense of the State, with those threats emanating from other States) or the newer concept of 'human security'."[10]

For these reasons, public health has become a matter of international concern that often cannot be addressed exclusively by one State, but must instead be addressed by the international community as a whole.

However, there are no legally binding instruments that address the specific issue of collaboration and coordination by the international community in the event of a global health crisis. Likewise, there are no provisions in existing regional and international treaties that provide for specific interventions of international or national actors in situations of State failure or when a failed State is unable to address global health emergencies.

To be certain, there is already a degree of collaboration between States on certain matters related to public health. For example, at the regional level, several existing organizations collaborate on health issues. Moreover, in general, several international organizations, including the World Health Organization ("WHO") and the UN Children Fund ("UNICEF"),[11] assume

---

Heymann affirmed: "Several recent events suggest that emerging and epidemic-prone diseases are being taken seriously as a threat to national and global security. In a an unprecedented step, a U.S. government-supported study concluded in 1995 that emerging and reemerging infectious diseases, especially AIDS, constituted a national security threat and foreign policy challenge. In 1996, the U.S. Department of Defense established the Global Emerging Infectious Surveillance and Response Systems, based on a network of domestic and overseas military laboratories, as an explicit acknowledgement that emerging disease can threaten military personnel and their families, reduce military readiness, and present a risk to U.S. national security. The threat posed by microbial agents to the security of the U.S. was further acknowledged in 2000 be an equally unprecedented report from the U.S. Central Intelligence Agency's National Intelligence Council. Citing the 'staggering' and 'destabilizing' number of deaths caused by AIDS in sub-Saharan Africa." In L. Heymann, *Evolving Infectious Disease Threats to National and Global Security*, in L. Chen et al., Global Health Challenges for Human Security 111 (2003).

10 *See* UNAIDS, *Security and Humanitarian Response to AIDS*, http://www.unaids.org/en/policyandpractice/securityhumanitarianresponse/default.asp (last visited 4 Sept. 2009).

See also International Crisis Group, *AIDS as a Security Issue* (19 June 2001), *available at*: http://www.unaids.org/NetTools/Misc/DocInfo.aspx?LANG=en&href=http://gva-doc-owl/WEBcontent/Documents/pub/Topics/Security/ICGreport_en.pdf.

11 UNICEF was established by a Resolution of the U.N. General Assembly on 11 December 1946. UNICEF is a semi-autonomous agency of the U.N. system. It is headed by a 30-member Executive Board and an Executive Director elected by the U.N. Economic and Social Council. Its "purpose is to help developing countries improve the condition of their children and youths. It aids country projects, preferably those which form part of national programs of development." It assists countries only at the request of their government. *See*

coordinating and facilitating roles in international public health matters. For example, every year at the beginning of the Fall, epidemiologists from across the world meet at the WHO Headquarters in Geneva to discuss which flu vaccine is more likely to be effective for the coming flu season. The agreed vaccine is then produced and distributed internationally. Also, in situations of humanitarian crises, which are often situations of conflict and State failure, the international community intervenes in support of national health sectors. Several existing international, national and non-governmental organizations are geared towards health emergencies and in such cases provide basic healthcare.[12]

However, work remains to be done. The recent example of the SARS virus epidemic is significant in this regard.[13]

SARS was first diagnosed in China in November 2002. However, the Chinese authorities did not initially report the existence of the disease and attempted to conceal its existence. Only on 26 March 2003, in light of media and political pressure, China revealed the extent of the epidemic, and on 2 April 2003, five months after the first breakout, allowed a WHO team to enter its territory and assess the situation.

The alarm, however, had already spread, and WHO had issued a global alert on 12 March 2003. With the support of reports from national health monitor systems and several governments, WHO was able to release daily updates on the progress of the epidemic and describe its controlling efforts. On 2 April, WHO also issued a travel alert discouraging travel to several countries in Asia and to Canada. Such a vigorous and coordinated response bore fruit, and by 5 July the epidemics had stopped.[14]

The SARS crisis highlights the need for a coordinated intervention by international actors in situations of global health emergencies. It also provides both positive and negative lessons.

On the positive side, the international reaction to the spreading of SARS demonstrates that the WHO has the capability to successfully manage and

---

Amos Jenkins Peaslee, *UNICEF*, in II International Governmental Organizations, Part I, 1398 (revised 3d ed. 1979).

[12] These include UNICEF, UNDP, the U.N. Office for the Coordination of Humanitarian Affairs ("OCHA"), the European Commission Humanitarian Office (ECHO), U.S. Aid International Development Office ("USAID"), Médicines Sans Frontières, Oxfam, and many others. Their programs, often jointly carried out, typically include the establishment of field health clinics and monitor centers, mother-and-child care, the provision of water and food, vaccination and sanitation campaigns.

[13] *See* D. Fidler, SARS, Governance and the Globalization of Disease (2004).

[14] M. Poulin, *La Gestion par l'OMS des Situations d'Urgence de Portée Internationale. L'exemple du Syndrome Respiratoire Aigu Sévère*, Actualité et Droit International (Nov. 2003), *available at*: www.ridi.org/adi.

control a potential global crisis. It also shows that the international community as a whole can exercise pressure and show cohesion when necessary. In fact, it should be noted that the first alert of the outbreak was reported by individuals and non-governmental groups that alerted other members of the international community. WHO verified the reports and requested more information from the Chinese government. Moreover, once the epidemic was confirmed, WHO issued several global alerts, including travel restrictions. This was the first time that such actions were taken by WHO. It is significant to note that although WHO does not have a clear mandate to issue such alerts, Member States generally complied with them (only the Canadian government protested the inclusion of Toronto on the list of places where travel was discouraged).[15]

On the negative side, the response to the SARS crisis also shows the limitations of the current system. In fact, had China declared the emergency sooner, the result of the epidemic would have been far less serious, and effective control measures could have been implemented sooner. Instead, China imposed the State secret on any news relating to the epidemic and denied any access for several months. This not only aggravated the situation, but also epitomized the limitation of the present legal system, which allows for little international action without State consent.

2. *Health Systems in Failing States*

The dangers brought by the spread of viruses, the emergence and re-emergence of diseases and the security implications of health emergencies are magnified in developing countries and in failing States.

Many developing countries still struggle in their efforts to ensure appropriate health standards for their citizens. The conditions of national public health systems, especially in certain low income and highly indebted countries, have hardly improved since independence. In most developing countries, social and economic conditions and environmental problems benefit opportunistic microbes.[16] Further, several diseases are becoming drug-resis-

---

[15] *See* Fidler, *Development Involving SARS, International Law, and the Infectious Disease Control at the Fifty-Sixth Meeting of the World Health Assembly*, ASIL Insights (June 2003).

[16] D.P. Fidler, International Law and Public Health, Materials on and Analysis of Global Health Jurisprudence 22 (2000) (internal citations omitted). Fidler identifies the following public health risks: "1. international trade and travel as effective channels for infectious diseases spread; 2. deteriorating or nonexistent public health capabilities, including the declining effectiveness on antimicrobial drugs; 3. the failure of the

tant, including diseases such as tuberculosis and malaria, which have grown antimicrobial resistance. As a consequence, public health systems remain inadequate and often incapable of coping with health emergencies like epidemics and the discovery of new infectious diseases.[17]

The situation of failing and collapsed States is particularly daring. In fact, by definition, such States are unable to provide basic political and social goods to their people. Often, their healthcare systems are all but completely collapsed. Moreover, the spreading of disease and new epidemics cannot be properly monitored and controlled.

Rotberg highlights one of the defining characteristics of State failure as a State's growing inability to provide basic healthcare, which results in a decline in health indicators like infant mortality and life expectancy. Based on this accepted definition, former Director General of WHO Gro Brundtland suggests that almost a third of the population of sub-Saharan Africa lives in countries that can be defined as weak and failed States, or which are ravaged by complex emergencies.[18]

The consequences of State failure on public health emergencies are severe. On one side, failed States become reservoirs for diseases that can spread internationally. On the other, they are unable to cope with disease outbreaks.

---

internationalization of public health; 4. the development of unprecedented levels of deeply rooted social, economic, and environmental problems that provide pathogenic microbes with fertile conditions."

[17] WHO further affirms: "Newly recognized and familiar pathogens have reasserted their epidemic potential as: 1. Development gaps have widened, leaving many countries unable to provide adequate basic services such as safe water, adequate nutrition, waste disposal and health care for their populations. 2. Governmental and public health care systems in many countries have collapsed due to civil strife and war. 3. Poverty, urbanization and population displacement have led to concentration of human populations in conditions that favour major outbreaks (e.g. refugee camps, urban slums). 4. Exploitation of pristine environments is exposing human populations to new infectious agents. 5. Diseases within animal populations cross into human populations. 6. Environmental change may alter the endemicity and transmission patterns of pathogens. 7. Ineffective vector control programmes have led to a proliferation of vectors, including resistant vector populations. 8. The development of antimicrobial resistance now threatens to make once curable diseases incurable. 9. The potential for accelerated spread of disease has increased markedly with globalization of travel and trade. 10. The situation is further compounded by inappropriate social, political and economic responses to epidemics with implementation of misguided measures to control disease spread." WHO Department Of Communicable Disease Surveillance And Response, *A Framework for Global Outbreak Alert and Response*, WHO/CDS/CSR/2000.2, *available at*: http://www.who.int/csr/resources/publications/surveillance/whocdscsr2002.pdf.

[18] Gro Harlem Brundtland, *Failed States and Global Security: How Health Can Contribute to a Safer World* (address to the Brookings Institute of 26 September 2002), *available at*: http://www.brook.edu/comm/events/20020926.pdf.

First, failed States become reservoirs for infectious diseases, such as poliomyelitis, malaria, and sleeping sickness. In fact, failed States lack a properly working health system that can appropriately sustain public health functions, prevent disease outbreaks, participate in disease eradication programs and create conditions that reduce disease transmission and promote health for all.

Second, certain areas within failed States become neglected and populations are left to fend health emergencies for themselves during health emergencies. Diseases spread as a result of a reduced effort and ability to control them, while health systems are weakened and have no financial and medical means to be effective.

Brundtland takes Ebola as an example, and suggests that:

> So far it has been contained because it has been confined to small villages far from big cities. Health systems like that of Uganda have done a fine job in isolating patients and restricting spread. They could do this with the help of international specialists from WHO and CDC [Center for Disease Control] Atlanta because the security situation in the area was good.
>
> What if an outbreak takes place in a devastated Central African country where there is no local health care? What if the security situation was so bad that we could not send in international experts to advise and assist in containing the outbreak? What if infected people start fleeing into cities, to neighboring countries, and eventually out of the region?[19]

What Dr. Bruntland envisions is indeed a risk that needs to be addressed. What can be done if an international health emergency occurs in a State incapable of controlling it or effectively dealing with it?

Health emergencies in failed States are not only problematic for the States themselves and their people, but they also present a risk and a challenge for the entire international community, which needs to act and effectively address global emergencies. Assessing the mechanisms that already exist and that can be usefully employed to address these emergencies is therefore vital to the international community. At the same time, it is important to identify possible lacunae that need to be filled to face possible emergencies.

Several strategies exist to support the health systems of failing states, both at the international and national levels. Internationally, several international organizations have been mandated to address specific aspects of international health emergencies. These include the WHO, UNICEF and the World Bank. Nationally, several donor countries include funding for health emergencies in their emergency and humanitarian programs. These are mostly channeled

[19] Gro Harlem Brundtland, *Failed States and Global Security: How Health Can Contribute to a Safer World* (address to the Brookings Institute of 26 September 2002) at 5, *available at*: http://www.brook.edu/comm/events/20020926.pdf.

through international organizations like WHO and UNICEF and other U.N. Agencies.

The most relevant mechanisms to deal with emergencies derive from either the normative or directive powers of the World Health Organization: the International Health Regulations ("IHR"), and the recently approved 2005 Amendments, are a fitting example of the first; the Global Outbreak Alert and Response Network ("GOARN") is a good example of the latter. Further, at a general level, the international community supports the health systems of failed or failing States in several ways, through several international organizations, including by providing worldwide vaccination campaigns and humanitarian interventions that target health needs.

Each of these mechanisms will be analyzed in detail below.

3. *International Effort to Confront Global Health Emergencies*

The main international organization dealing with health-related issues is the WHO, which was established on 7 April 1948 and soon thereafter became the specialized agency of the United Nations for health issues.[20] Nowadays, the WHO has 192 Member States, which means that it enjoys virtually universal membership. Its governing structure is constituted by a World Health Assembly, the main governing body of WHO, which is composed of delegates representing members; an Executive Board, made up of 32 members, elected by the Health Assembly for a period of three years; a Secretariat, headed by a Director General, and *ad hoc* committees established by the Board following a proposal by the Assembly or the Director General.

On a global scale, WHO

> plans and coordinates health actions on a global basis. At the request of members, it assists them in planning and carrying out health programs, strengthening their health services and training health workers. It promotes medical research and exchange of scientific information. Makes health regulations for international travel, keeps communicable disease under constant surveillance, collects and disseminates data on health matters and sets standards for the quality control of drugs, vaccines, and other substances affecting health. It gives health assistance to members in emergencies or natural disasters.[21]

---

[20] *See generally* G.L. Burci and C-H. Vignes, World Health Organization (2004); C-H. Vignes and H.J. Schelzka, *World Health Organization*, in V Encyclopedia of Public International Law, Installment 406–409 (Bernhardt ed. 1981); A.J. Peaslee, *World Health Organization*, III International Governmental Organizations Constitutional Documents, 449–451 (revised 3d ed. 1979).

[21] A.J. Peaslee, *World Health Organization*, III International Governmental Organizations Constitutional Documents 450 (revised 3d ed. 1979).

As in all international organizations, the WHO is constituted of sovereign subjects, the Member States, that have invested certain powers upon WHO. The extent and limits of these powers are enshrined in the WHO Constitution. The WHO Constitution provides no withdrawal mechanisms and no expulsion mechanisms against Members that do not behave according to its Constitution.

WHO's stated objective is "the attainment by all peoples of the highest possible level of health,"[22] defined, in the preamble of the WHO Constitution, as "a state of complete physical, mental and social well-being." Its role in global health emergencies is therefore fundamental. Yet, health is a dynamic concept and it is an "intrinsically complex and multi-faced topic, which straddles many areas of human activity and which has undergone a deep technical and philosophical evolution during the last few decades."[23] Health is also interlinked to many other basic issues that are at the center of the international agenda, including economic and social development, human rights, children and women's rights, environment and food policies. Thus, WHO acts in conjunction with many other international organizations, such as UNICEF, the UN Development Program, the Food and Agriculture Organization, and the UN Environmental Program. Although WHO retains the directing and controlling role within the field of health.

To reach its objective, WHO was given both normative and directing powers. The Organization can, *inter alia*, act as a coordinator and coordinating authority on international health work. Upon request, it can assist governments to strengthen health services and the United Nations to provide and assist in supplying health services and services to special groups (such as the peoples of trust territories). Further, WHO can stimulate and advance work to eradicate epidemics, endemics and other diseases, it can provide information, counsel and assistance in the field of health, standardize diagnostic procedures and generally take all necessary actions to attain its objective.[24]

---

[22] WHO Const. Art. 1, *available at*: http://www.who.int/en.

[23] G.L. Burci and C-H. Vignes, World Health Organization 108 (2004).

[24] WHO Const. Art. 2, *available at*: http://www.who.int/en. The Article enumerates the functions of the Organization. The full Article states: "In order to achieve its objective, the functions of the Organization shall be: (a) to act as the directing and co-ordinating authority on international health work; (b) to establish and maintain effective collaboration with the United Nations, specialized agencies, governmental health administrations, professional groups and such other organizations as may be deemed appropriate; (c) to assist governments, upon request, in strengthening health services; (d) to furnish appropriate technical assistance and, in emergencies, necessary aid upon the request or acceptance of governments; (e) to provide or assist in providing, upon the request of the United Nations, health services and facilities to special groups, such as the peoples of trust territories; (f) to establish and maintain such administrative and technical services as may be required, including

Member States of WHO have explicitly recognized the link between health and global security and, in 2001, the Health Assembly approved a resolution recognizing that "any upsurge in cases of infectious disease in a given country is potentially of concern for the international community."[25] The resolution highlights a strategy to address 'global health security.' This strategy has three main components:

1. specific programmes for the prevention and control of known epidemic threats such as influenza, meningitis or cholera;
2. detection and response to health emergencies resulting from unexpected circumstances or unknown causes;
3. improving preparedness through the strengthening of national infrastructures for diseases surveillance and response.[26]

Specifically, the Resolution requested the Director-General to:

> Provide technical support to Member States for developing intervention programmes that prevent epidemics and respond to communicable disease threats and emergencies, particularly with regards to epidemiological investigations, laboratory diagnoses, and community and clinical management of cases;

---

epidemiological and statistical services; (g) to stimulate and advance work to eradicate epidemic, endemic and other diseases; (h) to promote, in co-operation with other specialized agencies where necessary, the prevention of accidental injuries; (i) to promote, in co-operation with other specialized agencies where necessary, the improvement of nutrition, housing, sanitation, recreation, economic or working conditions and other aspects of environmental hygiene; (j) to promote co-operation among scientific and professional groups which contribute to the advancement of health; (k) to propose conventions, agreements and regulations, and make recommendations with respect to international health matters and to perform such duties as may be assigned thereby to the Organization and are consistent with its objective; (l) to promote maternal and child health and welfare and to foster the ability to live harmoniously in a changing total environment; (m) to foster activities in the field of mental health, especially those affecting the harmony of human relations; (n) to promote and conduct research in the field of health; (o) to promote improved standards of teaching and training in health, medical and related professions; (p) to study and report on, in co-operation with other specialized agencies where necessary, administrative and social techniques affecting public health and medical care from preventive and curative points of view, including hospital services and social security; (q) to provide information, counsel and assistance in the field of health; (r) to assist in developing an informed public opinion among all peoples on matters of health; (s) to establish and revise as necessary international nomenclatures of diseases, of causes of death and of public health practices; (t) to standardize diagnostic procedures as necessary; (u) to develop, establish and promote international standards with respect to food, biological, pharmaceutical and similar products; (v) generally to take all necessary action to attain the objective of the Organization."

[25] Res. WHA54.14 (Global Health Security: epidemic alert and response) (21 May 2001), *available at*: http://policy.who.int.

[26] G.L. Burci and C-H. Vignes, World Health Organization 141 (2004).

Make appropriate arrangements for the development of regional preparedness and response plans;
Provide support to Member States for strengthening their capacity to detect and respond rapidly to communicable disease threats and emergencies, especially by developing the laboratory skills needed for diagnosis and providing training in epidemiological methods for use in the field, particularly in the most exposed countries.[27]

Although under the Constitution of WHO, Assembly Resolutions are not legally binding instruments, the Health Assembly determines the policies of the organization (Art. 18, WHO Constitution), and these acts have a directive function. Moreover, the strategy envisioned by the Resolution is applicable to all health emergencies situations, and is well suited to deal with some situations arising from State failure.

The implementation of the resolution relies on WHO's Epidemic and Pandemic Alert and Response Operation ("EPR"), which is the main operational tool to accomplish the effort to address global health security. EPR responds to a series of diseases of international importance including: Anthrax, Avian influenza, Crimean-Congo hemorrhagic fever ("CCHF"), Dengue/dengue hemorrhagic fever, Ebola hemorrhagic fever, Hepatitis, Influenza, Lassa fever, Marburg hemorrhagic fever, Meningococcal disease, Plague, Rift Valley fever, SARS, Smallpox, Tularaemia and Yellow fever.[28]

EPR is based on the use of two important instruments, which are analyzed in details below: the International Health Regulations ("IHR") and the Comprehensive Event Management for International Outbreak and Response ("CEMIOR").

IHR control international outbreaks of certain diseases with the collaboration of Member States. They strive for a balance between controlling the spread of disease and minimum interference with trade and people movement. IHR are mandatory for Member States that have not expressly made a reservation to them.

CEMIOR manages critical data on outbreaks and ensures communication between key international public health professionals. This is based on a voluntary scheme.

The difference between the two instruments is fundamental: IHR are the product of the normative prerogatives of the Health Assembly. Instead, CEMIOR results from the directing and coordinating functions of WHO. However, certain prerogatives of CEMIOR can be used for situations controlled by the IHR.

---

[27] Res. WHA54.14 ¶ 3 (21 May 2001), *available at*: http://policy.who.int.

[28] WHO, *Diseases Covered by GAR*, http://www.who.int/csr/disease/en/ (last visited 4 Sept. 2009).

3.1. *The Framework Established by the International Health Regulations*

IHR are the first instruments for EPR. They are the product of a unique normative power in the context of international disease control, enshrined in Articles 19 and 21 of WHO's Constitution.

Article 19 provides that the Health Assembly may adopt conventions or agreements in matters for which the organization is competent. However, the recently adopted Framework Convention on Tobacco Control[29] is the only example of such conventions or agreements.

Article 21 provides for the Assembly to adopt regulations concerning five specific areas, including "sanitary and quarantine requirements and other procedures designed to prevent the international spread of disease."[30] These regulations are particularly relevant because they provide a significant tool to address the international spread of infectious diseases.

Regulations can be adopted by a simple majority of the Assembly[31] and "shall come into force for all members after due notice has been given of their adoption by the Health Assembly except for such members as may notify the Director-General of rejection or reservations within the period stated in the notice" (Art. 22, WHO Constitution). Thus, all Member States are bound by the regulations once adopted, provided they have not expressly announced a reservation to them.

So far, the Assembly has adopted only two sets of international regulations under Article 21.

The first (Regulations Regarding Nomenclature No. 1) adopted on 22 May 1967, is not relevant in addressing global health emergencies. In fact the 'Regulations' deal with the harmonization of statistical classifications of

[29] WHO, *WHO Framework Convention on Tabacco Control*, http://www.who.int/tobacco/framework/en/ (last visited 4 Sept. 2009).

[30] The other areas are: (b) nomenclatures with respect to diseases, causes of death and public health practices; (c) standards with respect to diagnostic procedures for international use; (d) standards with respect to the safety, purity and potency of biological, pharmaceutical and similar products moving in international commerce; (e) advertising and labeling of biological, pharmaceutical and similar products moving in international commerce.

[31] Article 60 of the WHO Constitution states: "(a) decision of the Health Assembly on important questions shall be made by a two-thirds majority of members present and voting. These questions shall include: the adoption of conventions or agreements; the approval of agreements bringing the Organization into relations with the United Nations and inter-governmental organizations and agencies in accordance with Articles 69, 70 and 72 [all relating to Relations with other Organizations]; amendments to this Constitutions. (b) Decisions on other questions, including the determination of additional categories of questions to be decided by a two-thirds majority, shall be made by a majority of the members present and voting. (c) voting on analogous matters in the Board and in committees of the Organization shall be made in accordance with paragraphs (a) and (b) of this article.

morbidity and mortality by Members States following WHO recommendation for purpose of easier comparability.[32]

The second set of regulations, the IHR, however, could be a very effective tool to assist States, including failing States, in addressing health emergencies. It was adopted under Article 21 of the Constitution by a Resolution of the Assembly of 25 May 1951.[33] This set of regulations provides unique powers to WHO to address specific infectious diseases, in all States Members. IHR are an important aspect of WHO's strategy to address global health security.

It is worth noting that, historically, internationally coordinated actions to control the spread of certain infections predated the creation of WHO. In fact, when WHO was created, it inherited the responsibility of controlling the international spread of diseases,[34] which was based on a series of international agreements and conventions dating back to 1851, with the first International Sanitary Conference in Paris in 1851. Between then and the end of the century, eight conventions on the spread of infectious diseases across national boundaries were negotiated, and multilateral institutions established to enforce these conventions, including the precursor of the present Pan American Health Organization ("PAHO").

Since its creation in 1948, WHO proceeded with the consolidation of the diverse conventions relating to public health, and in 1951, at its Fourth Health Assembly, adopted the International Sanitary Regulations, which constitute the "only international health agreement on communicable diseases that is binding on Member States."[35] The regulations declare that they replace, between the parties, all earlier conventions and agreements. Their objective is "to ensure the maximum security against the international spread of diseases with a minimum interference with world traffic." At first, they covered the so-called "quarantinable diseases": plague, cholera, yellow fever, smallpox, louse-borne typhus and louse-borne relapsing fever.

---

[32] The text of the Nomenclature Regulations is *available at*: http://www.who.int/classifications/icd/docs/en/NOMREGS.pdf.

[33] Res. WHA4.75 (25 May 1951), 764 U.N.T.S. 3–105 (1971), *available at*: http://www.who.int/csr/ihr/current/en.

[34] G.L. Burci and C-H. Vignes, World Health Organization 134–135 (2004). *See also* A.J. Peaslee, *World Health Organization*, III International Governmental Organizations Constitutional Documents 409–451 (revised 3d ed. 1979).

[35] D.P. Fidler, International Law And Public Health, Materials on and Analysis of Global Health Jurisprudence 129 (2000) (internal citations omitted).

The regulations were revised several times since 1948, mostly as a result of improved knowledge of the spreading of epidemic diseases.[36] For example, louse-borne typhus and louse-borne relapsing fever were removed from the scope of the list in 1969. In the same year, the regulations were renamed to the presently known International Health Regulations.[37] Moreover, following its eradication, smallpox was also removed from the Regulations in 1981.[38]

IHR are unique mechanisms to control the international spreading of certain human diseases.[39] They are an international, legal instrument binding on all WHO Member States who have not rejected them or have made specific reservations, as well as on all Non-Member States of WHO that have agreed to be bound by them. Because WHO enjoys quasi-universal membership, IHR are applicable widely.

IHR require Member States to notify WHO for any single case of cholera, plague or yellow fever that occurs in humans in their territories. WHO reports the notification of each case on the Weekly Epidemiological Record, a widely available publication. Member States are also required to give further notification when an area is free from infection. Significantly, Article 2 of the Regulations expressly affirms that "each State recognizes the rights of the Organization to communicate directly with the health administration of its territory or territories." It is therefore not necessary for WHO to go through official diplomatic channels, as it can directly initiate dialogue with health administrators.

IHR also specifically directs the kind of measures that should be implemented. For example, once a Member State has identified a case of one of the three controlled diseases, the State is required to implement measures like deratting, disinfecting, and disinsecting international carriers at ports and other points of arrival and departure. State Members are also required to provide specified sanitary conditions, facilities and certain services at seaports and airports. In certain circumstances, examinations or other similar measures may be performed on travelers, transportation systems and trade.

Importantly, Article 24 of the IHR provides that "health measures permitted by these regulations are the maximum measures applicable to international traffic which a State may require for the protection of its territory against diseases subject to the Regulations." IHR prohibits the use of other

[36] For example, special provisional provisions relating to the Mecca pilgrimage were repealed in 1956. *See* G.L. Burci and C-H. Vignes, World Health Organization 135 (2004).

[37] Res. WHA22.46 (25 July 1969), ISCD/WP.70.3, *available at*: http://whqlibdoc.who.int/hq/pre-wholis/ISCD_WP_70.3_and_Add.1.pdf.

[38] Res. WHA34.13 (20 May 1981), WHAD/34/1981/REC/1.

[39] For an instructive overview of IHR, *see* WHO, *What Are the International Heath Regulations?*, http://www.who.int/features/qa/39/en/index.html (last visited 4 Sept. 2009).

and different measures. IHR also provides for a State to apply limited measures in respect to certain non-quarantinable diseases, such as the destruction of malaria vectors, or certain measures predicated upon a grave danger to public health.

A fundamental characteristic of IHR is its unique reservation mechanism. In fact, Articles 88 and 91 of IHR contain provisions for which the Assembly reviews all reservations before they come into effect. The Assembly has the power to reject a reservation, which means that the Regulations do not enter into force for the reserving Member State. The authority of the Assembly is unique and "distinguishes the special regime of the regulations from that applicable to reservations to multilateral treaties under general international law and Article 19 to 23 of the Vienna Convention on the Law of Treaties."[40]

IHR thus provide a powerful tool to the WHO Assembly to control the spreading of certain epidemics. As such, in fact, its normative powers can impose obligations even on all its Member States, without their express consent, through a mechanism of implied consent and restricted reservation possibilities.

The IHR mechanisms have, however, never fully developed their potential given by their legal-binding status and have, in fact, not been effective measures to control the global spreading of disease. Several reasons explain this failure.

First, Member States are reluctant to notify outbreaks of diseases subject to HIR for several reasons. Certain States fear disproportionate reactions from WHO Member States and their consequences on trade and tourism. Others are reluctant due to internal political reasons, sometimes linked to a perceived dishonor in experiencing disease outbreaks. Finally, some States simply lack the surveillance systems necessary to recognize and report outbreaks under HIR.[41]

Second, IHR do not contain any enforcement provision.[42] There are no available sanctions for failure to comply with the binding regulations approved under article 21 of the WHO Constitution. Similarly, there is no enforcement provision within IHR themselves, although a dispute resolution mechanism for questions concerning the interpretation or application of IHR does exist.

---

[40] G.L. Burci and C-H. Vignes, World Health Organization 137 (2004).

[41] *See* D.P. Fidler, International Law and Infectious Diseases 133 (1999); *see generally id.* at 129–135.

[42] *See* D.P. Fidler, International Law And Public Health, Materials on and Analysis of Global Health Jurisprudence 134 (2000).

This mechanism, however, does not provide a solid enforcement instrument for failure to comply with IHR mandatory rules.[43]

Third, some of IHR measures have proven ineffective at preventing the spreading of diseases. In fact, in 1968, even the WHO Deputy Director-General himself observed that "the International Sanitary Regulations had failed to contain the international spread of cholera and smallpox – two of the diseases then subject to those regulations."[44]

Fourth, Members States have often adopted excessive measures to control the spreading of certain diseases. They adopted measures that were either prohibited by the regulations or not justified under the epidemiological circumstances of the time.[45] For example, in the wake of the AIDS pandemic, some States imposed restrictive travel measures, including requiring travelers to carry certain health documents.[46] Although this violated IHR regulations, the WHO could not take any enforcement actions.

Fifth, the fact that IHR only concern limited, named diseases is a major limitation. IHR only provide for the control of three specific diseases: yellow fever, cholera and plague. Member States have been reluctant to include new diseases in the list. In fact, while several diseases were removed from the list of the Regulations, including smallpox, which was removed from the list following its eradication in 1981, no new disease has ever been included. Thus, IHR do not provide a general mechanism to control the spreading of all diseases. Historically, this choice was linked to the fact that these diseases are more likely to substantially affect international trade. Moreover, this choice could also be explained by the fact that IHR were first approved in 1948 (and as indicated above it has older historical roots), when little was known about other diseases that are significant now and when the movement of people, goods and pathogens was not as rapid as it is now.

In sum, despite their great potential, IHR failed to provide a generally effective mechanism to assist the international community in addressing global health emergencies and controlling the spreading of disease. The lack of enforcement measures, the mixed track record, the unwillingness of States to comply with its rules and its limited application have barred IHR from

---

[43] Art. 93 of the IHR.

[44] D.P. Fidler, International Law And Public Health, Materials on and Analysis of Global Health Jurisprudence 133 (2000) (internal citations omitted).

[45] G.L. Burci and C-H. Vignes, World Health Organization 137–139 (2004).

[46] G.L. Burci and C-H. Vignes, World Health Organization 138 (2004). Fidler also reports as an example of unnecessary health measures taken under IHR, the EU ban on Fish Exports from Countries in East Africa during a cholera outbreak. *See* D.P. Fidler, International Law And Public Health, Materials on and Analysis of Global Health Jurisprudence 136–139 (2000).

becoming a comprehensive and powerful tool to assess and address global health emergencies.

WHO Members States identified this lost opportunity and, through the WHO Assembly, requested, in May 1995, a revision of the IHR through the adoption of a Resolution on the Revision and Updating of the International Health Regulations.[47] The new draft had the purpose of reflecting the significant changes in disease patterns brought by the emergence and re-emergence of disease, the advancement of medical science, and the changes of communications technology and shipping methods for goods and cargoes since the adoption of the previous version of the IHR in 1969.[48]

3.2. *A New Approach: The Approval of New International Health Regulations*

Recognizing the limitation of IHR, since 1995, several WHO technical committees and the Committee on International Surveillance of Communicable Diseases have worked on the development of a new set of IHR.[49]

The initial central purpose of the New International Health Regulations ("NIHR") was to replace the list of diseases included in the IHR with the concept of 'syndrome notification'. The technical groups working on NIHR first identified five syndromes that could cover all the diseases considered of public health importance. However, after undertaking a pilot project in 22 countries, it was found that syndromes were too difficult to report and could not be linked to pre-determined rules that could properly control the spread of infectious diseases. The syndrome-approach was therefore dropped from NIHR and different ideas pursued.[50]

The SARS epidemics renewed the willingness of the international community to successfully conclude a revision of IHR in the form of a general description of a disease, rather than a named disease. It also stressed the importance of some key points, particularly in terms of WHO's role in

---

[47] World Health Assembly, *Revision and Updating of the International Health Regulations*, Res. WHA48.7 (12 May 1995). *See*, generally, WHO, *International Health Regulations (2005)*, (2nd ed. 2005), *available at*: http://whqlibdoc.who.int/publications/2008/9789241580410_eng.pdf.

[48] As reported in G.L. Burci and C-H. Vignes, World Health Organization 139 (2004). For an American prospective on the new regulations, *see* PAHO, *International Health Regulations: Perspectives From The Region Of The Americas* (1 Aug. 2004), *available at*: http://www.paho.org/English/GOV/CD/cd45-12-e.pdf.

[49] For some negotiating insides, World Health Organization, Regional Office for South-East Asia, *The New International Health Regulations Revision Process* (4 July 2003), SEA/RC56/4; D. Fidler, *Revision of the World Health Organization's International Health Regulations*, ASIL Insights (Apr. 2004), *available at*: http://www.asil.org/insights/insigh132.htm.

[50] G.L. Burci and C-H. Vignes, World Health Organization 139 (2004).

addressing international emergencies relating to infectious diseases. Namely, in a Resolution related to the Revision of IHR and adopted during the SARS emergency, the Health Assembly requested the Director General:

> To take into account reports from sources other than official notification, to validate these reports [on infectious diseases] according to established epidemiological principles;
> To alert, when necessary and after informing the government concerned, the international community to the presence of a public health threat that may constitute a serious threat to neighboring countries or to international health on the basis of criteria and procedures jointly developed with Member States;
> To collaborate with national authorities in assessing the severity of the threat and the adequacy of control measures and, when necessary, in conduction on-the-spot studies by a WHO team with the purpose of ensuring that appropriate control measures are being employed.[51]

The Health Assembly's recommendations are very important because they recognize the importance of collaboration with non-State actors and the need to assess the adequacy of control measures implemented by national authority.

On 23 May 2005, the Health Assembly approved a revision of the International Health Regulations.[52] The purpose and scope of the regulations is stated in Article 2 and are "to prevent, protect against, control and provide a public health response to the international spread of disease in ways that are commensurate with and restricted to public health risks, and which avoid unnecessary interference with international traffic and trade."

NIHR became legally binding on all WHO Member States, except for those Members that have rejected them or have submitted reservations, in June 2007, 18 months after the notification of their adoption. If a Member State submits a reservation, the Regulations enter into force for the reserving State, subject to the reservation, only if the Health Assembly estimates that the reservation is compatible with the object and purpose of the NIHR and has not been objected to by at least one third of the other States within six months of its notification. Non-Member States of WHO may also notify the Director-General of WHO if they agree to be bound by the Regulations (Article 62).

State Parties must meet the requirements set forth in the NIHR as soon as possible and no later than five years after its entry into force. The implemen-

[51] Res. WHA56.28, Revision of the International Health Regulations (28 May 2003), *available at*: http://www.who.int/gb/ebwha/pdf_files/WHA56/ea56r28.pdf.

[52] Res. WHA58.3, *available at*: http://www.who.int/gb/ebwha/pdf_files/WHA58/WHA58_3–en.pdf.

tation phase is divided into two parts: the first two years, until June 2009, will focus on the assessment of existing national structures, resources and the development of a national plan of action. The following three years, until June 2012, will focus on the implementation of the action plans and the need to meet the core requirements capacity.[53]

NHIR represent a significant step forward in WHO's ability to control and prevent health emergencies of an international nature.

First, Article 1 of NIHR adopts a larger and more comprehensive definition of public health emergency than IHR. It defines a "public health emergency of international concern" using two concomitant elements. Such an emergency must "constitute a public health risk to other States through the international spread of disease" AND "potentially require a coordinated international response."[54]

This new definition of a public health emergency is of paramount significance. In fact, it addresses one of the main problems of IHR, and allows the application of NIHR to a wide range of diseases that can not presently be known. In fact, this definition covers all existing, new and re-emerging diseases, including emergencies caused by non-infectious disease agents. As such, it significantly enlarges the applicability of IHR and thus overcomes one of the most important limits of IHR – that it previously was only applicable to three determined diseases.

Moreover, it is based on two facts that have a high potential impact to efficiently coordinate a response in situations of State failure: first, a 'public health emergency' must pose a risk to other States. Thus, the cross-boundary character of present day health emergencies has become a central feature of NIHR. NIHR are only applicable if the disease has the potential to spread internationally and poses a risk to other States. Second, the new definition also recognizes that a health emergency requires an international coordinated response. This is further recognition that, increasingly, States cannot cope by themselves in health (and other) emergencies but need to coordinate a joint response.

To analyze the relevance of an event as an international public health risk, a series of factors must be taken into consideration, including geographical setting, time, size of outbreak, closeness to an international border or airport, the speed of spreading and mode of transmission. Article 12 provides the

---

53 WHO, *International Health Regulations (2005): Areas Of Work For Implementation* (June 2007), WHO/CDS/EPR/IHR/2007.1, *available at*: http://www.who.int/ihr/finalversion-9Nov07.pdf.

54 Res. WHA58.3, Revision of the International Health Regulations Art. 1, *available at*: http://www.who.int/ipcs/publications/wha/ihr_resolution.pdf.

criteria upon which the Director General of WHO, in consultation with the State Party concerned, may determine the existence of a health emergency of international concern.[55]

Importantly, Annex 2 of the Regulations provides States with a decision instrument (a 'decision tree' or algorithm) to assess events occurring in their territory. The occurrence of certain diseases, such as SARS, polio and Yellow Fever, needs to be reported directly. However, when other unspecified and unknown diseases are found, the decision instrument is used. Once the conclusion that the event qualifies as an international public health risk is reached, the State must notify WHO. The 'decision tree' contains four criteria:

1. Seriousness of the public health impact of the event;
2. Unusual or unexpected nature of the event;
3. Potential for the event to spread internationally; and/or
4. The risk that restrictions to travel or trade may result because of the event.

NIHR also provides for the establishment of an independent Emergency Committee to inform this process by advising the Director-General of WHO and to help determine when a particular event constitutes a public health emergency of international concern.

Further, the new framework is a significant step forward in terms of applicability of legally binding measures to international situations that qualify as health emergencies and that pose a public risk.

The new Regulations require all States to notify WHO of any event that may constitute a public health emergency of international concern within 24 hours from the event (Article 6). The notification can be kept reserved. Importantly, States must respond to WHO's requests for verification of information regarding health emergencies events, so that appropriate technical collaboration for effective protection of such emergencies can be ensured and, if necessary, other States can be informed of the public health risks that may require their attention. Further, each State is required to establish national IHR focal points to ensure continuous contacts with WHO, which must be known to all States (Article 4).

WHO Member States have further agreed to provide routine inspection and control activities at international airports, ports and some ground crossings to prevent international disease transmission. States are also bound to develop, strengthen and maintain the capacity to detect and report health emergencies as defined by NIHR.

---

[55] *Id.* Art. 12.

Moreover, in the event of a health emergency, States must respond to public health risks which may spread internationally. States must also provide the public health rationale and scientific justification for any additional measures that significantly interfere with international traffic adopted in accordance with Article 43 of the NIHR and to review such measures as required under that provision.

Additionally, the new regulations enhance the role of WHO. In the event of an emergency, WHO itself may recommend measures to be adopted by States affected by a public health emergency of international concern. Other States and operators of international transport WHO will also have to assist all Member States in assessing and controlling outbreaks, thus increasing the credibility of each Member's response. WHO may make temporary recommendations on an *ad hoc*, time-limited, risk-specific basis (Article 15).

WHO can also produce standing recommendations that indicate the appropriate measures to be applied for specific ongoing public health risks at certain international airports, ports and ground crossings and are for routine or periodic application. These can be directed at persons, baggage, cargo, containers, ships, aircraft, road vehicles, goods or postal parcels (Article 16).

In sum, NHIR represent a major step forward in controlling the global spread of disease. However, as for any international agreement, NIHR represent a consensus among WHO Member States on the balance between their sovereign rights and shared commitment to prevent the international spread of disease. The compromise between the varying interests permeates the Regulations.

First, similarly to IHR, NIHR do not include any enforcement mechanism to be used against a State that fails to comply with NIHR provisions. Although there are soft mechanisms that may stimulate compliance, there are no mandatory tools to enforce it.

Second, NIHR contain no provisions that allow WHO to act upon an emergency in the absence of State's action. Thus, only countries with a working health system will be able to fully participate in the NIHR system. The establishment of the national focal points may be relevant, especially coupled with a State's obligation to respond to WHO requests for verification of information regarding health emergencies events. However, the fact that no enforcement mechanisms exist undermines the stringency of the rule.

Third, NHIR are still only focused on monitoring health situations and WHO can only issue recommendations for the adoption of measures.

To conclude, NIHR represent an important step forward for a global action on health emergency. The two-prone definition of international health emergency is important: it indeed can encompass all international threats and it is based on the risk that it may cause to other States. Moreover, it is also important that one of the requirements that must be met is the fact that it potentially requires a coordinated international response. This underlines the importance of a common reaction. Moreover, States must nominate focal points and must respond to WHO's enquiry.

However, the use of the NIHR in a situation of State failure is limited. In fact, neither WHO, other States or organizations can monitor or officially be mandated to monitor, through NHIR, the health situation of failing States and report on possible public health emergencies. It is possible that national focal points, when they are established, take up this role and communicate directly with WHO. However, this would still be a peculiar circumstance, and not a power derived from NIHR. Similarly, neither WHO nor any other actor can officially control the outbreak of disease in sovereign areas that lack the national capacity to control disease spreading.

Thus, the most vulnerable and serious situations of health emergencies have not been addressed by Member States in the NIHR. Global health emergencies will remain a security threat in failing States under the regimen provided by the NIHR.

3.3. *Directing and Coordinating Powers of WHO: Epidemic and Pandemic Alert Response*

The second instrument created by the WHO to deal with global outbreak of disease is the Global Outbreak Alert and Response Network (GOARN).[56] GOARN provides a more comprehensive and flexible instrument than IHR to address health emergencies. Moreover, GOARN can also be applied in conjunction with IHR to cover the three IHR diseases and operate under the new NIHR regime. It will also be useful in coordinating the ground response with NIHR.

GOARN derives from the directing and coordinating powers of WHO and therefore is not binding on all its Member States. In fact, "generally, WHO has preferred to set norms or standards by non-binding recommendations which entails a duty of members to report on any action taken."[57] The coordinating and directing powers of WHO are enshrined in article 2 of the WHO Constitution, which affirms that "in order to achieve its objective, the functions of the Organization shall be: (a) to act as the directing and

[56] For a description of the Network and of its history. *See* WHO Department Of Communicable Disease Surveillance And Response, *A Framework for Global Outbreak Alert and Response*, WHO/CDS/CSR/2000.2, *available at*: http://www.who.int/csr/resources/publications/surveillance/whocdscsr2002.pdf.

[57] *World Health Organization*, 3 Encyclopedia of Public International Law 406–409 (Bernhardt ed. 1997).

coordinating authority on international health work." Article 23 and 62 of WHO's Constitution further give the Assembly the power to issue recommendations and the Member States the duty to report on their actions with respect to the recommendations.[58]

The creation of GOARN is recent and is the product of technical collaboration of several institutions and networks (it has 110 technical members) that combine human and technical resources with the goal of rapid identification, confirmation and response of outbreaks of international importance.[59] The Network provides an operational framework that links expertise and skills with the purpose of keeping the international community alert to any threat of outbreaks so as to be ready to respond to them.

GOARN was the outcome of a meeting held in Geneva in April 2001 that was called to discuss the necessity and feasibility of responding to global outbreaks. Participants include several U.N. agencies – including WHO and UNICEF – the International Committee of the Red Cross, the International Federation of the Red Cross and Red Crescent Societies, several NGOs (such as Médecins Sans Frontières, the International Rescue Committee) as well as scientific institutions in Member States, regional networks and laboratories.

GOARN implements the 'Global Health Security Resolution' in which the Health Assembly expressed its support for the "collaboration between WHO and all potential technical partners in the area of epidemic alert and response, including relevant public sectors, intergovernmental organizations, non-governmental organizations and the private sector."[60] GOARN also implements the Assembly's request, included in the same Resolution, to the Director-General to provide technical support to all Member States to develop intervention programs to prevent and strengthen their capacity to respond to epidemics and communicable disease threats and emergencies.[61] This Resolution is fundamental in the effort to control the spread of diseases. First, it recognizes the importance of collaboration with technical partners, including NGOs. Second, it mandates that the Director-General strengthen WHO's assistance to Member States in matters of epidemics prevention and control.

---

[58] Article 23 reads: "The Health Assembly shall have authority to make recommendations to Members with respect to any matter within the competence of the Organization." Article 62 monitors the implementation of the recommendations. It states: "Each Member shall report annually on the action taken with respect to recommendations made to it by the Organization and with respect to conventions, agreements and regulations."

[59] WHO, *Global Outbreak Alert & Response Network*, http://www.who.int/csr/outbreaknetwork/en/ (last visited 4 Sept. 2009).

[60] Res. WHA54.14, ¶ 1(3), *available at*: http://www.amun.org/final/03/WHA_II_1.pdf.

[61] Res. WHA54.14, ¶ 3(4), *available at*: http://www.amun.org/final/03/WHA_II_1.pdf.

WHO provides the secretarial service for GOARN, which is guided by a Steering Committee. WHO also coordinates international outbreak response through the use of resources from within the network.

In the field of global health security, GOARN's objective is to combat the international spread of disease outbreaks and to ensure that affected States receive appropriate technical assistance rapidly. GOARN also aims at contributing to long-term epidemic preparedness and capacity building. GOARN covers the outbreak of all diseases included in EPR strategy, including also the three IHR diseases.[62]

Since its creation, GOARN has worked on the development of agreed-upon standards for international epidemic response and has adopted Guiding Principles for International Outbreak Alert and Response. These principles aim to improve the coordination of international assistance in support of local efforts by partners of GOARN and seek to "improve the delivery of international assistance in support of local efforts by partners in the Global Outbreak Alert and Response Network, and seek to promote the highest standards of professional performance in the field."[63] Moreover, GOARN members have also agreed on several operational protocols that standardize epidemiological, laboratory, clinical management, research, communications, logistics support, security, evacuation and communications systems.

Ten Guiding Principles for International Outbreak Alert and Response express the consensus between partners of GOARN on how to respond to and evaluate outbreaks of diseases of international importance, how to coordinate field activities and how to secure international support. The Guiding Principles are sustained by detailed standard operating protocols. They are the following:

1. WHO ensures outbreaks of potential international importance are rapidly verified and information is quickly shared within the Network. There is a rapid response coordinated by the Operational Support Team to requests for assistance from affected State(s).
2. The most appropriate experts reach the field in the least possible time to carry out coordinated and effective outbreak control activities.
3. The international team integrates and coordinates activities to support national efforts and existing public health infrastructure.

[62] The diseases included in the EPR strategy are: Anthrax, Avian influenza, Crimean-Congo haemorrhagic fever (CCHF), Dengue/dengue haemorrhagic fever, Ebola haemorrhagic fever, Hepatitis, Influenza, Lassa fever, Marburg haemorrhagic fever, Meningococcal disease, Plague, Rift Valley fever, Severe Acute Respiratory Syndrome (SARS), Smallpox, Tularaemia and Yellow fever.

[63] WHO, *Guiding Principles for International Outbreak Alert and Response*, http://www.who.int/csr/outbreaknetwork/guidingprinciples/en/print.html (last visited 5 Sept. 2009).

4. There is a fair and equitable process for the participation of Network partners in international responses.
5. There is strong technical leadership and coordination in the field.
6. Partners make every effort to ensure the effective coordination of their participation and support of outbreak response.
7. There is recognition of the unique role of national and international non-governmental organizations (NGOs) in the area of health, including in the control of outbreaks. NGOs providing support that would not otherwise be available, particularly in reaching poor populations. While striving for effective collaboration and coordination, the Network will respect the independence and objectivity of all partners.
8. Responses will be used as a mechanism to build global capacity by the involvement of participants from field-based training programmes in applied epidemiology and public health practice [...].
9. There is commitment to national and regional capacity building as a follow up to international outbreak responses to improve preparedness and reduce future vulnerability to epidemic prone diseases.
10. All Network responses will proceed with full respect for ethical standards, human rights, national and local laws, cultural sensitivities and traditions.[64]

These principles are general, but appear to provide an effective way of addressing disease breakouts. In fact, since its creation, GOARN has been operational in several countries, including several failed States. Principle 2, relating to carrying out coordinated and affective outbreak control activities, is particularly relevant. Operations by GOARN in support of the delivery of international assistance and to support local efforts include intervention in Afghanistan, Burkina Faso, Côte d'Ivoire, Ethiopia, Kosovo, Republic of the Congo, Sierra Leone, and Sudan.[65]

A key feature of GOARN is the Global Alert and Response Team ("GART") which is in charge of assessing the epidemiological significance of any reported outbreak and of deciding whether any action is needed. The team is composed of members from WHO Country Offices, WHO sub-regional Response Teams, WHO Regional Offices, the Alert and Response Operations Centre team in Geneva and disease specialists. Every day, in Geneva, GART deals with reports of possible outbreaks and reports of unknown disease.[66] Once

---

[64] *Id.*

[65] WHO, *Containing Outbreaks in the Field*, http://www.who.int/csr/alertresponse/field/en/index.html (last visited 5 Sept. 2009).

[66] WHO, *Event Verification*, http://www.who.int/csr/alertresponse/verification/en/ (last visited 5 Sept. 2009).

verified, the reports of disease outbreaks are reported in widely accessible publications.[67]

GART developed six criteria to assess the seriousness of the reports for global health:

1. Whether the disease is unknown;
2. The potential for its spreading beyond national borders;
3. The seriousness of the health impact or of unexpectedly high rates of illness or death;
4. The potential for interference with international travel or trade;
5. The strength of national capacity to contain the outbreak;
6. Whether the disease is a suspected accidental or deliberate release.[68]

The second and last criteria are especially relevant for actions in situations of health emergencies in failing States. The fact that the seriousness of a report is assessed on its potential of spreading beyond national borders clearly underlines the preoccupation of global, rather than localized, emergencies. Similarly, the assessment of the strength of national capacity to contain the outbreak signals that GOARN anticipates the possibility of an outbreak and is willing to taking action when a State is incapable to do so.

Once the seriousness of the outbreak is confirmed, WHO provides targeted technical advice and supplies to the affected States. Importantly, WHO, through GOARN, can coordinate investigations and responses.[69]

The SARS outbreak provided an important testing ground for the efficacy of GOARN. In fact, GOARN was instrumental in dealing with the epidemics. First, the initial unofficial reports of an unknown disease in China were received and verified through GOARN. Second, GOARN was shown to be an available instrument to control the epidemics, with the effort to control the epidemics coordinated, in part, through GOARN.

GOARN's role in successfully dealing with the epidemic was recognized by the health community. In May 2003, the Health Assembly approved a

---

[67] These publications include the WHO Outbreak Verification List (OVL), a weekly publication targeted at public health professionals with information on verified or under-verification disease outbreaks of international public health importance so that timely actions can be taken. The Disease Outbreak News provides public information regarding officially confirmed outbreaks of international importance. The Weekly Epidemiological Record covers epidemiological information on cases and outbreaks of diseases under the IHR and also on other communicable diseases of public health importance. WHO, *Information Management and Dissemination*, http://www.who.int/csr/alertresponse/infomanagement/en/print.html (last visited 5 Sept. 2009).

[68] WHO, *Event Verification*, http://www.who.int/csr/alertresponse/verification/en/print.html (last visited 5 Sept. 2009).

[69] WHO, *Coordinated Rapid Outbreak Response*, http://www.who.int/csr/alertresponse/rapidresponse/en/print.html (last visited 5 Sept. 2009).

resolution on SARS requesting the Director-General "to strengthen the function of WHO's Global Outbreak Alert and Response Network."[70] Moreover, in another Resolution approved in the same session, the Assembly requested that the Director General, in the revision process of IHR, take into account reports from sources other than official notifications and collaborate with national authorities to assess the adequacy of their control measures.[71] Importantly, these resolutions show the support by the Assembly to the activities carried out by GOARN and the methodologies it applies.

So far, in the first eight months of 2009 alone, GOARN has already reported more than one hundred outbreaks.[72] Of these, sixty-four of the reported outbreaks relate to the swine flu pandemic (H1N1) and twenty-two concern avian flu in Egypt.

The most recent outbreak concerned avian flu in Egypt. The case was reported on 31 August 2009 by the Ministry of Health of Egypt. The report states that two new human cases of avian influenza A (H5N1) were confirmed by the Egyptian Central Public Health Laboratories. The report also contained information on the possible sources of the disease and how it was cured.[73]

Another recent report was released related to the outbreak of cholera in Zimbabwe. On 9 June 2009, the report confirmed that in the last ten months, the Ministry of Health and Child Welfare of Zimbabwe had reported 98,424 suspected cases of cholera, including 4,276 deaths. The Report also specified that WHO and its GOARN partners had been working with the Ministry of Health of Zimbabwe with cholera control efforts across the country.[74]

These two cases exemplify the different options available to GOARN members when confirming and reacting to a disease outbreak. In the case of Egypt, the verification of the virus was performed by the Egyptian Ministry of Health. In the case of Zimbabwe, GOARN partners have worked with the Ministry of Health to control the spread the disease.

Interestingly, GOARN's activities also play a role in the implementation of NIHR. For example, China reported at the beginning of May 2008, the outbreak of hand, foot and mouth disease ("HFMD") due to enterovirus

[70] Res. WHA56.29 ¶ 2, Severe Acute Respiratory Syndrome (SARS) (28 May 2003).

[71] Res. WHA56.28, Revision of the International Health Regulations (28 May 2003).

[72] *See* WHO, *Global Alert and Response*, http://www.who.int/csr/don/archive/year/2009/en/index.html (last visited 5 Sept. 2009).

[73] WHO, *Avian Influenza – Situation in Egypt* (31 Aug. 2009) http://www.who.int/csr/don/2009_08_31/en/index.html (last visited 5 Sept. 2009).

[74] WHO, *Cholera In Zimbabwe – Update 4* (9 June 2009), http://www.who.int/csr/don/2009_06_09/en/index.html (last visited 5 Sept. 2009).

71 ("EV71") in Fuyang City in China.[75] The outbreak counted several thousand cases, of which about twenty were fatal. On 21 May 2008, the Chinese Center for Disease Control and Prevention, in collaboration with the WHO Representative Office in China, released a preliminary report on the outbreak which stated that

> As part of the efforts to implement the International Health Regulations [NIHR] China will further strengthen the early warning system by immediate notification of clustering of clinically abnormal and severe cases, as well as increasing international collaboration and information exchange.[76]

GOARN has also shown its viability in situations where the support of the State is completely lacking, for example, including several outbreaks in Somalia, even when the security situation raised concerns during its operations.

In January 2007, the WHO reported 100 suspected cases of Rift Valley Fever, including 48 deaths, in Somalia. Several actors were involved in the process of detection, confirmation and containment: one case was confirmed by laboratory analysis in the Kenyan Institute of Medical Research and the Centers for Disease Control and Prevention/International Emerging Infectious Program in Kenya. Médecins sans Frontières facilitated the transport of samples and the WHO country office held training sessions with Somali medical officers on how to detect and contain the disease. However, it was also reported that the deteriorating security situation hampered control measures in the affected area.[77]

Further, in 2002, the Ministry of Health of Somalia reported an outbreak of meningitis, later confirmed by the WHO Collaborating Centre for Reference and Research on Meningococci, National Institute of Public Health in Oslo. As a result of the outbreak, a crisis committee was set up by the Ministry of Health, the Somali Red Crescent Society ("SRCS"), Médecins sans Frontières, UNICEF and WHO. The Committee strengthened surveillance and prepared

[75] WHO, *Enterovirous in China* (1 May 2008), http://www.who.int/csr/don/2008_05_01/en/index.html (last visited 5 Sept. 2009). Two further updates were also issued on May 20th: WHO, *Yellow Fever in the Central African Republic* (20 May 2008), http://www.who.int/csr/don/2008_05_20/en/index.html (last visited 5 Sept. 2009) and May 21st: WHO, *Enterovirus in China – Update 2* (21 May 2008), http://www.who.int/csr/don/2008_05_21/en/index.html (last visited 5 Sept. 2009).

[76] WHO, *Enterovirus in China – Update 2* (21 May 2008), http://www.who.int/csr/don/2008_05_21/enl (last visited 5 Sept. 2009).

[77] WHO, *Rift Valley Fever in Kenya and Somalia – Update 3* (31 Jan. 2007),http://www.who.int/csr/don/2007_01_31/en/index.html (last visited 5 Sept. 2009).

a mass vaccination campaign.[78] The campaign vaccinated 67,681 people in the first few weeks.[79]

Again, on 2 May 2000, WHO reported 2,232 confirmed cases of cholera in certain regions of Somalia. WHO carried out cholera control coordination activities through the cholera task force, whose membership includes UNICEF, Action Internationale Contre la Faim, the International Medical Corps, Médecins sans Frontières, the Coordinating Committee of the Organization for Voluntary Services and the Somali Red Crescent Society.[80]

To conclude, it seems that GOARN is able to provide effective assistance in cases of a disease outbreak and to control the spread of disease. Although it is based on a voluntary mechanism, GOARN is effective in reporting, managing and – to a certain extent – controlling the spreading of disease even in failed States, where health systems do not exist or do not properly function. Moreover, the fact that reports are assessed on the basis of the capability of a national health system to contain the outbreak ensures that proper action is taken in situations of State failure. However, as highlighted above, deteriorating security situations also play a role in the ability to control the spread of diseases in failed States.

GOARN is an elastic system based on collaboration between national and international healthcare professionals. The assistance provided by GOARN depends upon the threat that the disease outbreak poses on the international community and on international travel and trade, the knowledge of the specific disease, the seriousness of the health impact and the viability of the affected national health system. If a State is capable of controlling and reporting disease outbreak, it will do so. Otherwise, WHO's personnel in the field or other healthcare professionals will report the outbreak. WHO always coordinated the response, as possible, with the competent Health Ministry. WHO and the Network will take a larger role if national authorities do not possess the required expertise and capacity to control the outbreak. This 'elastic' solution seems to be particularly fitting for failed States.

GOARN also has some important limitations. The main limitation is that it is based on a voluntary system of coordination and is not a legally binding instrument. This means that it does not contain enforcing measures. Thus, for example, GOARN was powerless in the SARS epidemic until China let the inspection team into its territory. It is possible, however, that GOARN has been effective in many circumstances because it is, indeed, based on a loose rela-

---

[78] WHO, *Meningococcal Disease in Somalia – Update* (18 Jan. 2002), http://www.who.int/csr/don/2002_01_18/en/print.html (last visited 5 Sept. 2009).

[79] WHO, *Meningococcal Meningitis in Somalia – Update 1* (28 Jan. 2002), http://www.who.int/csr/don/2002_01_28/en/print.html (last visited 5 Sept. 2009).

[80] WHO, *Cholera in Somalia* (2 May 2000), http://www.who.int/csr/don/2000_05_02/en/print.html (last visited 5 Sept. 2009).

tionship between different actors that are not competing against each other. GOARN's strength is based on the fact that its membership is varied; it includes governmental and non-governmental actors as well as international organizations. Moreover, GOARN's members only include health professionals, not politicians or negotiators. As such, it does not hurt sovereignty sensibilities.

As shown above, the Health Assembly has suggested integrating NHIR within the GOARN framework. This will enhance the efficiency of both systems. In fact, on one side, GOARN will be involved in a normative structure. Presumably, this will enhance its reach in scope of operation. Alternatively, some part of NIHR will be implemented through a proven efficient methodology, thus probably eliminating some of the weaknesses of the previous IHR system.

3.4. *Directing and Coordinating Powers of WHO: The Polio Eradication Campaign*

Within its directing and coordinating powers, WHO is also active in the prevention of diseases through vaccination campaigns. This instrument is particularly interesting because it focuses on preventing the occurrence of diseases that may pose a serious threat to its people. This is a good example of the general strategy adopted by the international community to support health systems in failing and failed States. The most relevant example of such vaccination campaign is the Polio Eradication Program which is carried out by WHO in conjunction with other international actors.

In May 1988, the 41st Health Assembly WHO's Members States and WHO committed to the global eradication of poliomyelitis and emphasized that eradication "should be pursued in ways that strengthen the development of the Expanded Programme on Immunization as a whole, fostering its contribution, in turn, to the development of the health infrastructure and primary health care."[81] The Health Assembly mandated WHO develop a Polio Eradication Program. WHO maintains a coordinating and monitoring role. The United Nations Children's Fund (UNICEF) assists WHO in implementing the program on the ground, and it is an essential partner on the ground. Rotary International and the Center for Disease Control and Prevention (CDC) are also involved in the coordination, vaccines procurement and funding. The U.S. Government – through the CDC – USAID, the World Bank and other governmental donors are the main sponsors of the campaign.[82]

---

[81] Res. WHA41.28, Global eradication of poliomyelitis by the year 2000 (13 May 1988), *available at*: http://www.who.int/csr/ihr/polioresolution4128en.pdf.

[82] Is it estimated that once eradication occurs, the savings in economic, health care and related costs will amount to USD 1 billion per year. *See* WHO, *Global Polio Eradication Initiative –*

The eradication programs have been quite successful. By the end of 2003, polio had been eliminated from all but 6 countries in the world as a result of the Global Polio Eradication Initiative.[83] Polio transmission has been interrupted in the Americas, Europe and Western Pacific, and 175 countries are certified polio-free.

However, the campaign also faced some setbacks. For example, in 2003, Kano, in Northern Nigeria, suspended vaccinations for a year as a result of concerns by traditional and religious leaders over the safety of the oral polio vaccine. This resulted in a substantial increase in polio cases in 2004 over the same period in 2003 in Sub-Saharan Africa, including in locations previously declared polio-free.[84] It is estimated that because of this event, the entire eradication program has been delayed by at least a couple of years. Twenty-one previously polio-free countries were re-infected from 2003 through 2005. However, as of 2008, the outbreaks in these countries either stopped or are nearing eradication. The polio virus is now endemic in only four countries (Afghanistan, India, Nigeria and Pakistan).[85]

The implementation of polio-eradication programs is mostly carried out by UNICEF professionals, as polio vaccination targets at children, while WHO is involved in the strategic development of the eradication program. UNICEF's main implementation tool for vaccination campaigns is the organization of National Polio Immunization Days ("NIDs") and Sub-National Polio Immunization Days ("SNIDs"). In general, NIDs and SNIDs are conducted around the world, a few times a year and are coordinated through an Interagency Coordinating Committee, which includes representatives of national health authorities, international organizations, donors, and, often, of civil society.[86]

UNICEF identified the major challenge for a successful polio eradication campaign as access to children in conflict areas. In fact, ongoing conflicts in certain countries make implementation of vaccination and surveillance activities particularly challenging, especially when compounded with a destroyed/

Strategic Plan (2004–2008) 4 (2003), WHO Doc. WHO/Polio/00/05 (2001–2005), *available at*: http://www.unicef.org/immunization/files/global_polio_erad_int_plan_2001_2005.pdf.

83 *Id.*

84 Global Polio Eradication Initiative, *Statement/4 Global Polio Eradication Initiative Welcomes Immunization Campaign in Kano, Nigeria* (3 Aug. 2004), www.polioeradication.org/content/pressreleases/20040803_press.pdf (last visited 5 Sept. 2009).

85 Global Polio Eradication Initiative, *Wild Poliovirus Weekly Update* (2 Sept. 2009), http://www.polioeradication.org/casecount.asp (last visited 5 Sept. 2009).

86 WHO et al., Communication for Routine Immunizations and Polio Eradication: A Synopsis of five sub-Saharan Country Case Studies 7 (June 2000), *available at*: http://www.afro.who.int/socialmobilisation/pdf/synopsis-fivesubsaharan.pdf.

weakened healthcare system.[87] Moreover, in situations where national authorities are not able to assist in the initiative, intervention can be difficult. UNICEF identified several priority countries[88] where the situation is particularly urgent.

In 2004 in Afghanistan, for example, UNICEF supported the national efforts to eradicate polio. Together with the Ministry of Health and WHO, UNICEF increased polio immunization of children. Two rounds of National Immunization Days ("NIDs") were held in March and April, targeting all children below five years of age, reaching an estimated 6.6 million children. Sub-National NIDs were also conducted and follow-up actions planned.[89]

Subsequently, cease-fires and Days of Tranquility have been negotiated with national authorities in, among others, the DRC and Peru, to guarantee access for vaccinations, which demonstrates the feasibility of working successfully in conflict-affected areas.[90]

Similarly, in Somalia, which had been declared polio-free, UNICEF organized NIDs with the assistance of local communities. On 13 September 2005, however, one case of poliomyelitis was reported in Mogadishu. As a result, the Global Polio Eradication Initiative – led by the WHO, Rotary International, CDC and UNICEF – launched a new series of polio immunization campaigns to prevent the re-establishment of the disease in the Horn of Africa.[91]

Another significant example is that of Southern Sudan. In 2004, all international humanitarian activities in Southern Sudan were coordinated with the Secretariat of Health ("SOH") of the Sudan Peoples' Liberation Movement (SPLM), which is a representative of the rebel group in charge of power in Southern Sudan, and not of the Khartoum government. Polio is on the verge of eradication in Southern Sudan, with no new cases reported from 2001 to early 2004.[92] However, following the events in Nigeria, some new

---

[87] UNICEF, *UNICEF's Role in Emergencies* (20 Apr. 2006), http://www.unicef.org/emerg/index_33296.html (last visited 5 Sept. 2009).

[88] UNICEF, *UNICEF In Emergencies: Reaching the Vulnerable* (24 June 2009), http://www.unicef.org/emerg/index.html (last visited 5 Sept. 2009).

[89] UNICEF, *Afghanistan Donor Update* (30 Sept. 2004), http://www.unicef.org/emerg/files/Emergencies_Afghanistan_Donor_Update_300904.pdf (last visited 5 Sept. 2009).

[90] UNICEF, *Machel Study 10-Year Strategic Review Children And Conflict In A Changing World* 124 (Apr. 2009), *available at*: http://www.unicef.org/publications/files/Machel_Study_10_Year_Strategic_Review_EN_030909.pdf.

[91] WHO, *Poliomyelitis in Somalia* (13 Sept. 2005), *available at*: http://www.who.int/csr/don/2005_09_13/en/print.html (last visited 5 Sept. 2009).

[92] United Nations, *Southern Sudan Consolidated Donor Report 2004*, 9 (31 Mar. 2005), *available at*: http://www.unicef.org/emerg/files/SouthernSudanAnnualDonorReport2004.pdf (last visited 5 Sept. 2009).

cases were diagnosed in Southern Sudan, in late 2004, which were genetically traced back to Nigeria. UNICEF was concerned that the resurgence of polio in Sudan could become a threat to neighboring countries and re-infect them. Thus, it launched an extensive vaccination campaign. First, in 2004, UNICEF supported SOH to establish the first Expanded Program of Immunization office in Rumbek. Moreover, in a joint WHO-UNICEF effort, 1.9 million children under five were vaccinated during the first Sub National Immunization Day. Other campaigns were conducted in 2005 "as part of synchronized attempts to bring the national outbreak under control."[93]

Both practitioners and scholars recognize the importance of directly engaging regional leaders. In fact, WHO acknowledged that the role international and national organizations "in establishing access, cease-fires, and "Days of Tranquility" for NIDs in Afghanistan, Democratic Republic of the Congo, Peru and elsewhere has demonstrated the feasibility of working successfully in conflict-affected areas. These efforts must be expanded, drawing upon the strengths of the U.N. Secretary-General's office, many U.N. agencies, the International Red Cross and Red Crescent movement, and other new and existing partners who can operate in countries affected by conflict."[94]

This policy paid off. In fact, on 10 November 2005, WHO announced that the spread of polio had been stopped in 10 countries in West and Central Africa,[95] with only a maintenance immunization program necessary to achieve complete eradication.[96]

The successes of the vaccination campaigns demonstrate the efficacy of certain instruments set up by the international community. This is a preventive instrument rather than a response to an actual emergency threat. However, it is important to show that such instruments exist and that collaboration between different organizations has been tested. Moreover, the polio eradication effort is financed mostly by polio-free countries and non-governmental organizations. This also shows that once a health related mat-

[93] *Id.*

[94] WHO, Global Polio Eradication Initiative – Strategic Plan (2004–2008) 7 (2003), WHO Doc. WHO/Polio/00/05 (2001–2005), *available at*: http://www.unicef.org/immunization/files/global_polio_erad_int_plan_2001_2005.pdf.

[95] Benin, Burkina Faso, Cameroon, Central African Republic, Chad, Côte d'Ivoire, Ghana, Guinea, Mali and Togo.

[96] Press Release, WHO/UNICEF/ Rotary International/CDC, Massive international effort stops polio epidemic across 10 West and Central African countries (11 Nov. 2005), http://www.who.int/mediacentre/news/releases/2005/pr60/en/print.html (last visited 5 Sept. 2009). Also reported in *Polio spread halted across Africa*, BBC News, 11 Nov. 2005, http://news.bbc.co.uk/1/hi/world/africa/4426836.stm (last visited 6 Sept. 2009).

ter is identified as being of global importance, the international community is capable of delivering efficient instruments.

WHO/UNICEF's success in dealing with sub-regional and rebel groups shows their effectiveness in working in situation of conflict and State failure. Paradoxically, the 2003 difficulties of implementing vaccination programs in Nigeria show the limitations still faced by international organizations in relation to recalcitrant sovereign States.

3.5. *Other General Mechanisms in Support of Health Systems of Failed States: Interventions in Situations of Humanitarian Crises*

A second example of a broad and general mechanism adopted by the international community to support the health systems of failing and failed States are humanitarian programs. In fact, failing States are often conflict countries or countries with severe humanitarian needs. The international community, and particularly the United Nations, has created important mechanisms for intervention in such situations. In situations of humanitarian crises, the Office for the Coordination of Humanitarian Affairs ("OCHA"), a special section of the U.N. Secretariat, coordinates all operations, while other agencies and organizations implement their programs as per their mandate.

These interventions are a fundamental mechanism for failed and failing States to deliver health care to their populations, as it provides targeted support to populations in need. Equally, it is a mechanism by which the international community can ensure that minimum health standards are maintained.

OCHA is active in twenty nine countries[97] in Africa, Asia, Europe and the Americas. It coordinates the activities of several fields, including health, food distribution, shelter and protection.

UNICEF is an operational agency and has several projects on the ground. It also created a special program for its actions in Countries in Crises.[98] The program is specifically targeted at countries experiencing emergency situa-

---

[97] *See* OCHA, *OCHA Offices Around the World*, http://ochaonline.un.org/Geographic/tabid/1084/Default.aspx (last visited 6 Sept. 2009).

[98] UNICEF includes in his countries in crises program the following countries: Afghanistan, Angola, Bangladesh, Benin, Burundi, Caribbean, Central African Republic, Central America, Chad, Colombia, Côte d'Ivoire, DPR Korea, Democratic Republic of Congo (DRC), Eritrea, Ethiopia, Georgia, Ghana, Guinea, Guyana, Haiti, Indian Ocean Tsunami, Indonesia, Iran, Kenya, Liberia, Madagascar, Malawi, Mauritania, Mozambique, Namibia, Niger, Northern Caucasus (Russian Federation), occupied Palestinian territory, Peru, Philippines, Sierra Leone, Somalia, Southern Africa, Sri Lanka, Sudan, Tajikistan, Timor-Leste,Uganda, Venezuela, Zimbabwe. *See* UNICEF, *Donor Alerts and Field Reports*, http://www.unicef.org/emerg/index_fieldreports.html (last visited 6 Sept. 2009).

tions, especially during particularly critical periods. UNICEF's stated goal is to reach the most vulnerable in humanitarian crises, where access to vulnerable populations is often delayed because of inaccessibility, armed combat, or weather conditions.[99] UNICEF also developed a Core Commitments for Children in Emergencies (CCCs) specifically targeting children.[100]

The activities of UNICEF in Crises Countries vary.

For example, in Sierra Leone – the least developed among 177 countries according to the UNDP Human Development Report 2004 – UNICEF distributed essential drugs for case management of common communicable disease and medical supplies to cover an estimated population on 870,000. It instructed several local organizations on how to monitor the delivery and promote the use of child survival systems.[101]

In the DRC, UNICEF developed a program to provide vaccines, materials and support for the vaccination of 6,000,000 children against measles, and for 683,000 children and pregnant women against the five key vaccine-preventable diseases. UNICEF is also involved in water and sanitation programs that can protect local populations from other common diseases.

Although humanitarian programs cannot provide all the services of an effective health system, they are important interventions of the international community in crises countries. These efforts provide preliminary and targeted support to national health systems. They are important to guarantee a minimum standard of health to populations living in situation of State failure. They also provide the international community with an opportunity to monitor the status of certain health indicators and, if necessary, provide the necessary means to counter possible crises and threats.

---

99 UNICEF affirmed that "the consequences (of such emergencies) are usually devastating, leaving entire communities deprived of the most basic assistance and protection. Most of those who die in wartime, for instance, do not die as a direct result of violence but from the loss of basic health services, food, safe water or adequate sanitation. This is especially true for children. The countries with the highest rates of preventable deaths among children are countries which have experienced protracted periods of armed conflict: India, Nigeria, China, Pakistan, Democratic Republic of Congo, and Ethiopia." UNICEF, *UNICEF in Emergencies*, http://www.unicef.org/emerg/index.html (last visited 6 Sept. 2009).

100 *See* UNICEF, *Commitments*, http://www.unicef.org/emerg/index_commitments.html (last visited 6 Sept. 2009).

101 In UNICEF Humanitarian Action, *Sierra Leone, Donor Update* (13 Dec, 2004), *available at*: http://www.unicef.org/emerg/files/Emergencies_Sierra_Leone_Donor_Update_131204.pdf.

4. *Conclusion*

Global public health emergencies have become a major concern and an important part of the defense policies of many States. This chapter focused on the instruments available to the international community to control the spread of infectious diseases and health emergencies, within the context of State failure. In fact, failed and failing States are particularly ill-equipped to combat the spread of disease because their health systems are typically malfunctioning.

WHO is the main actor in the international arena dealing with health emergencies. Other organizations acting in this field include UNICEF, the World Bank and several regional and national governmental and non-governmental organizations.

WHO has both normative and directive powers. The International Health Regulations are the most relevant legally binding instruments. They are binding on all Member States. They provide a mechanism that Member States and WHO must apply in certain health emergencies situations. However, their application is limited to only three diseases and there is no enforcing mechanism for Member States. In emergency situations, these applications are limited when the State is absent.

Developments in global health, epitomized by the SARS epidemic, pushed the Health Assembly to pursue new International Health Regulations. The new Regulations were adopted in 2005 and entered into force in 2007. They represent a major development in international health law: the definition of health emergencies was substantially enlarged and their application relies on the seriousness of the outbreak, whether the disease is known, its potential for spreading cross-border and its likely consequences for travel and trade. The definition of health emergency is also based on the potential capability of the affected State to deal with it. However, similarly to the previous IHR, the new Regulations are based on State consent and have no enforcement mechanism. Their application in situations of health emergencies in failed States is likely to be modest.

WHO's directive and coordinating powers provide significant examples of instruments that are applicable in situations of health emergencies. These instruments provide viable alternatives to normative ones and have shown to be capable of being effective. Two instruments are particularly significant.

The first one, the Global Outbreak Alert and Response (GOARN) is an alliance of health specialists working with international organizations, non-governmental organizations and national health institutes. GOARN, whose Secretariat is provided by the WHO in Geneva, collects, verifies and confirms outbreaks reports to the international community. Once a disease outbreak is confirmed, GOARN coordinates and manages actions to control its spread. These actions are normally coordinated with the national governments. However, in situations of State failure, GOARN has been capable of collaborating with field personnel from international organizations and NGOs. Gian Luca Burci, WHO's Legal Counsel, defined GOARN as "an effective and powerful" mechanism to address global health emergencies.[102]

GOARN's success has been praised by several Resolutions of the Health Assembly, and the international community has given its support and backing. GOARN's role during the SARS epidemic is emblematic. Although it was not possible to enter China until the Government allowed WHO to do so, even before these field visits, GOARN was instrumental in collecting and confirming information on the outbreak and in issuing alerts. As a result, the international community was capable, and willing, to put pressure on the Chinese government to allow WHO to verify outbreak reports.

GOARN's success signals a development in the international dealings with health crises and indicates an intention of States to collaborate in certain domains and to take global health crises seriously. In fact, GOARN is a model of the new global governance.[103]

The second non-binding instrument is WHO's effort to prevent the spread of communicable diseases before outbreaks. This is a part of a general strategy, espoused by the international community through several international organizations, to support health systems in failing and failed States.

In this context, the Polio Eradication Campaign is particularly important. The Campaign is managed by WHO, and implemented on the ground by UNICEF. Support and funding is provided by several organizations, including Rotary International, USAID, CDC and other national governments. The campaign has proved a success, although it suffered a set-back in 2003 because of the refusal of some regional authorities in Nigeria to provide the vaccine. Despite international public pressure, the boycott of the vaccine continued and the eradication program was delayed. However, the campaign is now back on track and vaccination days are held throughout Western and Eastern Africa. UNICEF has also created a special operating procedure for special situations in crises and conflict countries whereby access to the population for vaccination campaigns is negotiated directly with local authorities. This happens, for example, in Southern Sudan where vaccination campaigns are coordinated with the Sundan People's Liberation Movement ("SPLM"). The WHO has recently confirmed that the eradication of polio is again a

[102] Interview with Gian Luca Burci, Counsel, World Health Organization, in Geneva, Switz. (17 Nov. 2005).

[103] *Id.*

reachable short-term goal. Several failing States are the location for extensive vaccination campaigns, and some have been declared free of polio. The collaboration between different international and non-governmental organizations, as well as the support of several Member States, has made it possible to achieve these results and has proven to be an efficient instrument to prevent global health emergencies.

The success of these instruments is important for several reasons. First, they demonstrate a renewed interest by the international community to take global health emergencies seriously. WHO's role in monitoring and controlling the spread of both the Swine and Avian Flu further demonstrates this trend. Second, although they are not based on legally binding provisions, these instruments have been respected and enforced by the great majority of States. It may be appropriate for these actions to be taken through non-binding instruments as the only workable and possible agreement. In fact, binding instruments entail long and difficult political negotiations, which often do not reach satisfactory results. Third, support for these instruments has also been shown publicly through resolutions of the Health Assembly. These resolutions are not binding, however, they signal the direction that the Member States wish the WHO to take and give mandates to organs of the WHO. Finally, although these resolutions are not binding, they are based on a sense of comity: a strong link between countries which may prove significant in putting the interest of the international community in halting the spreading of disease before parochial and less pressing interests.[104]

In sum, some imperfect, non–legally binding instruments exist that can address global health emergencies, even in situations of State failure. These instruments are not perfect, but have shown to be effective in some situations. Moreover, operationally, the success of non-binding instruments has surpassed that of binding instruments.

---

[104] *See* American Society of International Law, *A Hard Look at Soft Law*, 82ND ANNUAL MEETING PROCEEDINGS 373–387 (1988). *See also* A.E. Boyle, *Some Reflections on the Relationship of Treaties and Soft Law*, 48 INT'L & COMP. L. Q. 901 (1999).

Chapter Six

Environmental Emergencies in Failed States

1. *Introduction*

It is estimated that every three weeks a disaster happens that exceeds the response capacities of the most affected country.[1] The problem is magnified in failed States. For these reasons, the inability of failed States to efficiently address environmental emergencies poses serious risks to the international community and must be comprehensively addressed.

This chapter analyzes the means available, to States and to the international community as a whole, when an environmental calamity of international magnitude occurs in a failed State. It assesses what international actors can do to prevent the inability of a State to perform certain actions necessary to confront an international emergency, while respecting the sovereignty of the 'unable' State and implementing measures needed in case of emergencies. To properly evaluate the options that the international community has to address this issue, both existing principles of international law and treaty provisions dealing with cross-border environmental emergencies are relevant.

International calamities are environmental emergencies of a significant magnitude that may cause significant transboundary harm to the territory and residents of one or more States, including to the location of the event itself. Examples of such emergencies include both manmade and natural emergencies, and they range from the Chernobyl nuclear reactor disaster to the 2005 Asian Tsunami. Both kinds are considered in this study.

The environment is "the complex of physical, chemical, and biotic factors (as climate, soil, and living things) that act upon an organism or an ecological community and ultimately determine its form and survival."[2] It has become a primary concern of the international community, and the protection of the

---

[1] Les Aspects Internationaux des Catastrophes Naturelles et Industrielle – The International Aspects of Natural And Industrial Catastrophes (David D. Caron and Charled Leben eds., 2001).

[2] *Environment*, in Merriam-Webster Online Dictionary, http://www.m-w.com (last visited 10 Sept. 2009).

environment has become a highly legalized and regulated field:[3] many rules and principles of international law relating to the protection of the environment exist and can be easily identified.[4] Existing international and regional conventions cover all of the many facets of the environment, including the biosphere, lithosphere, hydrosphere and the atmosphere. These provisions include measures related to hazardous substances and activities, waste, air pollution (such as climate change and ozone depletion), oceans and seas, freshwater resources, biological diversity and particular habitats and species.[5]

However, despite the numerous international environmental provisions, available case law is limited. Most States show a preference to address environmental differences in diplomatic settings and have only rarely referred them to international courts. As Professor Brunnée concludes:

> In principle, it is accepted that a State that violates international environmental law incurs in State responsibility. But there is strikingly little State practice and most transnational environmental concerns are resolved through negotiations or adoption of an agreement that regulates the issue at hand. Only in a hand-

---

3 Koskenniemi remains skeptical on the effectiveness of increased regulatory activities. He states that "the massive increase in international legislation during the last quarter of a century, particularly in the environmental field, has not created a new world order. In fact, the gap between law in books and how states act may now appear wider than at any other time in history – the more rules there are, the more occasion there is to break them. After years of active standard-setting, global and regional organizations stand somewhat baffled in front of a reality that has sometimes little in common with the objectives expressed in the inflated languages of their major conventions and declarations." Marti Koskenniemi, *New Institutions and Procedures for Implementing Control and Reaction*, Greening International Institutions 236 (J. Wersmann ed., 1996).

4 *See generally* Philippe Sands, Principles of International Environmental Law (2d ed., 2003); Alexandre Kiss and Dinah Shelton, International Environmental Law (3d ed. 2003); P.W. Birnie and A.E. Boyle, International Law and the Environment (2d ed. 2002).

5 Perrez identifies four distinct periods in the evolution and emergence of international environmental law. Specifically: "The first period stretched from a series of bilateral fisheries treaties in the nineteenth century thought the creation of the new international organizations in 1945. During that period, people and nations began to understand the necessary of limiting the exploitation of certain natural resources. The second period endured between the creation of the United Nations (U.N.) in 1945 and the 1962 Stockholm Conference on the Human Environment. This period was shaped by the creation of international organizations with competence in environmental matters and the adoption of legal instruments to address environmental problems. The third period occurred between the 1972 Stockholm Conference and the 1992 Rio Conference on Environment and Development (UNCED). During that period the U.N. sought to coordinate responses to international environmental problems. Finally, the post-UNCED period has sought to integrate environmental concerns into all international activities." Franz Xaver Perrez, *The Relationship Between "Permanent Sovereignty" And The Obligations Not To Cause Transboundary Environmental Damage*, 26 Envt'l. L. 1187, 1197 (1996).

ful of cases have environmental concerns actually given rise to formal dispute settlement.[6]

Moreover, although many environmental regulations exist, there are no comprehensive, general provisions that address environmental emergencies in situations of State failure.

Addressing international catastrophes is, "in comparison to other far less certain areas of international affairs, both relatively underdeveloped in practice and under-examined in the academic legal literature."[7]

The International Law Commission ("ILC") began exploring the possibility of codifying general principles applicable to environmental emergency situations in 1978. The efforts of the ILC resulted in the elaboration of Principles on the Prevention of Transboundary Harm and Co-operation, which included several existing general international law principles.

Initially, the ILC began addressing environmental injuries as an issue of international liability arising out of activities not prohibited by international law, and involving a risk of causing significant transboundary harm. In 1997, however, the ILC decided to split the matter and to address, first, the issue of risk prevention and, second, the issue of reparation and liability.[8] A Draft Convention on the Prevention of Transboundary Harm from Hazardous Activities was adopted in 2001, and recommended to the U.N. General Assembly for elaboration as a Convention.[9] The draft Convention in effect "codifies existing international obligations of environmental impact assessment, notification, consultation, monitoring, harm prevention, and diligent control of activities likely to cause transboundary harm to other States,"[10] as the articles included are "more securely based on existing precedents."[11]

---

[6] Jutta Brunnée, *Of Sense and Sensibility: Reflections On International Liability Regimes As Tools For Environmental Protection*, 53 Int'l & Comp. L. Q. 351, 355 (2004).

[7] Les Aspects Internationaux des Catastrophes Naturelles et Industrielle (David D. Caron and Charled Leben eds., 2001).

[8] *See* International Law Commission, *First Report on Prevention of Transboundary Damage From Hazardous Activities*, U.N. Doc. A/CN.4/487 (18 Mar., 1998); *see also* U.N. Doc. A/CN.4/487/Add.1 (3 Apr. 1998).

[9] *See* International Law Commission, *Report – International Liability for Injurious Consequences Arising Out of Acts not Prohibited by International law* (Prevention of Transboundary Hard From Hazardous Activities), Ch. 5, U.N. Doc. A/56/10 (53rd Sess. 23 Apr.–1 June 2001; 2 July–10 Aug. 2001). *See also* International Law Commission, *Report International Liability for Injurious Consequences Arising Out of Acts not Prohibited by International law* (International Liability In Case Of Loss From Transboundary Harm Arising Out of Hazardous Activities), Ch. VI, U.N. Doc. A/CN.4/528 (55th Sess. 5 May–6 June 2003; 7 July–8 Aug. 2003).

[10] P.W. Birnie and A.E. Boyle, International Law and the Environment 106 (2d ed. 2002).

[11] *Id.*

The Draft applies to activities within the jurisdiction of a State that risk causing significant transboundary physical and environmental harm to other States. The ILC stresses the procedural obligations of States in cases where there is significant and foreseeable risk of transboundary harm. The Draft Convention includes a general obligation of good-faith collaboration and prevention of significant environmental harm (Articles 3 and 4), and a duty to provide information in the event of an environmental emergency to States that are at risk of being affected by the emergency (Article 7).[12] The Principles, however, are limited to risk-prevention and are of limited applicability to ongoing emergencies.

These principles are significant as they seek to provide a general framework of actions for all environmental emergencies. However, they mostly deal with the issue of providing appropriate measures to prevent and minimize risk accidents. They stress cooperation on risk avoidance with States and international organizations, through implementation legislative and other actions, and provide a system of prior authorization for all relevant activities.

However, as clearly stated by the ILC Special Rapporteur himself, they have a primary preventive function. The Rapporteur concluded that:

> the obligation not to cause damage to the environment of other States or of areas beyond the limits of national jurisdiction is a clear directive to States to employ their best possible efforts to prevent such transboundary damage. Prevention is preferable because compensation in case of harm can often not restore the situation prevailing prior to the event or accident, i.e. the status quo ante. […] Prevention is any way better than cure.[13]

The Principles elaborated by the ILC are, therefore, of only limited use in ongoing emergency situations because they focus on risk-avoidance. As such, they lack specific provisions directing States on action they should perform after accidents have occurred. Moreover, no attention is given to situations where a State is incapable of performing the required actions and needs assistance in confronting emergencies. Thus, it is necessary to look specifically at other alternative provisions which may be applicable.

Preliminary, it is important to note that this is not an issue of State liability ensuing from a State's inability to perform certain obligations in times of environmental emergencies. As Oppenheim convincingly asserts

[12] International Law Commission, *Draft Principles of Prevention of Transboundary Harm from Hazardous Activities*, 372, U.N. Doc. A/56/10 (53rd Sess., 2001). *See also* art. 9 (Consultation on Preventive Measures), art. 10 (Factors Involved in an Equitable Balance of Interests), and art. 1 (Exchange of Information).

[13] *See* International Law Commission, *First Report on Prevention of Transboundary Damage From Hazardous Activities* ¶ 32, U.N. Doc. A/CN.4/487 (18 Mar. 1998).

> In any event the whole matter [of ensuring protection of the environment] raises a serious legal question whether the international community can afford to go on attempting to deal with those problems by adapting, and supplementing by treaty, a legal system based essentially on establishing the delictual liability of certain respondents and assessing appropriate compensation. This, by itself at least, seems an inadequate way of tackling what is basically a question of public order, and accidents are likely to have results not compensable by damages. A delictual system is hardly designed to deal with things that ought not to be allowed to happen at all.[14]

What is needed are principles that can be concretely used by the international community to address environmental emergencies in failed States. Thus, this chapter will first examine general principles of international environmental law that are applicable to situations of cross-border emergencies and frame the general law applicable to these situations.[15] It will then appraise existing treaty-based mechanisms and examine which ones may be used in emergency situations in failing States. Finally, it will explore the role of the United Nations, as the operational instrument of the international community as a whole, to face environmental emergencies.

---

[14] OPPENHEIM'S INTERNATIONAL LAW 415 (Sir Robert Jennings and Sir Arthur Watts eds., 9th ed. 1992).

[15] It is also interesting to note the concept of shared responsibility for shared resources as proper in international environmental law. In fact, many types of environmental resources are shared among two or more states. To properly protect them, international environmental lawyers have developed specific concepts that entail common responsibility for two or more states. Shared resources include the outer space and the moon, certain animal and vegetal species (like fish, wild animals or certain plants). Another concept that is proper in international environmental law is that of resources that are of 'common concern of humankind. The Climate Change Convention affirms that "change in the Earth's climate and its adverse effects are common concern of humankind." United Nations Framework Convention on Climate Change, Preamble (1992), *available at*: http://unfccc.int/not_assigned/b/items/1417.php. Similarly, the 1992 Biodiversity Convention defines biological diversity as "a common concern of humankind." Convention on Biological Diversity, Rio de Janeiro, Braz., Preamble, 5 June 1992, *available at*: http://www.biodiv.org/convention/articles.asp?lg=0&a=cbd-00. Moreover, certain spaces have been singled out as 'global commons' and enjoy particular status in international law. These spaces fall outside the sovereign territory of any State and no state has exclusive jurisdiction over them. They include the high seas and their seabed and subsoil, outer space and the Antarctic. The existence of the concept of shared resources and shared responsibility is useful to this analysis because it provides a background to assess emergency situations that may require the involvement of more than one State.

2. *The Overall Framework Given by General Principles of International Environmental Law Applicable to Emergencies Situations*

General principles of law relating to environmental rights and obligations of States provide the general framework that States must adhere to in situations of environmental emergency in their relation with each other.[16] They are therefore relevant as general guidelines to the legal understanding and appraisal of cross-border operations in failed States, in the event of environmental emergencies. In fact, although they do not prescribe specific actions that States must perform, they provide guidelines of behavior that States must follow.

Established general principles of international environmental law include the principles of sovereignty over natural resources; the responsibility not to cause damage to the environment of other States or to areas beyond national jurisdiction; the principle of preventive action; the principle of cooperation; the precautionary principle; the polluter-pays principle; the principle of common but differentiated responsibility and the sustainable development principle.

Two of these principles are particularly relevant to the issue of State failure: first, the principle of a general duty of cooperation between States to mitigate transboundary environmental risk and emergencies. Second, the prevention principle, which mandates States work to prevent, reduce and control pollution and environmental harm that may cause transboundary injury to the territory of another State.

As Birnie and Boyle effectively affirm:

> International law does not allow states to conduct activities within their territories, or in common spaces, without regards for the rights of other states or for the protection of the global environment. This point is sometimes expressed by reference to the maxim *sic utere tuo, ut alienum non laedas* or 'principles of good neighborliness', but the contribution of customary law in environmental matters is neither as modest nor as vacuous as these phrases suggest. Two principles enjoy significant support: duties to prevent, reduce, and control pollution and environmental harm, and a duty to co-operate in mitigating environmental risks and emergencies.[17]

These principles provide a general guidance that direct States' behaviors in emergency situations. Both are now recognized as principles of international

---

[16] OPPENHEIM'S INTERNATIONAL LAW 410–415 (Sir Robert Jennings and Sir Arthur Watts eds., 9th ed. 1992).

[17] PATRICIA W. BIRNIE AND ALAN E. BOYLE, INTERNATIONAL LAW AND THE ENVIRONMENT 89 (1992).

customary law and, therefore, must be applied by all States. Each will be analyzed in detail below.

2.1. *The Duty of Cooperation*

The duty to cooperate is "the building block on which rests all of the other international environmental principles."[18] This principle establishes a general duty for States to act in a cooperative manner and to take each other's legitimate interest into account when making decisions. As such, the duty gives an indication of how States should act and sets a general framework for States' decisions, rather than setting specific behavior.[19]

The duty to cooperate first exists as a general principle of international law, and as such "the obligation for States to cooperate generally with their neighbors in addressing international issues is a binding principle of international law."[20] It is found in the U.N. Charter[21] and in several resolutions of the General Assembly including the – particularly significant – Resolution 2625.[22] This resolution approves the Declaration on Principles of International Law Concerning Friendly Relations and Cooperation Among States in Accordance with the Charter of the United Nations. The principle relating to 'Duty of States to Co-operate With One Another In Accordance With the Charter' affirms:

> States have the duty to co-operate with one another, irrespective of the differences in their political, economic and social systems, in the various spheres of international relations, in order to maintain international peace and security and to promote international economic stability and progress, the general welfare of nations and international co-operation free from discrimination based on such differences.

The purpose of the duty to cooperate is, therefore, to guarantee peace and security and to encourage international stability and the welfare of nations. It thus coincides with the general purposes of international law, and its respect is essential for the progress of international law.

---

18 Ved P. Nanda and George Pring, International Environmental Law and Policy for the 21st Century 20 (2003).

19 *See generally* Franz Xaver Perrez, Cooperative Sovereignty, From Independence to Interdependence in the Structure of International Environmental Law (2000).

20 David Hunter, James Salzman and Durwood Zaelke, International Environmental Law and Policy 428 (2d ed. 2002).

21 For example, *see* Arts. 1(1)–(3), 11, 13, 55, 56 and 74 as well as the Preamble of the U.N. Charter.

22 G.A. Res. 2625 (XXV), U.N. Doc. A/2625, 13 U.N.R. 337 (24 Oct. 1970).

The duty of cooperation has also been expressly recognized as a general principle of international environmental law. It is found in many international treaties, including the seminal Stockholm and Rio Declarations, and it is also supported by State practice.

The 1972 Stockholm Declaration has played a pivotal role in the development of international environmental law. The Declaration was approved during the United Nations Conference on the Human Environment, convened by the United Nations in Stockholm in June 1972, the first major conference dealing with environmental issues.[23] Participants included more than one hundred States, as well as a large number of international institutions and non-governmental organizations. Although not binding, the Declaration reflects, in many instances, existing principles of environmental law and general political commitment by participating States.[24] Article 24 affirms

> International matters concerning the protection and improvement of the environment should be handled in a cooperative spirit by all countries, big and small, on an equal footing. Cooperation through multilateral or bilateral arrangements or other appropriate means is essential to effectively control, prevent, reduce and eliminate adverse environmental effects resulting from activities conducted in all spheres, in such a way that due account is taken of the sovereignty and interests of all States.[25]

Similar words of endorsement are found in the 1992 Rio Declaration on Environment and Development, which was adopted by consensus at the United Nations Conference of Environment and Development 1992.[26] The Rio Declaration is, like the Stockholm Declaration, not a binding instrument of law. However several of the principles that it contains are considered part of customary law, including the duty of cooperation.

Principle 27 of the Rio Declaration states

---

[23] *See Report of the United Nations Conference on the Human Environment*, Stockholm, Swed., U.N. Doc. A/CONF.48/14/Rev.1 (5–16 June 1972).

[24] F. Perrez notes that "although the Stockholm Declaration did not seek to formulate legally binding provisions, but to provide inspiration and guidelines for the governments and peoples of the world, it was regarded as the "first step" in establishing the basic rules of international environmental law." Perrez, *The Relationship Between "Permanent Sovereignty" And The Obligations Not To Cause Transboundary Environmental Damage*, 26 Envt'l L. 1187, 1212 (1996).

[25] *Report of the United Nations Conference on the Human Environment*, Stockholm, Swed., U.N. Doc. A/CONF.48/14/Rev.1 (5–16 June 1972), *available at*: http://www.unep.org/Documents.multilingual/Default.asp?DocumentID=97&ArticleID=1503.

[26] The Rio Declaration is *available at*: http://www.unep.org/Documents.multilingual/Default.asp?DocumentID=78&ArticleID=1163.

> States and people shall cooperate in good faith and in a spirit of partnership in the fulfillment of the principles embodied in this Declaration and in the further development of international law in the field of sustainable development.

The obligation to cooperate – also sometimes referred to as the principle of good-neighborliness – is also affirmed in "virtually all international environmental agreements of bilateral and regional application and global instruments."[27]

For example, the Preamble of the 1992 Convention on the Transboundary Effects of Industrial Accidents underlines the need to:

> promote active international cooperation among the States concerned before, during and after an accident, to enhance appropriate policies and to reinforce and coordinate action at all appropriate levels for promoting the prevention of, preparedness for and response to the transboundary effects of industrial accidents.[28]

Similarly, the 1986 Convention on Assistance in the Case of Nuclear Accident or Radiological Emergency, adopted after the Chernobyl incident,[29] creates an international framework for cooperation among State Parties and the International Atomic Energy Agency ("IAEA") to facilitate assistance and support in the event of nuclear accidents or radiological emergencies. Article 1 requires States to "cooperate between themselves and with the International Atomic Energy Agency" in accordance with the provisions of the Convention "to facilitate prompt assistance in the event of a nuclear accident or radiological emergency to minimize its consequences and to protect life, property and the environment from the effects of radioactive releases."[30]

In general, the cooperation principle calls for 'prompt assistance' to minimize possible consequences of environmental disasters.

---

[27] Philippe Sands, Principles of International Environmental Law 249 (2d ed. 2003).

[28] *Id.*

[29] The Convention entered into force on 26 February 1987, as of 27 January 2006, the Convention had 96 parties and 68 signatories, *available at*: http://www.iaea.org/Publications/Documents/Infcircs/Others/inf336.shtml.

[30] As seen above, the ILC also approved Draft Articles on Prevention of Transboundary Harm From Hazardous Activities, which were endorsed by the UN General Assembly. Article 4 (Cooperation) provides that "States concerned shall cooperate in good faith and, as necessary, seek the assistance of or more competent international organizations in preventing significant transboundary harm or at any event in minimizing the risk thereof." *Report of the International Law Commission*, U.N. Doc. A/56/10 (53rd Sess. 23 Apr.–1 June 2001; 2 July–10 Aug. 2001). *See also* Article 17, which prescribes that "The State of origin shall, without delay and by the most expeditious means, at its disposal, notify the State likely to be affected of an emergency concerning an activity within the scope of the present articles and provide it with all relevant and available information."

The validity and extent of the principle has also been tested and confirmed in many international cases dealing with environmental law. One of the first international cases to address environmental matters specifically explores this issue. In the *Lac Lanoux arbitration*,[31] the arbitral Tribunal was called to decide over a dispute between France and Spain over the use of shared water resources by France for energy production purposes, which Spain claimed would affect the quantity of water it would receive as the downstream State. In its opinion, the Tribunal reasoned that every State had an obligation to consider the interests and respect the rights of another State when exercising its rights. It then concluded that

> France is entitled to exercise its rights, but she cannot ignore Spanish interests. Spain is entitled to require that her rights are respected and that her interests are taken into consideration.[32]

In the end, the Tribunal held that France had complied with its international obligations under treaty and customary law to consult and negotiate in good faith with Spain before diverting a river's waters.

International practice has emphasized that prior notification, consultation and negotiation must occur on the basis of adequate information, and result in an obligation to negotiate in good faith. The conclusions reached in *Lac Lanoux* for freshwater resources are now applicable, by practice, to other sources, including nuclear installations close to a border, continental shelf operations and other sources of marine pollution, including dumping and land-based activities, long-range transboundary air pollution and industrial accidents.[33]

More recently, similar conclusions were reached on a matter concerning the alleged discharge of pollutants into the Irish Sea and related movement of radioactive materials through the Irish Sea in the *Mox Plant Case* (Ireland v. United Kingdom). Pending the constitution of a Tribunal under the Annex VII of the 1982 United Nations Convention on the Law of the Sea ("UNCLOS"), Ireland requested some provisional measures to the Interna-

---

[31] *Lac Lanoux arbitration (France v. Spain)*, 16 Nov., 1957, 12 RIAA. 12, 281 (1957). *See also* Astrid Epiney, *Lac Lanoux Arbitration*, Max Planck Encyclopedia of Public International Law (R. Wolfrum ed., on line edition, 2009). For a good overview that also includes case background, aftermath and assessment, *see* Cesare Romano, The Peaceful Settlement of International Environmental Dispute, A Pragmatic Approach 219–231 (2000).

[32] *Lac Lanoux arbitration* 316. The French original reads: "La France peut user de ses droits, elle ne peut ignorer les intérêts espagnols. L'Espagne peut exiger le respect de ses droits et la prise en considération de ses intérêts."

[33] Patricia W. Birnie and Alan E. Boyle, International Law and the Environment 126–127 (1992).

tional Tribunal for the Law of Sea ("ITLOS").[34] In dismissing the specific measures requested by Ireland, the ITLOS Tribunal nonetheless directed parties to cooperate and to exchange information, monitor the risks and effects of the operation of the plans, and devise measures to prevent pollution of the marine environment, based on the consideration that

> the duty to cooperate is a fundamental principle in the prevention of pollution of the marine environment under Part XII of the Convention and general international law.[35]

To conclude, the duty of cooperation is well established in international environmental law, and is recognized both in doctrine and in practice. Because of its foundational character, "all of international environmental law flows from this one basic concept."[36] The duty, however, only prescribes that States must adopt a general behavior in their mutual relationship: States must cooperate in good faith and with a view of reaching an agreement. However, if reaching an agreement is impossible, States need not withdraw from their activities. The duty does not order specific obligations, but only requests a specific behavior to be adopted in dealing with other States.

Nonetheless, the duty of cooperation provides some guidance for States to be followed in cases of environmental emergencies in situation of State failure. It signals that all relations with other States must be built upon a principle of cooperation. As such, it is important because it underlines that, to obtain successful results, the goal to be reached is cooperation.

2.2. *The Duty Not to Cause Transboundary Environmental Harm*

The obligation not to cause transboundary environmental damage is a direct application of the 'good neighborliness' principle and it is another important general principle of international law.[37] The principle embodies the duty of every State to protect the interest of other States within their territory. Thus,

---

[34] *The Mox Plant Case (Ireland V. United Kingdom)*, Request For Provisional Measures, International Tribunal For The Law Of The Sea (3 Dec. 2001). The Tribunal on jurisdiction and the merits seats in The Hague, where the International Bureau of the Permanent Court of Arbitration functions as a Registry. Documents relating to the case are available on the PCA website (www.pca-cpa.org).

[35] *The Mox Plant Case (Ireland v. United Kingdom)*, Request For Provisional Measures, ¶ 82, International Tribunal For The Law Of The Sea (3 Dec. 2001), *available at*: www.itlos.org.

[36] Ved P. Nanda and George Pring, International Environmental Law and Policy for the 21st Century 19 (2003).

[37] Franz X. Perrez, *The Relationship Between "Permanent Sovereignty" And The Obligation Not To Cause Transboundary Environmental Damage*, 26 Envt'l. L. 1187, 1200–1203 (1996).

all States have an obligation under international law to prevent harm and to take adequate steps to control and regulate sources of serious environmental pollution within the territory under their jurisdiction. In fact,

> It is beyond serious argument that states are required by international law to take adequate steps to control and regulate sources of serious global environmental pollution or transboundary harm within their territory or subject to the their jurisdiction.[38]

The principle was one of the first principles on matters of environmental law to arise in international environmental law and it enjoys continued international support, both in legislative settings and judicial decisions. It is included as Principle 21 in the Stockholm Declaration on the Human Environment, which asserts that, though States have, in accordance with the Charter of the United Nations and the principles of environmental law, the sovereign right to exploit their own resources pursuant to their own environmental policies, they also have

> the responsibility to ensure that activities within their jurisdiction or control do not cause damage to the environment of other states or of areas beyond the limits of national jurisdiction.[39]

The importance of this principle was recognized during the Stockholm negotiations.[40] In fact,

> The totality of the provision, including its emphatic reference to responsibility for environmental damage, was regarded by many states present at the Stockholm Conference, and subsequently by the UN General Assembly, as reflecting customary international law.[41]

---

[38] Patricia W. Birnie and Alan E. Boyle, International law and the Environment 89 (1992).

[39] Report of the United Nations Conference on the Human Environment, U.N. Doc. A/Conf.48/14/rev.1 (1973), *available at*: http://www.nethics.net/nethics_neu/n3/quellen/voelkerrechtsverb_texte/stockholm_human-environment.html.

[40] The Working Group on the Declaration on Human Environment, working on the Stockholm Declaration, was unable to reach an agreement on Principle 21 during the group negotiations, and referred the matter to the Plenary. The Plenary approved the Declaration by acclamation. In the Plenary debate, the U.S. Representatives supported approval of the text and interpreted it as follows "the United States of America consider it obvious that nothing contained in this principle [21] or elsewhere in the Declaration, diminishes in any way the obligation of States to prevent environmental damages or gives rise to any right on the part of States to take actions in derogation of the rights of other States or of the community of nations. The statement on the responsibility of States for damage caused to the environments of other States or of areas beyond the limits of national jurisdiction is not in any way a limitation on the above obligation, but an affirmation of existing rules concerning liability in the event of default of the obligation." *Report Of The United Nations Conference on the Human Environment*, U.N. Doc. A/CONF.48/14/Rev.1, 66 (1973).

[41] Birnie and Boyle, International law and the Environment 90 (1992).

Principle 21 still remains "a highly influential statement in the post-Stockholm development of law and practice in environmental matters, notably in the U.N. resolutions, in UNEP principles and in multilateral treaties."[42]

The same basic principle is also reiterated – albeit with some modifications that are not relevant to this analysis- in Principle 2 of the Rio Declaration, which requires states to prevent harm to the environment of other States or of other common areas. It states that

> States have, in accordance with the Charter of the United Nations and the principles of international law, the sovereign right to exploit their own resources pursuant to their own environmental and developmental policies, and the responsibility to ensure that activities within their jurisdiction or control do not cause damage to the environment of other States or of areas beyond the limits of national jurisdiction.[43]

Most international environmental law experts affirm that as far as Principle 2 is concerned "the more convincing view is that the Rio Declaration is merely restating existing law."[44]

A similar principle is also found in several international conventions, including in Article 3 of the Convention on Biological Diversity, which holds that States have, together with the sovereign right to exploit their own resources pursuant to their own environmental policies and in accordance with the Charter of the United Nations and the principles of international law,

> the responsibility to ensure that activities within their jurisdiction or control do not cause damage to the environment of other States or of areas beyond the limits of national jurisdiction.

The Agreement by the Association of Southeast Asian Nations ("ASEAN") Agreement of 1985 on The Conservation Of Nature And Natural Resources provides a regional example of the same principle. Article 20, dealing with trans-frontier environmental effects, affirms:

---

[42] *Id.* at 111. They specifically refer to the London Dumping Convention, the Ozone Convention, the Basel Convention on the Transboundary Effects of Industrial Wastes, Articles 192–4 of the 1982 UNCLOS, and in the 1992 Convention on the Transboundary Effects of Industrial Accidents. *See also* UN General Assembly Resolution 2996, where the General Assembly stated that Principle 21 laid down "the basic rules governing this matter," G.A. Res. 2996 (XXVII), U.N. Doc. A/2996 (15 Dec. 1972).

[43] UNEP, *Rio Declaration on Environment and Development, Rio de Janeiro*, Braz. 3–14 June 1992, *available at*: http://www.unep.org/Documents.multilingual/Default.asp?DocumentID=78&ArticleID=1163.

[44] Patricia W. Birnie and Alan E. Boyle, International Law and the Environment 105 (1992).

1. Contracting Parties have in accordance with generally accepted principles of international law the responsibility of ensuring that activities under their jurisdiction or control do not cause damage to the environment or the natural resources under the jurisdiction of other Contracting Parties or of areas beyond the limits of national jurisdiction.
2. In order to fulfill this responsibility, Contracting Parties shall avoid to the maximum extent possible and reduce to the minimum extent possible adverse environmental effects of activities under their jurisdiction or control, including effects on natural resources, beyond the limits of their national jurisdiction.[45]

The same principle is also found in U.N. resolutions, including in General Assembly Resolution 2995 of 15 December, 1972, and relating to the Cooperation Between States In The Field Of The Environment, in which the General Assembly emphasizes that

> in the exploration, exploitation and development of their natural resources, States must not produce significant harmful effects in zones situated outside their national jurisdiction.[46]

The existence of the duty not to cause transboundary environmental harm as a principle of international environmental law is also well established in practice. In fact, it can be traced back to the *Trail Smelter* arbitration, one of the very first international environmental law cases.

In the *Trail Smelter* arbitration,[47] the arbitral Tribunal was asked to adjudge a dispute between Canada and the United States over noxious fumes originating in Canada and allegedly damaging certain communities and agricultural plots situated across the border from the smelter in American territory. The Tribunal, faced with the first case on this matter, concluded that

> Under principles of international law, as well as the law of the US, no state has the right to use or permit to use its territory in such a manner as to cause injury by fumes in or to the territory of another or to the properties or persons therein.[48]

The Tribunal therefore specifically affirmed that States themselves could not use or permit other entities to use their territory in a way that may cause

---

[45] Association of Southeast Asian Nations, Agreement On The Conservation Of Nature And Natural Resources, Kuala Lumpur, 9 July 1985 (not yet entered into force), *available at*: http://www.aseansec.org/1490.html.

[46] G.A. Res. 2995 (XXVII), U.N. Doc. A/2995 (15 Dec. 1972).

[47] *Trail Smelter Arbitration (United States v. Canada)* 3 R.I.A.A. 1903–1982 (1949). For a comprehensive overview, including case background, aftermath and assessment, *see* Cesare Romano, The Peaceful Settlement of International Environmental Dispute, A Pragmatic Approach 261–278 (2000).

[48] *Trail Smelter Arbitration* (United States v. Canada) 3 R.I.A.A. 1965 (1949).

damages to the territory of another State.[49] Although the decision of the Tribunal specifically relates to transboundary injury caused by fumes, the same conclusions are generally applicable to other sources of environmental injuries.

The International Court of Justice ("ICJ") also specifically addressed the existence of legal obligation to prevent transboundary harm in its recent Advisory Opinion on the Legality of Threat or Use of Nuclear Weapons. In this case, the ICJ was asked by the General Assembly to render an advisory opinion over whether the threat or use of nuclear weapons was permitted in any circumstance under international law.

In its opinion, the Court concluded that the threat or use of nuclear weapons would generally be contrary to the rules of international law applicable in armed conflict, and in particular, the principles and rule of humanitarian law. However, in view of the current state of international law, and of the elements of fact at its disposal, it could not definitively conclude whether the threat or use of nuclear weapons would be lawful or unlawful in an extreme circumstance of self-defense, in which the very survival of a State would be at stake.

In its decision, the Court specifically interpreted the question within the realm of international environmental law. It recognized that the environment is under daily threat and that the use of nuclear weapons could constitute a catastrophe for the environment. The Court reasoned that the environment was not an abstraction but represented the living space, the quality of life and the very health of human beings, including generations unborn. It concluded that

> The existence of the general obligation of states to ensure that activities within their jurisdiction and control respect the environment of other states or of area beyond national control is now part of the corpus of international law relating to the environment.[50]

The Court therefore explicitly confirmed that the prevention obligation constitutes a general principle of international law.

---

[49] In fact, the principle was also stated – though not in an environmental context – in the *Corfu Channel case* which was decided at approximately the same time. In *Corfu Channel*, the International Court of Justice held that Albania was responsible for certain damages suffered by some British warships because it had failed to warn the United Kingdom of the presence of mines in its territorial waters. The Court reasoned that every State had an "obligation not to allow knowingly its territory to be used for acts contrary to the rights of other States." *Corfu Channel Case (UK v. Albania)*, Decision, 1949 I.C.J. 4, ¶ 22 (9 Apr.).

[50] *Legality of the Threat or Use of Nuclear Weapons*, Advisory Opinion, 1996 I.C.J. 226, ¶ 29 (8 July).

The duty is not an absolute prohibition on environmental damage, but it is a recognition of the duty of States to take preventive measures to protect the environment. The Court held that States have an obligation to protect the natural environment against widespread, long-term and severe environmental damage in times of armed conflict and to refrain from methods of warfare or reprisals intended to cause such damage.[51]

This interpretation, coupled with the general obligation not to cause transboundary environmental injuries by fumes (or other means), provides a useful setting to evaluate the existing framework relating to trans-border environmental activities. The duty of prevention is particularly interesting because it sets the framework for assessing the rights of the affected State in case of environmental emergencies. In particular, read together with the obligation of cooperation, it establishes general principles applicable in all matters of environmental concerns, including emergencies, for both the States where an emergency occurred and States affected by the emergency. Specifically, States have an obligation to refrain from causing transboundary environmental damage, and must also cooperate in dealing with environmental emergencies.

2.3. *The Importance of These Principles*

The two general principles examined above constitute the general framework within which States must act in all matters related to international environmental law, including in cases of emergencies occurring in failed States.

These general principles specify two firm obligations that must be respected in all circumstances and provide a starting point for a legal appraisal.

These principles are particularly relevant because they provide a general framework of behavior for both States that are affected by environmental emergencies, and by States in whose territories the emergencies occurred. In general, all States must cooperate with each other in all matters related to environmental emergencies. This duty is specifically relevant in situations of State failure – where a State is typically not fully capable of coping with such emergencies – as it provides the general direction that all other States must follow. Thus, an action by a State in support of another State that is the victim of an environmental emergency which is or threatens to become a transboundary emergency, should be performed and interpreted as an application of the duty of international cooperation, and not as a violation of sovereignty. As such, the duty of international cooperation is an expression

[51] *Id.* ¶ 31.

of international comity, and a demonstration of the cohesion of the international community towards each member.

On the same ground, the duty to prevent environmental injuries remains significant in situations of State failure as a general principle that all States must respect. Although, as specified in the introduction, this chapter does not deal with liability for environmental injuries, it is important that a duty to prevent damages is recognized as a general principle of international environmental law that all States must consider. In situations of natural or man-made emergencies, failed States may comply with these duties by, as much as possible, providing information, notifying other States and cooperating with other affected States and the international community as a whole.

Thus, these principles are complementary, and both of them must be applied and respected. However, by their very nature, these principles are also general and non-detailed and are difficult to render actionable.

These principles also provide the foundations for the specific treaty obligations, analyzed below, that are applicable in cases of transboundary environmental emergencies.

3. *Specific Treaty-based Provisions Relating to Cross-boundary Environmental Emergencies*

This section explores and assesses existing treaty provisions applicable to transboundary emergencies situations. Their analysis is necessary and useful to properly assess provisions applicable to environmental emergencies in failed States.

As stated in the introduction of this chapter, there are no comprehensive and general provisions applicable to all emergency situations. However, several treaties and conventions exist that deal with emergencies either arising from specific activities (for example industrial or nuclear activities) or occurring in a specific ecosystem (for example land, the high seas or in rivers).

These agreements encourage international cooperation to prevent accidents.[52] Obligations included in these treaties vary. They include the duty of notification of an emergency situation, the obligation to prepare contingency plans, the obligation to provide assistance of demand, and – only when the emergencies occur in the high seas, the possibility of intervening without prior State's consent. Each will be considered below.

It should be noted at the outset that all these obligations require the – more or less – active participation of the State where the emergency occurred. They

[52] Philippe Sands, Principles of International Law 620–625 (2d ed. 2003).

are therefore of limited assistance to States that lack a functioning or fully functioning government. However, their analysis is still useful because it indicates the different obligations incumbent upon States. Moreover, because State failure is a gradual process, it is possible that certain duties and obligations continue to be respected, at least to a certain degree, even in situations of State failure.

Most importantly, moreover, this analysis provides useful examples of the types of duties, obligations and rights that are available to the States, the international community, as well as failing States, to address emergency situations. As such, therefore, they can provide a useful blueprint for the development of a comprehensive action plan for failed States.

3.1. *The Duty of Notification of Emergency Situations*

The most common provision found in emergencies treaties is the duty of the State where the emergency occurred to notify other States that might be affected by the emergency. The duty of notification also often includes a duty to notify the Secretariat that administers and oversees the implementation of the Conventions.

The purpose of the duty to promptly notify other countries in case of imminent danger is to enable other States to minimize environmental damage that may occur within their territory.[53] The information duty derives from, and is an application of, the general obligation not to cause transboundary harm.

Notification obligations are included in several biodiversity and biosafety conventions, conventions related to industrial accidents, conventions related to hazardous substances and activities, conventions dealing with civil use of nuclear energy and several conventions related to marine activities.

The duty to timely notify States at risk in case of accidents and emergencies likely to cause transboundary harm is also an application of the duty of cooperation, and is a principle of general international law.[54] In fact, the International Court found that a duty to inform and notify other countries

[53] These include the Convention on Early Notification of Nuclear Accidents, Article 11 of the 1976 Convention on the Protection of the Rhine Against Chemical Pollution, Article 13(1) of the Basel Convention, and the 1982 UNCLOS. *See* Birnie and Boyle, International Law and the Environment 136 (1992); Philippe Sands, Principles of International Law 841–847 (2d ed. 2003).

[54] On the duty of notification, *see* Philippe Sands, Principles of International Law 841–852 (2d ed. 2003); Birnie and Boyle, International Law and the Environment 126–137 (1992).

existed in the very first case it decided, the *Corfu Channel Case*, where it held that notification would benefit "shipping in general".[55]

This conclusion was further confirmed by a later decision, confronting Nicaragua versus the United States in the matter of illegal military and paramilitaries activities, in which the Court derived the substantive obligation of notification principles from international humanitarian law.[56]

As a principle of international environmental law, the information duty is also spelled out in its general format in Principle 18 of the Rio Declaration, which affirms that

> States shall immediately notify other States of any natural disaster or other emergencies that are likely to produce sudden harmful effects on the environment of those States.

Additionally, the international community is mandate to make "every effort" to help States so afflicted.

Most importantly, the duty of information is also found in treaties protecting marine resources, which are "among the most highly developed in the field of international environmental law."[57] In fact, together with the comprehensive UNCLOS, there are fourteen conventions and protocols (three global and eleven regional – including eight Protocols to UNEP Regional seas convention) that provide a framework for international cooperation to combat emergency situations in the marine environment.[58]

The most significant example of a notification obligation is found in Article 198 UNCLOS, which requires States, when they become aware of cases:

> in which the marine environment is in imminent danger of being damaged or has been damaged by pollution, [to] immediately notify other States it deems likely to be affected by such damage, as well as the competent international organizations.[59]

---

55 *Corfu Channel Case (UK v. Albania)*, 1949 I.C.J. 4, ¶ 22 (9 Apr.) (holding that "the obligations incumbent upon the Albanian authorities consisted in notifying for the benefit of shipping in general, the existence of a minefield in Albanian territorial waters and in warning the approaching British warship of imminent danger to which the minefield exposed them").

56 *Case Concerning Military and Paramilitary Activities in and against Nicaragua (Nicaragua v. US)*, Judgment, 1986 I.C.J. 112 (27 June), *available at*: http://www.icj-cij.org/docket/index.php?p1=3&k=66&case=70&code=nus&p3=4 (reasoning that "if a state lays mines in any waters whatever in which the vessels of another state have rights of access or passage, and fails to give any warning or notification whatsoever, in disregard of the security of peaceful shipping, it commits a breach of the principles of humanitarian law").

57 Philippe Sands, Principles of International Law 478 (2d ed. 2003).

58 *Id.* at 448–454.

59 The Convention entered into force on 27 October 1986. As of 17 January 2006, the Convention had 98 Parties and 70 signatories, including the five nuclear weapons States, *available at*: http://www.un.org/depts/los/convention_agreements/texts/unclos/part12.htm.

This provision was specifically tested in a recent case brought by Malaysia and Singapore in front of the ICJ and dealing with the sovereignty of certain islands.[60] In that case, the Court analyzed UNCLOS notification provision to assess whether Singapore had acted as a sovereign when it investigated and notified other Contracting States of certain hazards to the safety of navigation that occurred in the disputed area.[61] The Court concluded that Singapore's notification reports gave significant support to Singapore's case and, thus, supported the importance of fulfilling the notification obligation as well to as its international relevance.[62]

Similar provisions exist in regional agreements on the same matter. Biodiversity[63] and biosafety treaties also include an obligation to notify other States in case of an emergency.

The 1992 Biodiversity Convention, for example, requires parties (as far as possible, and where appropriate) when they face imminent or grave danger or damage to biological diversity in an area under the jurisdiction of other States or in areas beyond the limits of national jurisdiction, but when the emergency originates under their jurisdiction or control, to

> notify immediately the potentially affected States of such danger or damage, as well as initiate action to prevent or minimize such danger or damage.[64]

The Convention therefore places a double burden on countries that are or will experience grave danger to biological diversity to notify other potentially affected States and initiate action to prevent and minimize the damage. Importantly, the member States are required to notify other States when the threat originates in their territory and could have transboundary effects.

Several treaties include similar provisions, including bio-safety conventions related to the prevention of large-scale loss of biological material. The 2000 Cartagena Biosafety Protocol deals primarily with reducing the risk of alien viral or transgenic genes and prions, and with reducing the risk of food bacterial contamination.

---

[60] *Sovereignty Over Pedra Branca/Pulau Butu Puteh Middle Rocks and South Ledge* (Malaysia/Singapore), Judgment (23 May 2008), *available at*: http://www.icj-cij.org/docket/index.php?p1=3&k=2b&case=130&code=masi&p3=4.

[61] *Id.* ¶¶ 231–234.

[62] *Id.* ¶ 234.

[63] Biodiversity is defined as "the variability among living organisms from all sources including, *inter alia*, terrestrial, marine and other aquatic ecosystems and the ecological complexes of which they are part; this includes diversity within species, between species and of ecosystems." *Convention on Biodiversity*, Art. 2, *available at*: http://www.biodiv.org/convention/articles.asp?lg=0&a=cbd-14.

[64] *Id.* at Art. 14.

Art. 17(1) of the Protocol mandates Parties to take appropriate measures to notify affected or potentially affected States, the Biosafety Clearing-House and relevant international organizations

> when it knows of an occurrence under its jurisdiction resulting in a release that leads, or may lead, to an unintentional transboundary movement of a living modified organism that is likely to have significant adverse effects on the conservation and sustainable use of biological diversity, taking also into account risks to human health in such States. The notification shall be provided as soon as the Party knows of the above situation.[65]

Similarly, Article 17(4) further provides that each Party must immediately consult all others that are affected or will potentially be affected by the release of the modified organism to enable them to determine appropriate responses and initiate necessary action, including emergency measures.[66]

Further, Article II of the 1959 Agreement Concerning Cooperation in the Quarantine of Plants and Their Protection Against Pests and Diseases also mandates that Contracting parties regularly exchange information concerning the spread of dangerous pests and diseases, as well as the measures taken for their control. In the event of the outbreak of especially dangerous quarantinable plant pests and diseases, Contracting Parties are also obligated to immediately transmit information related to the centers of infection discovered for the first time.[67]

Similar provisions are also found in a series of conventions and agreements dealing with industrial accidents.[68]

---

[65] Cartagena Biosafety Protocol (2000), *available at*: http://www.biodiv.org/biosafety/articles.asp?lg=0&a=bsp-17. The Protocol has 147 ratifications and entered into force on 11 Sept. 2003.

[66] Art. 17 (4) affirms that "Each Party shall take appropriate measures to notify affected or potentially affected States, the Biosafety Clearing-House and, where appropriate, relevant international organizations, when it knows of an occurrence under its jurisdiction resulting in a release that leads, or may lead, to an unintentional transboundary movement of a living modified organism that is likely to have significant adverse effects on the conservation and sustainable use of biological diversity, taking also into account risks to human health in such States. The notification shall be provided as soon as the Party knows of the above situation." Cartagena Biosafety Protocol, 2000, *available at*: http://www.biodiv.org/biosafety/articles.asp?lg=0&a=bsp-17.

[67] Agreement Concerning Cooperation in the Quarantine of Plants and Their Protection Against Pests and Diseases, 14 Dec. 1959, *available at*: http://sedac.ciesin.columbia.edu/entri/texts/quarantine.of.plants.1959.html.

[68] *See* also, as general conventions, the ILO Code of Conduct on Major Industrial Accidents and the ILO Convention for the Prevention of Major Industrial Accidents, ILO Convention No. 174, 1993. They establish responsibilities for the employer and public authorities in the conduct of activities and the preparation of emergency preparedness arrangements.

In this context, two European regional agreements are particularly relevant: first, the Convention of the United Nations Economic Commission for Europe on the Transboundary Effects of Industrial Accidents;[69] and, second, the EC Seveso Directive, first enacted in 1982 and replaced in 1996 ("Seveso II Directive") and 2003 ("Seveso III Directive").[70]

First, the United Nations Economic Commission for Europe ("UNECE") Convention on Industrial Accidents was signed in Helsinki on 18 March, 1992 and entered into force on April 19, 2000. Presently, there are 34 Contracting States including the EU itself.[71] The Convention aims at preventing, reducing and mitigating the effects of transboundary industrial accidents and protecting both human beings and the environment. Article 10 specifically requests parties to cooperate and to share information in the event of an industrial accident. It requires Parties to create an efficient industrial accident notification system. It further obligates the Party of origin, in the event of an industrial accident capable of causing transboundary effect, or an imminent threat of one, to ensure that "affected Parties are without delay, notified at appropriate levels through the industrial accident notification systems."

Second, and similarly, the Seveso Directives aim at *preventing* major-accident hazards involving dangerous substances and limiting the consequences of accidents for both humans and the environment when they occur. The Directives focus on the presence of certain hazardous substances in establishments, both as storage and as a component of industrial activities. The Convention specifically excludes nuclear materials and the transport and temporary storage of substances. Similarly to the UNECE Convention, the Seveso Directive provisions mandate Member States to inform the Commission of major accidents. Member States must ensure that major operators take all possible preventive measures and draw up emergency plans.

Similar provisions relating to the duty of information are also found in international conventions relating to waste and hazardous materials. For example, the 1976 Agreement for the Protection of the Rhine Against Chem-

---

[69] The text is *available at*: http://www.unece.org/env/teia/text.htm.

[70] The First Seveso Directive was enacted as Council Directive 82/501/EEC on the major-accident hazards of certain industrial activities of 24 June, 1982 (OJ No. L 230 of 5 August 1982). Seveso Directive II revised and supplemented Seveso I, it was enacted as Council Directive 96/82/EC on the control of major-accident hazards involving dangerous substances (OJ No. L 10 of January 14, 1997). The Seveso II Directive 96/82/EC was extended by the Directive 2003/105/EC of the European Parliament and of the Council of 16 December 2003 amending Council Directive 96/82/EC (OJ of 31 December 2003), *available at*: http://europa.eu.int/cgi-bin/eur-lex/udl.pl?REQUEST=Seek-Deliver&COLLECTION=oj&SERVICE=eurlex&LANGUAGE=en&DOCID=2003l345p0097.

[71] The list of Contracting Parties as of 10 Oct. 2005 is *available at*: http://www.unece.org/env/teia/parties.htm.

ical Pollution[72] includes in Article 11 the requirement to inform potentially exposed Contracting Parties of any future threat. Specifically, it requires a Contracting Party to "immediately inform" the International Commission for the protection of the Rhine against pollution and other Parties that may be affected when it becomes aware of an accident that could result in a serious threat to the quality of the waters of the Rhine or it discovers a sudden large increase of certain dangerous substances.[73]

The Basel Convention on the Control of Transboundary Movements of Hazardous Wastes and Their Disposal also contains similar provisions.[74] Article 13(1) requires parties to ensure that States are "immediately informed" in the case of an accident occurring during movement of hazardous or other wastes or their disposal across borders, which are "likely to present risks to human health and the environment in other States."

Similar notification obligations are applicable in the situation of nuclear accidents. Such principles were developed in the aftermath of the Chernobyl accident, first by the International Atomic Energy Agency, in the form of Guidelines,[75] then in the form of a full-fledged Convention on Early Notification of a Nuclear Accident ("Early Notification Convention"),[76] which was based upon the principles developed by the Guidelines. The Early Notification Convention applies in the event of an accident that involves facilities or activities of a Contracting Party or of persons or legal entities under its jurisdiction or control "from which a release of radioactive material occurs or is likely to occur" and which may result in "an international transboundary release that could be of radiological safety significance for another State."[77]

The informing Party must provide a series of information, including: the time, location and the nature of the nuclear accident; the facility or activity involved; the assumed or established cause and its foreseeable transboundary developments and information necessary to forecast the transboundary release of the radioactive materials; the general characteristics of the

---

72 Agreement for the Protection of the Rhine Against Chemical Pollution, 3 Dec. 1976, *reprinted in* DOCUMENTS IN INTERNATIONAL ENVIRONMENTAL LAW 652–662 (P. Sands et al. eds., 1994).

73 These substances include organohalogen, organophosphorous and organotin compounds, heavy metals, mineral oils, and inorganic compounds. For a complete list, *see* DOCUMENTS IN INTERNATIONAL ENVIRONMENTAL LAW 660–662 (P. Sands et al. eds, 1994).

74 Basel Convention on the Control of Transboundary Movements of Hazardous Wastes and Their Disposal, 5 May 1992, *available at*: http://www.basel.int/text/con-e-rev.doc.

75 Guidelines on Reportable Events, Integrated Planning and Information Exchange in Transboundary Release of Radioactive Materials, IAEA Doc. INFCIRC/321 (1985).

76 Convention on Early Notification of a Nuclear Accident, 27 Oct., 1986, a*vailable at*: http://www.iaea.org/Publications/Documents/Infcircs/Others/infcirc335.shtml.

77 *Id.* at Art. 1.

radioactive release, the offsite protective measures taken or planned; and the predicted behavior over time of the radioactive release.[78]

These provisions are only applicable to civil use of nuclear energy and do not include any kind of military use.[79] Importantly, it is the prerogative of the State where the accident occurred to evaluate whether the accident may be of radiological safety significance to another State.[80] This limits the possible relevance of this provision in times of State failure.

* * *

To conclude, the duty of information is present in various forms in most international treaties relating to the protection of environmental resources. The specific content of the duty is flexible and depends on the treaty provision it is found in. Certain characteristics appear to be common.[81]

First, information obligations are activated by an emergency situation. The thresholds that trigger the duty are varied and range from 'imminent or grave danger' to 'serious threat'. Second, the duty of information is triggered when the danger has a potential transboundary impact, and when there is danger that may 'affect or potentially affect' other countries or pose 'risks to human health and environment' of neighboring States. Third, information must be timely, comprehensive and accurate so that the purpose of the provision – to allow actions to be taken by potentially affected countries – is respected.

The implementation of the duty of information, however, shows mixed results. In the case of the 1986 Sandoz chemical spill in the Rhine,[82] for

---

[78] *Id.* at Art. 5.

[79] Although the five nuclear weapons states declared that they will voluntarily apply the Convention to all nuclear accidents. *See* PHILIPPE SANDS, PRINCIPLES OF INTERNATIONAL ENVIRONMENTAL LAW 846 n. 169 (2d ed. 2003).

[80] Also, Sands considers some of the reservations over-reaching, including China's choice not to apply the Convention to cases caused by 'gross negligence.' *See generally* PHILIPPE SANDS, PRINCIPLES OF INTERNATIONAL ENVIRONMENTAL LAW 846–947 (2d ed. 2003).

[81] *See* NINA NORDTRÖM, THE STATE DUTY TO INFORM ON TRANSBOUNDARY ENVIRONMENTAL ACCIDENTS 153–180 (1996). She claims that the duty of information may have reached a customary level: "The State duty to inform on transboundary environmental accidents appears to be well anchored in international law. Although the great number of treaties including the accident information duty could be seen as a reflection of a lack in general international law of an equivalent norm, this would be a view which distorts the full picture drawn by all relevant legal sources seen together. Besides treaty law on all levels, customary international law shows plenty of proof of the existence of such a duty. The 1992 Rio Declaration stands out as the most recent and most widely accepted evidence." *Id.* at 177–178.

[82] For a brief overview on the accident, *see 1986: Chemical Spill Turns Rhine Red*, BBC NEWS, *available at*: http://news.bbc.co.uk/onthisday/hi/dates/stories/november/1/newsid_4679000/4679789.stm (last visited 10 Sept. 2009).

example, Switzerland had an obligation under the 1976 Convention for the Protection of the Rhine (examined above) to inform other riparian States of the accident. However, it did so late and its delay precluded other Contracting Parties to take measures that could have potentially minimized the damage of the spill.[83]

Conversely, Romania, acting under the UNECE Convention on the Transboundary Effects of Industrial Accidents (in which 100,000 cubic meters of liquid and suspended waste containing about 50 to 100 tons of cyanide was accidently spilled in several rivers, ultimately reaching the Black Sea), informed Hungary of the 2000 Baia Cyanide Spill about ten hours after it occurred.[84] Although the time elapsed could have been minimized, Hungary had sufficient time to put in place some preventive measures, for example in relation to drinking water, that reduced the impact of the accident. Furthermore, Hungary informed Yugoslavia on the spill and collaborated with Yugoslavia to reduce the spill's effects.[85]

Moreover, although the existence of the information duty is prevalent in many environmental treaties, a study of the practice by States show that they have mostly chosen not to exercise their right to request reparations at the failure of notification. In fact, States have been reluctant to refer their grievances to the appropriate courts for a party's failure to inform other parties. For example, no action was taken against Switzerland in the Sandoz chemicals accident.

The duty of information indicates that States that experience an environmental emergency must not isolate themselves from the international community. Their duties toward other States and the international community as a whole include an obligation to provide information. The duty of information is particularly important because it allows other States that are possibly affected, and the international community as a whole, to assess the nature and gravity of the emergency and to provide assistance.

The applicability of this duty to the situation of failed States must be assessed on a case-by-case situation. Even in situations of State failure, the existence of an information obligation is important. First, this is because, in

---

83 Nina Nordtröm, The State Duty to Inform on Transboundary Environmental Accidents 160–161 (1996).

84 For a background on the accident, *see* UNEP/OCHA, *The Cyanide Spill at Baia Mare, Romania* (June 2000), *available at*: http://www.rec.org/REC/Publications/CyanideSpill/ENGCyanide.pdf (last visited 10 Sept. 2009).

85 S. Stec, et al., *Transboundary Environmental Governance and The Baia Mare Cyanide Spill*, 27 Rev. Cent. & Eur. L. 639, 642–645 (2002). *See also* Cedric Lucas, *The Baia Mare and Baia Borsa Accidents: Cases of Severe Transboundary Water Pollution*, 31 Envtl. Pol'y & L. 106, 107–108 (2001).

most instances, a certain degree of public authority will still be functioning in failing States and thus competent authorities in certain circumstances will be able to provide relevant information together with a request of assistance. Second, this is because the duty could become actionable by other actors, including U.N. agencies or NGOs present on the ground.

Moreover, in the development of a framework applicable to failing States, the respect of the information duty could have two important consequences. First, giving priority to the fulfillment of this duty would reduce the overall impact of the emergency, as it would allow other potentially impacted States to take appropriate measures to limit damages. Second, it could trigger the delivery of assistance to States that are unable to properly react to the emergency. The later result could be explicitly stipulated in conjunction with other obligations and duties. Presently, it can be seen as an aspect of the obligations to prepare a contingency plan and to provide assistance upon request, both of which are analyzed below. In the absence of third-party assistance, the information duty would be limited to assisting potentially affected countries, but not the countries at the heart of the emergency.

3.2. *Obligation to Prepare Contingency Plans*

A second obligation common to several treaties dealing with environmental emergencies is the duty to develop and have in place contingency plans that can be set in motion in the event of an environmental emergency. The obligation is an application of the duty of cooperation.

Article 199 of UNCLOS, for example, asserts that when a State becomes aware of cases in which the marine environment is in imminent danger of being damaged or has been damaged by pollution,

> States in the area affected, in accordance with their capabilities, and the competent international organizations shall cooperate, to the extent possible, in eliminating the effects of pollution and preventing or minimizing the damage. To this end, States shall jointly develop and promote contingency plans for responding to pollution incidents in the marine environment.[86]

Similarly, the UN Convention on the Law of the Non-navigational Uses of International Watercourses Adopted by the UN General Assembly in resolution 51/229 of 21 May 1997[87] requires Contracting Parties notify other

---

[86] UNCLOS, Agreement Relating to the Implementation of Part XI of the Convention, Art. 199, 10 Dec. 1982, *available at*: http://www.un.org/Depts/los/convention_agreements/texts/unclos/closindx.htm.

[87] U.N. Convention on the Law of the Non-navigational Uses of International Watercourses, 21 May 1997, *available at*: http://untreaty.un.org/ilc/texts/instruments/english/conventions/8_3_1997.pdf.

potentially affected States and competent international organizations of any emergency originating within its territory. Article 28 requires watercourse States in the territory where an emergency occurs to immediately take all practicable measures, in cooperation with potentially affected States and appropriate international organizations, to prevent, mitigate and eliminate harmful effects of the emergency. Further, when necessary, watercourse States are required to "jointly develop contingency plans for responding to emergencies, in cooperation, where appropriate, with other potentially affected States and competent international organizations."

Similarly, UNEP Regional Sea Convention[88] often include a series of protocols[89] dealing with emergencies and calling for cooperation in situations of grave and imminent danger to the marine environment and the establishment of contingency plans in case of emergencies. These treaties contain similar provisions relating to cooperation in cases of grave and imminent dangers to the marine environment caused by oil or other harmful substances

---

88 *See generally* UNEP, *Regional Seas Conventions and Protocols*, http://www.unep.ch/regionalseas/legal/conlist.htm (last visited 10 Sept. 2009).

89 The Emergency Protocols are: Protocol Concerning Cooperation in Combating Pollution of the Mediterranean Sea by Oil and other Harmful Substances in Cases of Emergency, Arts. 1, 9, 10, 16 Feb. 1976, *available at*: http://www.unep.ch/regionalseas/main/med/medemer.html [hereinafter *Barcelona Protocol*]; Protocol Concerning Regional Co-operation in Combating Pollution by Oil and Other Harmful Substances in Cases of Emergency, Arts. I(2), X, XI, 1978, *available at*: http://sedac.ciesin.columbia.edu/entri/texts/combating.pollution.oil.emergency.1978.html [hereinafter *Kuwait Protocol*]; Protocol Concerning Cooperation In Combating Pollution in Cases of Emergency, Arts. 4, 6, 8, 1981, *available at*: http://www.sdnpbd.org/sdi/treaty/transboundary_air_pollution/ww74.htm [hereinafter *Abidjan Protocol*]; Agreement on Regional Cooperation in Combating Pollution of the South-East Pacific by Hydrocarbons or Other Harmful Substances in Case of Emergency, Arts. I, X, XI, 1981, *available at*: http://www.sdnpbd.org/sdi/treaty/oceans_their_living_resources/ww120.htm [hereinafter *Lima Protocol*]; Protocol Concerning Regional Co-Operation in Combating Pollution by Oil and Other Harmful Substances in Cases of Emergency, Arts. I, II, X, 1982, *available at*: http://www.persga.org/about/history/Protocol/Protocol.asp [hereinafter *Jeddah Protocol*]; Protocol Concerning Co-operation in Combating Oil Spills in the Wider Caribbean Region, Arts. 1(4), 3, 6, 1983, *available at*: http://www.cep.unep.org/pubs/legislation/oilspill.html [hereinafter *Cartagena Oil Spills Protocol*]; Protocol Concerning Co-operation in Combating Marine Pollution in Cases of Emergency in the Eastern African Region, 1985, Arts. 1(d), 3, 6, 7, *available at*: http://sedac.ciesin.org/entri/texts/combating.marine.pollution.emergency.east.africa.1985.html [hereinafter *Nairobi Emergency Pollution Protocol*]; Protocol Concerning Co-operation in Combating Pollution Emergencies in the South Pacific Region, Arts. 1(d), 6, 7, 1986, *available at*: http://beta.austlii.edu.au/au/other/dfat/treaties/1990/32.html [hereinafter *Noumea Pollution Emergency Protocol*]; Protocol on Cooperation in Combating Pollution of the Black Sea Marine Environment by Oil and other Harmful Substances in Emergency Situations, Arts. 1, 4, 1992, *available on*: http://eelink.net/~asilwildlife/ProtocolOil.html) [hereinafter *Black Sea*].

resulting from accidental causes or an accumulation of small discharges that are polluting or are threatening to pollute. Contracting States faced with a marine emergency situation can take every appropriate measure to avoid and reduce the effects of the pollution.[90] In general, the Emergency Protocols include obligations to cooperate in case of grave or imminent danger to a specified regional marine environment; obligations include the maintenance of contingency plans, the development and application of monitoring activities, the salvage and recovery of harmful substances released in the sea or lost overboard, the exchange of information and coordination of means of communication, the insurance of reporting specified incidents, the establishment of coordination centers.[91]

Similar provisions are found in the 1990 Co-operation Agreement for the Protection of the Coasts and Waters of the North-East Atlantic Against Pollution, which focuses on acting promptly and effectively in the event of a pollution incident at sea that could endanger the coasts or the related interests of a coastal State. Article 4(2) of the Agreement requires Parties to set up national systems to prevent and combat incidents of pollution at sea, and, in particular, a national plan of action to prevent and combat incidents of pollution at sea.[92]

Several bilateral agreements also contain provisions requesting each Party to prepare contingency plans. These include the 1983 Agreement between Canada and Denmark for Cooperation relating to the Marine Environment[93] that deals with pollution accidents resulting from offshore hydrocarbon exploration or exploitation, and from shipping activities.[94]

---

[90] For example, *see* Article 9 of the Barcelona Protocol, which instructs any Party faced with an emergency situation to "(a) Make the necessary assessments of the nature and extent of the casualty or emergency or, as the case may be, of the type and approximate quantity of oil or other harmful substances and the direction and speed of drift of the spillage; (b) Take every practicable measure to avoid or reduce the effects of pollution: (c) Immediately inform all other Parties, either directly or through the regional centre, of these assessments and of any action which it has taken or which it intends to take to combat the pollution." *See also* Article 10 of the Jeddah Protocol, Article X of the Lima Protocol and Article X of the Kuwait Protocol.

[91] Philippe Sands, Principles of International Law 453–454 (2d ed. 2003).

[92] Cooperation Agreement for the Protection of the Coasts and Waters of the North-east Atlantic Against Pollution, 17 Oct. 1990, *available at*: http://faolex.fao.org/docs/texts/mul34606.doc.

[93] Agreement For Cooperation Relating to the Marine Environment, Can.-Den., 26 Aug. 1983, 1348 U.N.T.S. 121 (1984), *available at*: http://untreaty.un.org/unts/60001_120000/12/2/00022093.pdf.

[94] *See also* Convention on Mutual Assistance in the Event of Disasters or Serious Accidents, Fr.-F.R.G., 3 Feb. 1977, 1214 U.N.T.S. 67.

The content of the duty is not uniform, and varies depending on each treaty. Two core requirements are, however, relevant: first, the duty is of a preventive nature and imposes obligations that exist before the situation of emergency actually occurs. Second, it is a common duty of several Contracting Parties and, as such, requires collaboration amongst them.

In situations of State failure, both characteristics are important. In fact, the obligations to set up contingency plans in case of emergency is an interesting tool to limit the damages ensuing from an emergency situation in failed or failing States.

The biggest limitation of this duty is that if it is not respected or is implemented poorly it may undermine actions that can be taken when emergencies occur.

Contingency planning is now a common feature of environmental regulations, however, there is little analysis of the implementation of this obligation in emergency situations, and it is therefore difficult to evaluate it properly. However, for situations of State failure this obligation may be useful and should be taken into consideration for further development of a comprehensive assessment of State failure.

3.3. *The Obligation to Provide Assistance on Demand*

Several treaties also contain the obligation for Contracting States to provide assistance when requested by another Contracting State under emergency. The obligation is an application of the duty of cooperation.

The obligation is often coupled with provisions that establish a duty to notify emergency situations, and it is also often linked to the obligation to prepare contingency plans examined above.[95]

The obligation to provide assistance on demand usually requires operations in the territory of the State requesting assistance, and it therefore requires specific arrangements between the State requesting assistance and the State providing it.

Conventions relating to the use of nuclear energy or the reduction of oil pollution often include this kind of obligation.

For example, Article 7(1) of the 1990 International Convention On Oil Pollution Preparedness, Response And Cooperation[96] contains provisions on international cooperation in pollution response. It states that:

---

[95] ALEXANDRE KISS AND DINAH SHELTON, INTERNATIONAL ENVIRONMENTAL LAW 194–197 (3d ed. 2003).

[96] International Convention On Oil Pollution Preparedness, Response And Cooperation, 30 Nov. 1990, *available at*: http://sedac.ciesin.columbia.edu/entri/texts/oil.pollution.preparedness.1990.html.

> Parties agree that, subject to their capabilities and the availability of relevant resources, they will co-operate and provide advisory services, technical support and equipment for the purpose of responding to an oil pollution incident, when the severity of such incident so justifies, upon the request of any Party affected or likely to be affected.

State to State assistance is based on a request formulated by the State requiring assistance. The request for assistance must specify the scope and kind of assistance required and must also provide the assisting party with necessary information to determine its ability to assist. A State Party that receives a request for assistance must promptly decide and notify the requesting State Party, directly or through the Agency, whether it is in a position to render the assistance requested, and the scope and terms of the assistance that might be rendered.[97] Assistance may be provided at no cost or on a reimbursement basis.[98]

Similarly, Article 15 of the 1992 Helsinki Convention on the Protection and Use of Transboundary Watercourses and Lakes[99] provides that if a critical situation arises "the Riparian Parties shall provide mutual assistance upon request." Specifically, the Riparian Parties must elaborate on and agree to procedures for mutual assistance that address several issues, namely:

> The direction, control, coordination and supervision of assistance;
> Local facilities and services to be rendered by the Party requesting assistance, including, where necessary, the facilitation of border-crossing formalities;
> Arrangements for holding harmless, indemnifying and/or compensating the assisting Party and/or its personnel, as well as for transit through territories of third Parties, where necessary;
> Methods of reimbursing assistance services.

The UNECE Convention on Industrial Accidents also requires Parties provide, upon request, mutual assistance in the event an accident. Article 12 of the Convention states that, in the event of an industrial accident, if a party needs assistance, it may ask for assistance from other Parties. The request for assistance must indicate the scope and type of assistance required. In turn, the Party that receives the request must reply promptly and decide and inform the requesting Party whether it is in a position to assist and how. Once the Parties agree, assistance must be given promptly and shall include "actions to minimize the consequences and effects of the industrial

---

97 *Id.* at Art. 2.

98 *Id.* at Art. 7.

99 Helsinki Convention on the Protection and Use of Transboundary Watercourses and Lakes, 17 Mar. 1992, *available at*: http://www.unece.org/env/water/pdf/watercon.pdf.

accident."[100] The Convention specifies that the Requesting Party maintains the overall direction, control, coordination and supervision of the assistance, and it is normally responsible for the overall cost of the assistance.

Several other Conventions contain similar provisions. The 1963 Nordic Mutual Emergency Assistance Agreement in Connection with Radiation Accidents,[101] for example, was agreed upon to assist each Party in the event of an incident involving damage from ionizing radiation. The provision of assistance is based on the request by a Contracting Party to another. The overall responsibility for the use of assistance remains with the Requesting State, including financial and personnel responsibilities and overall liability for assistance rendered in its territory. The Requesting State may demand the termination of the assistance in writing at any time, while the Assisting Party may terminate its assistance when it believes that it is no longer necessary, if domestic needs so require, or if the Requesting State fails to observe the terms of the Agreement. A written notice must be given in advance.

Several Conventions applicable to high seas and the marine environment also contain Assistance-On-Demand Provisions. For Example, article 7 of the 1969 Agreement For Cooperation In Dealing With Pollution Of The North Sea By Oil[102] provides that

> A Contracting Party requiring assistance to dispose of oil floating on the sea or polluting its coast may call on the help of the other Contracting Parties, starting with those which also seem likely to be affected by the floating oil. Contracting Parties called upon for help in accordance with this Article shall use their best endeavors to bring such assistance as is within their power.

Similarly, the 1983 Agreement For Cooperation In Dealing With Pollution Of The North Sea By Oil And Other Harmful Substances[103] aims to ensure cooperation between coastal States in providing personnel, supplies, equipment and scientific advice on short notice to deal with discharges of oil or other harmful substances in the North Sea. In addition to a duty of information, the Agreement provides, at Article 7, that a Contracting Party requiring assistance to deal with pollution or the prospective presence of pollution

---

[100] UNECE Convention on the Transboundary Effects of Industrial Accidents, 17 Mar. 1992, *available at*: http://www.unece.org/env/teia/text.htm.

[101] Nordic Mutual Emergency Assistance Agreement in Connection with Radiation Accidents, 17 Oct. 1963, *available at*: http://www.iaea.org/Publications/Documents/Infcircs/Others/infcirc49.shtml. Parties to the Agreement are: Denmark, Finland, Norway and Sweden.

[102] Agreement For Cooperation In Dealing With Pollution Of The North Sea By Oil, 8 June 1969, *available at*: http://sedac.ciesin.columbia.edu/entri/register/reg-049.rrr.html.

[103] Agreement For Cooperation In Dealing With Pollution Of The North Sea By Oil And Other Harmful Substances, 13 Sept. 1983, *available at*: http://sedac.ciesin.columbia.edu/entri/texts/pollution.oil.north.sea.1983.html.

at sea or on its coast "may call on the help of the other Contracting Parties". The Party that requires assistance shall specify the kind of assistance it requires, while the assisting Party must "use their best endeavors to bring such assistance as is within their power taking into account, particularly in the case of pollution by harmful substances other than oil, the technological means available to them."

The obligation to provide assistance on demand is a very important tool for the management of environmental emergency. Similarly to other obligations examined above, its contents vary, but two criteria remain fundamental: first, no action can be taken without an explicit request by a State where the emergency takes place. Assistance is given only as requested and specified by the Requesting State. Second, the requesting State remains in control of the assistance that is delivered, including financially. Thus, requesting parties continue to play the leading role when tackling an emergency.

These provisions allow Parties to certain treaties to request assistance to other Contracting Parties while maintaining the overall responsibility and direction of the assistance provided. Thus, they permit Parties in difficulties to voice their difficulties and obtain assistance in situations where they are not capable of fully addressing by themselves.

These provisions could be most relevant for failed States, though they remain problematic. In fact, the obligations rely entirely on the active role of the Party that needs assistance. However, in situations of State failure, this Party is often not in a position to clearly request assistance and maintain its direction. Although it is possible that at the early stages of State failure or in phases of recovery, failing States may be able to request specific and direct assistance and keep control and responsibility over it, in many other cases, this will not be possible. Thus, the main limitation of this type of obligation remains the fact that States may be incapable of requesting assistance, may decide not to request it and may not be capable of managing and controlling the assistance received. At the same time, they may still be incapable of confronting an emergency. In this situation, the consequence of environmental emergencies would escalate while little action could be taken by the other members of the international community. A solution must be found so that the delivery of assistance is triggered even without a specific request from the State under emergency, and requesting States are not held financially and managerially responsible for the assistance they receive.

3.4. *Unilateral Intervention in the Event of an Accident*

The fourth and last general obligation arising out of environmental treaties dealing with emergency situations is the possibility of acting unilaterally in the event of an environmental emergency.

The existence of this right is limited and only rarely found in treaties. Provisions relating to such a possibility are found in, for example, conventions concerning the protection of the high seas or the reduction of oil pollution.

The most important example is found in UNCLOS,[104] which provides that States may unilaterally intervene to avert accidental harm originating outside of their territory. Article 221 of UNCLOS describes measures to avoid pollution arising from maritime casualties. It states that

> 1. Nothing in this Part shall prejudice the right of States, pursuant to international law, both customary and conventional, to take and enforce measures beyond the territorial sea proportionate to the actual or threatened damage to protect their coastline or related interests, including fishing, from pollution or threat of pollution following upon a maritime casualty or acts relating to such a casualty, which may reasonably be expected to result in major harmful consequences.
> 2. For the purposes of this article, "maritime casualty" means a collision of vessels, stranding or other incident of navigation, or other occurrence on board a vessel or external to it resulting in material damage or imminent threat of material damage to a vessel or cargo.[105]

The applicability of this provision is limited to harmful consequences stemming from maritime casualties, as defined by the Convention, and intervention is only possible in international waters. This provision is nonetheless interesting, because it specifically allows action beyond the territory of a State. Moreover, UNCLOS is a widely ratified Convention and, thus, imposes obligations on most States.[106]

Article 1 of 1969 Brussels Convention Relating to Intervention on the High Seas in Cases of Oil Pollution Casualties,[107] adopted under the auspices of IMO, similarly provides that Parties to the Convention

[104] UNCLOS Convention, Agreement Relating to the Implementation of Part XI of the Convention, 16 Nov. 1994, *available at*: http://www.un.org/Depts/los/convention_agreements/texts/unclos/closindx.htm.

[105] *Id.*

[106] As of September 2009, 159 States ratified or acceded to UNCLOS, *see* UNCLOS, Chronological lists of ratifications of, accessions and successions to the Convention an the related Agreements (20 July 2009), *available at*: http://www.un.org/Depts/los/reference_files/status2008.pdf (last visited 11 Sept. 2009).

[107] Convention Relating to Intervention on the High Seas in Cases of Oil Pollution Casualties, 29 Nov. 1969, *available at*: http://sedac.ciesin.org/entri/texts/intervention.high.seas.casualties.1969.html. The Convention has 62 Contracting parties, representing 72.88 percent of the world's tonnage (*see* IMO, Summary of Status of the Convention (31 July 2009), *available at*: http://www.imo.org/Conventions/mainframe.asp?topic_id=247).

> may take such measures on the high seas as may be necessary to prevent, mitigate or eliminate grave and imminent danger to their coastline or related interests from pollution or threat of pollution of the sea by oil, following upon a maritime casualty or acts related to such a casualty, which may reasonably be expected to result in major harmful consequences.[108]

This provision is subject to several restrictions. First, measures must be proportionate to the damage actual or threat of damage, and they must not go beyond what is reasonably necessary to achieve the specified goals. Second, they must cease as soon as their purpose has been achieved. Third, these measures must not unnecessarily interfere with the rights and interests of other States or physical or legal persons.[109]

The right of the coastal State to intervene in cases of grave and imminent danger is further limited by other provisions of the Convention. First, Article 1 (2) specifically prohibits all measures against warships and ships owned or operated by a State and used only for governmental, non-commercial service. Further, besides cases of extreme urgency requiring immediate measures, before taking any measures, a coastal State must consult States affected by the maritime casualty, and in particular with the flag State. The coastal State must also notify without delay the proposed measures to any interested corporate or physical persons that may be affected by the measures and hear their views. States and all known physical and corporate persons concerned must be notified, as well as the Secretary-General of the IMO.[110]

A Protocol extending the types of substance to which the aforementioned measures are applicable was added in 1973.[111] The Protocol applies to substances other than oil listed in an Annex as well as other substances that are "liable to create hazards to human health, to harm living resources and

[108] Convention Relating to Intervention on the High Seas in Cases of Oil Pollution Casualties, Arts. 2, 29 Nov. 1969, *available at*: http://sedac.ciesin.org/entri/texts/intervention.high.seas.casualties.1969.html. (specifying that "'maritime casualty' means a collision of ships, stranding or other incident of navigation, or other occurrence on board a ship or external to it resulting in material damage or imminent threat of material damage to a ship or cargo.").

[109] *Id.* at Arts. 5–6.

[110] *Id.* at Art. 3.

[111] Protocol on Intervention of the High Seas in Cases of Marine Pollution by Substances Other Than Oil, 2 Nov. 1973, *available at*: http://sedac.ciesin.org/entri/texts/intervention.high.seas.casualties.protocol.1973.html. The Protocol has 48 State Parties representing 47.40 percent of the world's tonnage (*see* IMO, Summary of Status of the Convention (31 July 2009) *available at*: http://www.imo.org/Conventions/mainframe.asp?topic_id=247). The list of substances which may trigger interventions was revised in 1991, 1996 and 2002.

marine life, to damage amenities or to interfere with other legitimate uses of the sea."[112]

Before taking action, a coastal State must notify the flag State of the ship, consult independent experts and notify any person whose interests may reasonably be expected to be affected by such action. However,

> in cases of extreme urgency requiring measures to be taken immediately, the coastal State may take measures rendered necessary by the urgency of the situation, without prior notification or consultation or without continuing consultations already begun.[113]

In any case, the coastal State must endeavor to protect human life and assist persons in distress. Moreover, all measures taken must not go beyond what is reasonably necessary to achieve their goal and must be proportionate to the actual or threatened damage.[114] Article VI assigns responsibility to the acting State for any damage done to other Parties. Specifically, it states that a Party that takes measures in contravention of the provisions of the Convention causing damage to others, will have to pay compensation to the extent of the damage caused by measures which exceed those reasonably necessary.

The 1990 International Convention On Oil Pollution Preparedness, Response And Co-Operation[115] provides a further example of unilateral intervention in the event of an accident. The Convention mandates State Parties undertake, individually or jointly, all appropriate measures to prepare for and respond to an oil pollution incident originating from ships, offshore units, sea ports and oil handling facilities. Article 1 of the Convention provides that it does not apply to warships and other ships owned by a State or operated as governmental, non-commercial service, while Article 5 mandates Parties inform all other parties that may be affected by an oil pollution incident.

Parties may cooperate and provide services and support when a Party affected or likely to be affected requests it, as well as on their own initiative. Annex I of the Convention, to which Article 7 refers for the financing of the operational costs, provides that unless parties conclude a bilateral or

---

112 Protocol on Intervention of the High Seas in Cases of Marine Pollution by Substances Other Than Oil, Art. 1(2), 2 Nov. 1973, *available at*: http://sedac.ciesin.org/entri/texts/intervention.high.seas.casualties.protocol.1973.html.

113 *Id.* at Art. III.

114 *Id.* at Art. V.

115 International Convention On Oil Pollution Preparedness, Response And Co-Operation, 13 May 1995, *available at*: http://fletcher.tufts.edu/multi/texts/BH981.txt. The Convention entered into force on 13 May 1995. As of 31 Dec. 2005, the Convention had 86 Contracting Parties, representing 64.32% of the world's tonnage (*see* IMO, *Summary of Status of the Convention* (31 July 2009), *available at*: http://www.imo.org/Conventions/mainframe.asp?topic_id=247).

multilateral agreement "concerning the financial arrangements governing actions of Parties to deal with oil pollution incidents" prior to the pollution incident, the Party that takes action will bear the cost of the action taken by the Party at its own initiative. However, "if the action was taken by one Party at the express request of another Party, the requesting Party shall reimburse to the assisting Party the cost of its action."[116]

A 2000 Protocol on Preparedness, Response and Co-operation to Pollution Incidents by Hazardous and Noxious Substances[117] extended the provisions of the 1990 Convention to several hazardous and noxious substances.[118]

UNEP Regional Sea Conventions often have Protocols that relate to emergency measures. In general, these Emergency Protocols include diverse obligations to address emergencies. Article 1 of the 1976 Barcelona Emergency Protocol, for example, mandated that Contracting Parties:

> co-operate in taking the necessary measures in cases of grave and imminent danger to the marine environment, the coast or related interests of one or more of the Parties due to the presence of massive quantities of oil or other harmful substances resulting from accidental causes or an accumulation of small discharges which are polluting or threatening to pollute the sea.[119]

Existing caselaw on this matter generally refers to domestic litigation, between a State and the private actors, responsible for the pollution. There are no international decisions available applying any of these norms.

It is important to note that provisions related to unilateral assistance are only found in Conventions that relate to the high seas or sea pollution. The high seas are not subject to sovereignty, and sovereignty has traditionally been less prominent on sea resources. However, with the development of technology that makes it possible to reach resources in the high seas, these areas promise to become a more prominent focus of attention.

That said, provided that certain criteria are preserved, unilateral assistance may provide an essential tool for environmental emergencies in failing and failed States. Criteria that are essential for the implementation of unilateral

---

[116] *Id.* at Art. 7.

[117] Protocol on Preparedness, Response and Co-operation to Pollution Incidents by Hazardous and Noxious Substances, 15 Mar. 2000, *available at*: http://www.fog.it/legislaz/londra-2000.htm. For ratification information *see* http://www.imo.org/Conventions/contents.asp?topic_id=258&doc_id=683.

[118] These substances are defined by reference to lists of substances included in various IMO Conventions and Codes, and include oils; other liquid substances defined as noxious or dangerous; liquefied gases; liquid substances with a flashpoint not exceeding 60°C; dangerous, hazardous and harmful materials and substances carried in packaged form; and solid bulk materials defined as possessing chemical hazards.

[119] Barcelona Protocol, supra note 406.

assistance include proportionality and necessity. Proportionality ensures that the assisting State only reacts to the emergency with means that are adept to address the situation and that only necessary means are employed. The necessity criterion ensures that unilateral assistance is only provided in situations that will result or are likely to result in major harmful consequences. Unilateral assistance is a last resort method, and cannot be extended unnecessary.

If both of these criteria are respected, unilateral assistance could become an effective and cost-efficient method to address emergency situations in the most serious cases of State failure.

3.5. *Conclusion*

Existing treaty provisions concerning emergency situations include several principles that may be usefully transposed to situations of State failure. These principles are not mutually exclusive and could all be used to address different emergencies and during different stages of State failure.

First, the obligation to inform other States of emergency situations that may pose a serious threat to them could be implemented by most failing States who retain some form of representation and functioning government. Criteria included in the obligation comprise timely notice, and the obligation to provide detailed, clear and comprehensive information.

Second, the duty of developing contingency plans is an important preventive obligation that derives from the duty of cooperation. It is important because it places duties upon several members of the international community and not just one State. Its biggest limitation, however, derives from its very characteristic as it remains a preventive commitment. As such, it may not necessarily provide the right assistance in emergency situations.

Third, the duty to provide assistance upon request is another important provision included in several emergency treaties. However, it remains problematic as it relies heavily on the capacity of the requesting State to assess the emergency, request appropriate assistance and take charge of it.

Fourth, unilateral assistance represents the most interesting form of intervention and assistance to failing States in cases of emergency situations. Provided that certain criteria are respected, including proportionality and necessity, unilateral assistance could provide timely assistance in situations of emergency, while respecting the essential sovereign prerogative of the State.

These obligations, however, have been tested in practice only sparsely. Moreover, they remain limited to States that are parties to the relevant Treaties and Conventions.

However, these obligations remain important as guiding principles for the development of a principled approach to State failure.

4. *The Role of the United Nations in Environmental Emergencies*

Several agencies and programs of the United Nations play an important role in dealing with environmental emergency situations, both manmade and natural. The main body dealing with emergency is the Joint UNEP/OCHA Environment Unit ("Joint Unit"), an operational organization whose main goal is to provide assistance in situations of emergency.

Initially, the Joint Unit, then called the U.N. Centre for Urgent Environmental Assistance, was created on an experimental basis in 1992 for a period of 18 months.[120] As it exists now, the Joint Unit was established in 1995 by a collaboration between the United Nations Environment Programme ("UNEP") and the United Nations Department of Humanitarian Affairs ("OCHA"), with the aim of enhancing the international capacity to respond to environmental emergencies.[121] Because of its dual composition, the Joint Unit is governed by two high levels bodies: the U.N. General Assembly for OCHA and the UNEP Governing Council for UNEP.

The Joint Unit mobilizes and coordinates the international response to environmental emergencies and natural disasters with major environmental impacts. Its three main areas of operations are:

1. Providing environmental assistance;
2. Providing response preparedness assistance;
3. Acting as secretariat to Environmental Emergencies Partnership.

The Joint Unit supplies several essential functions to confront environmental emergencies. First, it makes available continuous monitoring with an international network of contacts specializing in early notification of environmental emergencies. Second, it can notify the international community of disasters when necessary, and can issue information and situation reports. Third, in the event of an environmental emergency it can provide rapid assessments of the impacts of the emergency and can recommend response actions. Fourth, it mobilizes multilateral assistance from the donor community based on its assessment. Fifth, it can act as a liaison between the country where the emergency occurred and governments that are willing to provide

[120] UNEP Governing Council Decision 16/9 (31 May 1991).
[121] UNEP Governing Council Decision 18/19 (Feb. 1995).

assistance, including information on maps, satellite images and other general information.[122]

However, assistance can only be provided at the specific request of the country affected. This limitation impacted the action of the international community in the aftermath of the tropical Cyclone Nargis that hit Myanmar in May 2008, where national authorities refused and limited most assistance.[123]

The Joint Unit relies on a network of more than one hundred National Focal Points established by the Join Unit itself. National Focal Points exist in more than one hundred countries in every region of the world, and provide information, advice and assistance to the Joint Unit.

In its fourteen years of existence, the Joint Unit mobilized assistance and deployed expert teams to respond to over seventy environmental emergencies and natural disaster events. In 2008, these interventions include a geohazards assessment in Honduras; an environmental assessment report for Turks and Caicos Islands for hurricanes and tropical storms and an assessment for a power outage crisis in Zanzibar.[124]

Additionally, the Joint Unit was also deployed in the aftermath of the Southeast Asia earthquake of October 2005, one of the worst natural disasters ever recorded. The Rapid Assessment Team arrived in Islamabad one day after the earthquake, on 9 October 2005, to assess life-threatening environmental issues in the disaster area and identify major impacts and risks caused by the earthquake. In a second phase, sectoral experts developed plans to address the problems identified by the Rapid Assessment Team, including waste management (especially from refugee camps), landslides and potential sources of risk from industrial sites.[125]

---

[122] *See* OCHA, UNEP and JEU, OCHA, *Guidelines for Environmental Emergencies* 7–17 (May 2009), http://ochaonline.un.org/ToolsServices/EmergencyRelief/EnvironmentalEmergenciesandtheJEU/ToolsandGuidelines/tabid/5094/language/en-US/Default.aspx; *see also* OCHA, *Environmental Emergencies and the Joint Environment Unit*, http://ochaonline.un.org/ToolsServices/EmergencyRelief/EnvironmentalEmergenciesandtheJEU/tabid/1276/language/en-US/Default.aspx (last visited 11 Sept. 2009).

[123] *See* OCHA, *Myanmar Tropical Cyclone Nargis Flash Appeal 2008* (9 May 2008), *available at*: http://ochaonline.un.org/humanitarianappeal/webpage.asp?MenuID=10860&Page=1665.

[124] For a complete list, *see*, OCHA, *Full List of Environmental Disaster Reports*, http://ochaonline.un.org/ToolsServices/EmergencyRelief/EnvironmentalEmergenciesandtheJEU/Reportsonemergenciesandactivities/tabid/1464/language/en-US/Default.aspx (last visited 11 Sept. 2009).

[125] OCHA, *Update to Partners on Environmental Aspects of the South Asia Earthquake* (11 Nov. 2005), *available at*: http://ochaonline.un.org/ToolsServices/EmergencyRelief/EnvironmentalEmergenciesandtheJEU/Reportsonemergenciesandactivities/tabid/1464/language/en-US/Default.aspx.

Further, the Joint Unit traveled to the DRC in 2004 to assess and report on the potential environmental impact of a mine collapse in Shinkolobwe, which was believed to cause radiological harmful consequences. The mission was established following a request by the Ministry of Solidarity and Humanitarian Affairs of the DRC to the Joint Environmental Unit. It consisted of representatives of UNEP, OCHA, WHO, the IAEA and the UN Mission in the DRC. The mission was mandated to assess the current state of the mine as well as to provide an evaluation of the causes of its partial collapse. Environmental, humanitarian and health concerns were assessed. The mission concluded that the collapse was due to artisanal and unsafe mining and that the site was contaminated by naturally accruing radioactive materials, which had no large-scale environmental consequences but were dangerous for miners because of continuous exposure. The mission suggested that the mine be closed and its access restricted.[126]

These examples demonstrate that the Joint Environmental Unit plays an important role in dealing with environmental emergencies.

First, it provides continuous monitoring and real-life information on any environmental emergencies. Further, it can deploy immediate assessment and operational assistance thanks to its web of National Focal Points. This is particularly important because timely and efficient action is crucial in environmental emergencies.

Second, because of its supra-national and independent character, the Unit can provide services to States without threatening their sovereignty. Multilateral assistance is often more easily welcomed than bilateral assistance in situations of emergencies. The Unit can also coordinate the deployment of bilateral assistance.

Third, the main weakness of the system is that assistance can only be provided upon explicit demand by the State affected by an emergency. Although this situation is the norm in international law, it raises the question of the role of the international community in situations where one country does not request or refuses to accept assistance. The question that needs to be answered, therefore, is whether States have an obligation to accept relief to reduce the overall impact of an environmental disaster for both its people and the international community, if their resources are inadequate.

---

126 Joint UNEP/OCHA Environment Unit, *Assessment Mission of the Shinkolobwe Uranium Mine Democratic Republic of Congo 5 November 2004, available at*: http://ochaonline.un.org/ToolsServices/EmergencyRelief/EnvironmentalEmergenciesandtheJEU/Reportsonemergenciesandactivities/tabid/1464/language/en-US/Default.aspx.

5. *Conclusions*

The need for collective actions in times of environmental emergencies has been demonstrated by several disasters, both manmade – like the Chernobyl nuclear accidents, and the Bopal and Seveso industrial disasters – and natural – like the East Asia Tsunami, the earthquake in Pakistan and more recently in 2008 the tropical cyclone that hit Myanmar.

This chapter assessed three types of instruments developed by the international community to address a situation of environmental emergency.

First, the general principles of international law applicable to emergency situations were assessed. Specifically, my analysis reviewed the obligation not to cause transboundary pollution and the duty of cooperation between States. These principles are relevant because they can provide guiding principles, and thus a framework, applicable to situations of environmental emergencies.

Second, several environmental treaties contain provisions that are applicable to emergency situations. Four relevant obligations have been identified and analyzed in this chapter: the obligation to provide information, the obligation to prepare contingency plans for environmental emergencies, the obligation to assist States experiencing environmental emergencies upon their request, and the obligation to act unilaterally in certain environmental emergencies. These obligations are found in numerous treaties covering many regions and dealing with different aspects of the environment. However, their applicability has rarely been tested in practice and assessing how they can work in situations of State failure remains a challenge. Moreover, although the environment is a highly regulated field, most treaties and conventions only cover specific regions (often in Europe) or specific sections of the environment. There is no comprehensive treaty dealing with environmental emergencies.

However, both treaty obligations and the general principles identified in this chapter provide an indication of the mechanisms that could be used and developed to guarantee assistance to failing and failed States in emergency situations. They indicate that actions are possible, and that provisions exist that can guide the actions of the international community.

The third instrument analyzed in this chapter is the Joint Environmental Unit, created under the auspices of two U.N. agencies to deal with environmental emergencies. Different than the previous two categories, the Unit has clear rules of engagement and has been operational for several years. The Joint Unit provides information and monitoring services, as well as coordination of assistance in emergencies situations. Assistance, however, may only be provided upon the request of the State where the emergency occurs.

In sum, in developing a comprehensive system that deals with emergencies in failed States, some lessons can be learned from the examples set up in the environment field. The three types of instruments examined here provide guidelines and a model for the development of a system that addresses the peculiarities faced by failing States. These different instruments are not mutually exclusive, but should be seen as providing several instruments to be used in different situations. Importantly, the instruments must be available through a prior agreement of all States, and should not require a specific request or action from a State facing failure.

Chapter Seven

United Nations Actions and the Use of Military Force to Provide Assistance to Domestic Populations in Failed States

This chapter explores the – limited – mechanisms available to the international community to address domestic human rights crises in failed States. In particular, three mechanisms are studied.

First, I will explore the activities of U.N. agencies and programs to provide assistance to needy domestic populations in crises countries, including the delivery of food, sanitation and health services. Then, I will appraise the use of force to protect populations in need under two different scenarios. First, I will analyze interventions by the international community using the delegated powers of the Security Council under Chapter VII of the U.N. Charter, which allows for a limited use of force in certain circumstances that threaten international security, including by providing humanitarian assistance. Second, I will examine unilateral interventions to stop gross violations of human rights by certain States and without the U.N. mandate.

These kinds of actions by the international community all address emergencies faced by the populations within the territory of countries in crisis. However, these crises also constitute an emergency for the international community and require coordinated actions. This is not only a basic, paramount question of humanity, it is also important for all States' stability, territorial integrity and to avoid cross-boundary crimes and population's influx.

1. *Actions of United Nations Agencies and Programs to Address Human Rights of Civilians in Conflict*

The human rights of domestic populations in failed or failing States are often neglected. Often people are displaced and become subject to human rights abuses. On many occasions, internal conflicts, violence and wars ensue. In general, agencies, funds and programs of the United Nations system have been at the forefront of providing assistance in situations of crisis and emergencies.

They normally act in coordination with NGOs and State agencies that are tasked with similar mandates.

In this section, I will explore in detail the activities of three specific U.N. bodies that are active in emergencies to assess the viability of their mandate. While none of these mandates directly include failing and failed States, their work touches on all the issues faced by failing and failed States, which often face emergencies and conflicts. First, I will analyze the activities of the United Nations Office for the Coordination of Humanitarian Affairs ("OCHA") which is tasked by the United Nations to coordinate actions in complex emergencies. I will then explore the activities of the World Food Program ("WFP"), which is mandated to provide food resources in situations of emergencies. Finally, I will look at the work of the United Nations Children's Fund ("UNICEF"), which directs its effort to the protection of children, including in emergencies.

1.1. *The United Nations Office for the Coordination of Humanitarian Affairs*

OCHA was created in 1991 to coordinate the actions of all humanitarian actors, including U.N. agencies, NGOs and donor countries working in complex emergencies. It does not *per se* implement projects, but it coordinates the interventions of different actors in complex situations and is therefore a key player in such interventions.[1]

OCHA was established by the U.N. General Assembly under Res. 46/182 of 19 December 1991.[2] The goal of the General Assembly was to strengthen the coordination of emergency humanitarian assistance and efficiently address emergency situations, specifically regarding "the loss in human lives, the flow of refugees, the mass displacement of people and the material destruction."[3] For this reason, it tasked OCHA (originally called Office For Disaster Relief) with, *inter alia*:

1. Processing requests from affected Member States for emergency assistance requiring a coordinated response;
2. Maintaining an overview of all emergencies [...] with a view to coordinating and facilitating the humanitarian assistance of the United Nations system to those emergencies that require a coordinated response;
3. Organizing, in consultation with the Government of the affected country, a joint inter-agency needs-assessment mission and preparing a consolidated

[1] The role of OCHA in health crises is discussed in depth in Chapter Five.

[2] G.A. Res. 46/182, U.N. Doc. A/RES/46/182 (19 Dec. 1991), *available at*: http://www.un.org/documents/ga/res/46/a46r182.htm.

[3] *Id.*

appeal to be issued by the Secretary-General, to be followed by periodic situation reports including information on all sources of external assistance;
4. Actively facilitating, including through negotiation if needed, the access by the operational organizations to emergency areas for the rapid provision of emergency assistance by obtaining the consent of all parties concerned, through modalities such as the establishment of temporary relief corridors where needed, days and zones of tranquility and other forms;
5. Managing, in consultation with the operational organizations concerned, the central emergency revolving fund and assisting in the mobilization of resources;
6. Serving as a central focal point with Governments and intergovernmental and non-governmental organizations concerning United Nations emergency relief operations and, when appropriate and necessary, mobilizing their emergency relief capacities, including through consultations in his capacity as Chairman of the Inter-Agency Standing Committee;
7. Providing consolidated information, including early warning on emergencies, to all interested Governments and concerned authorities, particularly affected and disaster-prone countries, drawing on the capacities of the organizations of the system and other available sources.[4]

OCHA is part of the Secretariat of the United Nations and is headed by an Under-Secretary General for Humanitarian Affairs, with offices in both New York and Geneva. In the field, OCHA Representatives are the U.N. Humanitarian Coordinators, and often the Head of the U.N. mission in one country. They have overall responsibility for ensuring coherence of relief efforts in the field.

OCHA executes its coordination function primarily through the Inter-Agency Standing Committee ("IASC"). Participants to this Committee include all humanitarian partners, from UN agencies and funds to other international organizations and NGOs. Interestingly, in fact, OCHA is explicitly mandated to coordinate not only with U.N. Agencies, but also with the International Organization for Migration, the International Committee of the Red Cross, the League of Red Cross and Red Crescent Societies and other relevant NGOs.[5]

OCHA has a budget of approximately USD 220 million, mostly from State donors, and a staff of about 1,500, of which 500 are internationals.

As a coordinating body, OCHA focuses specifically on issues associated with humanitarian assistance, including the protection of civilians in armed conflict, issues related to internally displaced persons and human security.[6]

---

[4] *Id.* ¶ 35.

[5] G.A. Res. 46/183 ¶ 36, U.N. Doc. A/RES/46/183 (19 Dec. 1991), *available at*: http://www.un.org/documents/ga/res/46/a46r183.htm.

[6] *See* OCHA, *Humanitarian Issues*, http://ochaonline.un.org/HumanitarianIssues/tabid/1081/Default.aspx (last visited 11 Sept. 2009).

OCHA works mainly on policies and advocacy strategies designed to ensure the protection of civilians in armed conflict and respect for international humanitarian law. Further, OCHA has in-house emergency response capacities, supported by a 24-hour monitoring and alert system, able to deploy staff to disaster areas at short notice.[7] Specifically, OCHA supports mechanisms that can provide relief, including:

1. The United Nations Disaster Assessment and Coordination System – which can dispatch teams within 12 to 24 hours of a natural disaster or sudden onset emergency to gather information, assess needs, and coordinate international assistance. UNDAC runs On-Site Operations Coordination Centers, which assist local authorities with coordinating international response teams during disasters.
2. The Environment Standby Experts, a joint venture with the UN Environment Programme, which focuses on environmental disasters.
3. The Civil-Military Coordination Section which ensure that military resources are effectively used to respond to humanitarian emergencies.

OCHA is currently active in twenty-nine countries, including the occupied Palestinian territories, and has five regional offices, covering the Asia-Pacific, Central and East Africa, Latin America and the Caribbean, Southern Africa and West Africa.[8]

For example, OCHA has been present in Indonesia since 1999 when the United Nations established a base for its assistance in East Timor. OCHA then strengthened its presence to assist the victims of violence and conflict in several regions of Indonesia, as well as the displaced people that resulted from the unrest. Later, when the conflict situations were almost resolved, Indonesia was hit by the 2004 tsunami, which resulted in extreme loss of life, massive destruction of property and environmental damages. Then again in 2005 and 2006, earthquakes shook the West coast of Sumatra and off the coast of Java, causing further severe damage. OCHA coordinated assistance to confront both manmade and natural disasters throughout these events.[9]

Further, OCHA has also a substantial presence in Sudan, where it has operated since 2004 in coordination with the United Nations and African Union Missions. OCHA in Sudan coordinates the efforts of the international community in Darfur and in other regions that are in need of assistance; it provides information and analysis for decision making and facilitates coordination amongst agencies. In particular, OCHA negotiated safe access to

[7] *See generally* http://ochaonline.un.org. (last visited 10 Sept. 2009)

[8] *See* OCHA, *OCHA Offices Around the World*, http://ochaonline.un.org/Geographic/tabid/1084/Default.aspx (last visited 10 Sept. 2009).

[9] *See* OCHA, *OCHA in Indonesia*, http://ochaonline.un.org/AboutUs/tabid/3333/Default.aspx (last visited 10 Sept. 2009).

populations in need with the Government and rebel groups and supported protection and return activities. OCHA-Sudan has central offices in Khartoum and Juba, a liaison office in Nairobi and field offices throughout Sudan and Darfur.[10]

OCHA has also been present in Zimbabwe since January 2006. In what can be easily called a government-caused emergency, OCHA works to alleviate human suffering caused by food insecurity, HIV/AIDS, and rapid decline in social services. It also promotes preparedness and prevention efforts to reduce future vulnerability to natural disasters.[11]

The creation and activities of OCHA have been instrumental in the coordination of assistance in many emergency situations. However, OCHA's mandate is limited to coordinating activities, and its operational impact in emergencies is limited.

Further, it is clear that any actions taken by OCHA are subordinated to the consent of the affected country. Res. 46/182, which created OCHA, states in no uncertain terms that:

> The sovereignty, territorial integrity and national unity of States must be fully respected in accordance with the Charter of the United Nations. In this context, humanitarian assistance should be provided with the consent of the affected country and in principle on the basis of an appeal by the affected country.[12]

Further, the same Resolution entrusts the State as the main actor responsible to assist needy populations. It states

> Each State has the responsibility first and foremost to take care of the victims of natural disasters and other emergencies occurring on its territory. Hence, the affected State has the primary role in the initiation, organization, coordination, and implementation of humanitarian assistance within its territory.[13]

In sum, although OCHA has an important coordinating role and has acquired the respect of many humanitarian actors, its role in failed States – i.e. States that may not be able to meaningfully appeal for assistance – is necessarily limited.

---

[10] *See* OCHA, *OCHA in Sudan*, http://ochaonline.un.org/sudan/AboutUs/tabid/3021/Default.aspx (last visited 10 Sept. 2009). OCHA has also been working in Ethiopia since 2001 and its efforts focus on the alleviation of human suffering caused by drought (*see* OCHA, *Ethiopia – Humanitarian Bulletin*, http://ochaonline.un.org/Default.aspx?alias=ochaonline.un.org/ethiopia (last visited 10 Sept. 2009)).

[11] *See* OCHA, *Zimbabwe*, http://ochaonline.un.org/Default.aspx?alias=ochaonline.un.org/zimbabwe (last visited 10 Sept. 2009).

[12] G.A. Res. 46/182, Guiding Principle 3, Annex, U.N. Doc. A/RES/46/182, (19 Dec. 1991).

[13] G.A. Res. 46/182, Guiding Principle 4, U.N. Doc. A/RES/46/182 (19 Dec. 1991).

1.2. *The World Food Program*

WFP was created in 1963 as a program of the United Nations to fight hunger. It performs both emergency and longer term activities, namely it: (1) provides food assistance in refugee crises and other emergencies; (2) improves nutrition for the world's most vulnerable (3) promotes longer term self-reliance of poor people and communities.[14]

Institutionally, WFP was established by the United Nations and the Food and Agriculture Organization of the United Nations ("FAO").[15] Article VII of the General Regulations provides that WFP is an autonomous joint subsidiary program of the United Nations and FAO, drawing on the legal personality of the United Nations, but with its own legal capacity to contract, acquire and dispose of movable and immovable property, and be party to judicial proceedings.[16]

In order to carry out its mandate in situations of emergency, the Executive Board of the WFP established several program categories, including:

1. Emergency Relief Program Category, for food assistance to meet emergency needs.
2. Protracted Relief Program Category, for food assistance to meet protracted relief needs.
3. Special Operations Program Category for interventions undertaken to:
   i. rehabilitate and enhance transport and logistics infrastructure to permit timely and efficient delivery of food assistance, especially to meet emergency and protracted relief needs;
   ii. enhance coordination within the United Nations system and with other partners through the provision of designated common services.[17]

Specifically in terms of emergencies, WFP is mainly involved in the distribution of food. In 2008, WFP was involved in 78 countries and distributed food to an estimated 62.3 million people in emergencies and relief operations.[18] All contributions are voluntary and the program does not receive any core funding from the United Nations.

Recent interventions by WFP include assistance to refugees and internally displaced persons, including in places like Darfur, the Democratic Repub-

---

[14] *See* World Food Programme, *Operations,* http://www.wfp.org/operations/introduction/index.asp?section=5&sub_section=1 (last visited 10 Sept. 2009).

[15] World Food Programme, *General Regulations General Rules, Art. 1*(2008 ed.), *available at*: http://www.wfp.org/~executiveboard/english/frontpage/index.asp?section=7&sub_section=1#.

[16] *Id.* at Art. VII.

[17] *Id.* at General Rule II.2.

[18] *See* World Food Programme, *WFP in Numbers,* http://www.wfp.org/wfp-numbers (last visited 10 Sept. 2009).

lic of Congo and Colombia. WFP is also active in the aftermath of natural disasters, such as the 2006 East Africa drought, the Pakistan earthquake and Hurricane Stan in 2005, the tsunami disaster and Bangladesh floods in 2004, the Iran earthquake in 2003 and Hurricane Mitch, which affected one million people in Honduras, Nicaragua, El Salvador and Guatemala in October 1998.[19]

Activities of the WFP are particularly noteworthy because, unlike in other U.N. programs, the U.N. Secretary-General can directly request food assistance on behalf of the WFP. Article IX spells out the eligibility criteria for food relief. It states:

> All States Members of the United Nations or Members or Associate Members of any specialized agency or of the IAEA shall be eligible to submit requests for consideration by WFP.
> WFP may also provide emergency food aid and associated non-food items and logistics support at the request of the Secretary-General.
> WFP assistance in such exceptional cases shall be fully coordinated with the United Nations system and efforts of governments, intergovernmental and non-governmental organizations in the areas concerned.

Thus, food relief can be given either by request of a Member State or at the request of the Secretary-General. In this second case, the only extra requirement is that assistance is fully coordinated with other humanitarian actors in the areas concerned.

Further, Art. X provides that governments, bilateral donors, U.N. agencies and NGOs can request emergency food assistance. The Article specifies that "governments can make a request for food aid programs and food assistance to meet emergency needs." Similarly, "bilateral donors, United Nations agencies and non-governmental organizations can also request WFP services for operations which are consistent with the purposes of WFP and which complement WFP's operations." The Article further specifies that

> Requests for assistance to country programs or development projects shall indicate that they have a clear relationship with the recipient country's development plans and priorities and include, as appropriate, a significant input of the recipient government's resources.[20]

---

[19] *See* World Food Programme, *Operations List*, http://www.wfp.org/operations/list (last visited 10 Sept. 2009).

[20] Art. X(3). Article II clearly differentiates between development programs and emergency relief.

Decisions on requests are made by the Executive Board, which has delegated authority to the Executive Director for certain smaller scale emergency relief operations.

The possibility for the Secretary General to directly ask for assistance without the need for an official request by the government may provide a very useful instrument for action in situations of State failure. There is no available date on the number of requests that the Secretary General has made to WFP, however, the very possibility of such instrument is very significant and should be kept in careful consideration for actions in situations of State failure.

1.3. *The United Nations Children Fund*

UNICEF is another active U.N. in emergency situations.

UNICEF was created in 1946 at the first session of the General Assembly of the United Nations, as the International Children's Emergency Fund and was tasked to address the needs of children and adolescents, particularly emergency food and healthcare, in countries which had been the victims of aggression during WWII and those receiving development assistance.[21] It became a permanent fund of the United Nations in 1953, with a particular mandate for children and adolescents.[22]

Interestingly, UNICEF's mission statement directly refers to the U.N. Convention on the Rights of the Child as a guiding principle for its work. The Convention provides many basic rights for children, and it has been ratified and accessed widely.[23] For its work, UNICEF also refers to the agreement 'A World Fit For Children' agreed upon by world leaders at the Special Session of the U.N. General Assembly in May 2002, which sets up time-bound goals

---

[21] UNICEF was established by G.A. Res. 57 (I), U.N. Doc. A/57 (11 Dec. 1946), *available at:* http://daccessdds.un.org/doc/RESOLUTION/GEN/NR0/033/08/IMG/NR003308.pdf?OpenElement.

[22] G.A. Res. 802 (VIII), U.N. Doc. A/802 (6 Oct. 1953), *available at*: http://daccessdds.un.org/doc/RESOLUTION/GEN/NR0/086/67/IMG/NR008667.pdf?OpenElement. The Resolution changed the name of the Fund to UN Children's Fund, still to be knows as UNICEF and confirmed the operating regulations of Res. 57(I).

[23] U.N. Convention on the Rights of the Child (20 Nov. 1989), *available at*: http://www2.ohchr.org/english/law/crc.htm. As of December 2008, 193 countries have ratified it, including every member of the United Nations except the United States and Somalia, see U.N. Treaty Collection, *Status of the Convention of the Rights of the Child*, http://treaties.un.org/Pages/ViewDetails.aspx?src=TREATY&mtdsg_no=IV-11&chapter=4&lang=en (last visited 13 Sept. 2009).

for the children's health, well-being and education.[24] These instruments, however, do not contain binding legal provisions for UNICEF and are only guiding principles for its actions.

UNICEF has a specific program addressing emergency situations, which works in over thirty countries. Its work focuses on protection and the prevention of disease, malnutrition and violence, all of which hit children particularly hard in times of emergencies. Further, UNICEF works on tracing and reunification programs for separated children and preventing the recruitment of children into armed groups. It also provides demobilization programs for children that have been recruited by local militias. UNICEF's work is widely respected by other humanitarian actors, and UNICEF always tries to work in collaboration with local and international partners, including governments, other U.N., agencies, and NGOs.[25] Within the U.N. system involved in emergency operations, UNICEF is also in charge of nutrition, water and sanitation, common data services, and education.[26]

More specifically, UNICEF has developed a very clear set of priorities and actions to be implemented in emergency situations. In 2003, it revised its Core Commitments for Children in Emergencies ("CCC")[27] and agreed that within the first six to eight weeks from the onset of an emergency and together with its national, U.N. and NGO partners, UNICEF will work to:

1. Assess, monitor, report and communicate on the situation of children and women.
2. Provide measles vaccination for children between 6 months and 14 years, vitamin A, essential drugs and nutritional supplements. Provide emergency supplies as appropriate.
3. Provide child and maternal feeding and nutritional monitoring: with WFP and NGO partners.
4. Provide emergency water supplies and safe drinking water, sanitation and hygiene.
5. Assist in preventing the separation and facilitate the identification, registration and medical screening of children separated from their families.
6. Initiate the resumption of schooling and other child learning opportunities.[28]

[24] *See* UNICEF, *Why We Do It, The World Has Set Goals for Children*, http://www.unicef.org/why/why_worldgoals.html (last visited 10 Sept. 2009).

[25] *See* UNICEF, *UNICEF in Emergencies, UNICEF's Role in Emergencies*, http://www.unicef.org/emerg/index_33296.html (last visited 10 Sept. 2009).

[26] *Id.*

[27] UNICEF, *Core Commitments for Children in Emergencies* (Mar. 2005), *available at:* http://www.unicef.org/emerg/files/CCC_EMERG_E_revised7.pdf.

[28] *See* UNICEF, *UNICEF in Emergencies, Commitments*, http://www.unicef.org/emerg/index_commitments.html (last visited 10 Sept. 2009).

After the initial period, UNICEF developed a series of actions to be implemented that focus on the longer-term provision of health and education assistance to children in emergencies.[29]

For example, UNICEF has provided emergency assistance to children who are victims of conflict in the Democratic Republic of Congo, where an estimated 4 million children were orphaned by the war that ended in 2003. Specifically, UNICEF provided shelter and household items to 100,000 families affected by armed conflict and/or natural disasters. It provided water and sanitation services to 200,000 people in 2005, set up 86 therapeutic feeding centers, and provided emergency nutrition to more than 45,000 children. At the same time, it immunized nearly 8 million children during a major campaign against measles. Together with its partners, it also rehabilitated classrooms and distributed school supplies to 200,000 internally displaced children, and trained hundreds of teachers and other non-formal educators. It also provided counseling to children affected by war and violence.[30]

Similarly, UNICEF has a strong presence in Darfur (Sudan), where an estimated 4.7 million people have been victims of a civil conflict. In Darfur, UNICEF assisted populations in gaining access to safe water, conducted immunization campaigns for polio, measles and vitamin A supplementation, trained health workers, distributed nutritional supplements and supplied health kits.[31]

Chad has also been affected by the war by a vast influx of refugees, 60 percent of whom are children. UNICEF has been very active in donating food and health supplies, distributing water chlorination supplies and beginning a routine vaccination program in the refugee camps to combat measles and polio after a reported polio case in eastern Chad, covering 94 percent of children less than one year old.[32]

All activities are done in partnership and collaboration with national authorities and other humanitarian actors. Guiding Principle 4 of the CCC specifically states that "responses will be based on nationally defined priorities and UNICEF comparative advantage."[33]

[29] *Id.*

[30] *See* UNICEF, *Democratic Republic of the Congo, Background* (Aug. 2006), http://www.unicef.org/infobycountry/drcongo_636.html (last visited 10 Sept. 2009).

[31] *See* UNICEF, *Sudan, Darfur – Overview* (Dec. 2008), http://www.unicef.org/infobycountry/sudan_darfuroverview.html (last visited 10 Sept. 2009).

[32] *See* UNICEF, *Chad, Background* (Aug 2006), http://www.unicef.org/infobycountry/chad_2477.html (last visited 10 Sept. 2009).

[33] UNICEF, *Core Commitments for Children in Emergencies, Guiding Principle 4*, at 2, *available at:* http://www.unicef.org/emerg/files/CCC_EMERG_E_revised7.pdf.

Paragraph 2(b) of Res. 57(I) also deals with the relation of UNICEF with host governments, and clearly states that

> The Fund in agreement with the Government concerned, shall take all measures as are deemed appropriate to ensure the proper distribution of supplies or other assistance it provides.[34]

Para. 2(c) further requires UNICEF not to engage in activity in any country "except in consultation with, and the consent of, the government concerned."

Thus, UNICEF is required to act in consultation and with the consent of the government concerned. The standard for action is lower than the operation requirement set out by OCHA rules of engagement, which require, in principle, "an appeal" from the concerned government.

In situations of State failure, therefore, UNICEF could still operate but would need to seek the consent of the State and operate in consultation with representatives of the government. This 'middle of the road' solution would probably allow UNICEF's activities in many situations of State failure.

2. *The Use of Force to Address Humanitarian Emergencies as a Threat to Global Security*

The desire of sectors of the international community to intervene and address humanitarian emergencies of foreign populations is not new. However, this willingness has – for the past decades – been in tension with other fundamental principles of international law, including self-determination, sovereignty and the general prohibition of the use of force. This tension is particularly strong vis-à-vis the principle that prohibits intervention in the internal matters of States. In fact, Art. 2(6) of the U.N. Charter clearly states that

> Nothing contained in the [U.N.] Charter shall authorize the United Nations to intervene in matters which are essentially within the domestic jurisdiction of any State or shall require the Members to submit such matters to settlement under the present Charter.[35]

The same article, however, also clearly states that the principle "shall not prejudice the application of enforcement measures under Chapter VII" which allows for intervention in situations that are considered threats to international peace and security.

---

[34] G.A. Res. 57(I), U.N. Doc. A/57 (11 Dec. 1946), *available at:* http://www.un.org/documents/ga/res/1/ares1.htm.

[35] U.N. Charter, *available at*: http://www.un.org/aboutun/charter.

A fundamental shift in international law now supports the principle that gross violations of human rights cannot be considered 'internal matters.' In fact, the definition of what are matters that are essentially domestic has changed, and international interventions to ease certain serious crises faced by domestic populations have become accepted practice in certain limited circumstances.[36]

For example, Levitt notes that there has been a progressive shift "from traditional prohibition against forcible intervention in the internal affairs of States, towards the recognition of a right to humanitarian intervention by groups of States and regional actors in internal conflict."[37] This has resulted in a developing practice of intervention by external actors to defend and uphold human rights.

As Professor Reisman concludes, although the United Nations Charter replicates the 'domestic jurisdiction-international concern' dichotomy "no serious scholar still supports the contention that internal human rights are 'essentially within the domestic jurisdiction of any State' and hence insulated from international law."[38] Further, Vukas also notes that

> there is a dominant view today that the respect for human rights (both of nationals as well as of foreigners) cannot be considered as a matter which is 'essentially within the domestic jurisdiction of any State'. The protection of human rights does not belong any more to the *domaine resérvé* of States. This is particularly clear in States where there is no central Government, or the Government is engaged in a civil war.[39]

The underlying basis for action by the international community is the principle that certain human rights obligations are *erga omnes*, and thus are owed to the international community as a whole.[40] Further, fundamental human

[36] For example, *see* A. Tanca, Foreign Armed Intervention in Internal Conflict (1993).

[37] Jeremy Levitt, *Humanitarian intervention by regional actors in internal conflicts: and the cases of ECOWAS in Liberia and Sierra Leone*, 12 Temp. Int'l & Comp. L.J. 333, 333 (1998).

[38] M. Reisman, *Sovereignty and Human Rights in Contemporary International Law*, 84 Am. J. Int'l. L. 866, 869 (1990).

[39] B. Vukas, *Humanitarian Intervention and International Responsibility*, in International Responsability Today: Essays in Memory of Oscar Schachter 235, 237 (M. Ragazzi ed., 2005).

[40] This principle was also clearly articulated by the International Court of Justice. First, in *Barcelona Traction*, the Court distinguished between obligations of a State vis-à-vis another State and obligations towards the international community. It concluded that "an essential distinction should be drawn between the obligation of a State towards the international community as a whole, and those arising vis-à-vis another State in the field of diplomatic protection. By their very nature the former are the concern of all States. In view of the important of the rights involved, all States can be held to have a legal interest in their

rights are considered peremptory norms, and as such are not derogable by treaty or otherwise.[41]

However, tensions between diverse *erga omnes* principles and peremptory norms remain. And the question of balancing different principles and interventions by the international community is still unresolved.

In the following paragraphs I will explore two separate options adopted by States to address humanitarian crises in another State by using force. First, I will appraise the use of force by the United Nations through the delegated

---

protection: they are obligations *erga omnes.*" *Barcelona Traction, Light and Power Company, Limited, Second Phase, (Belgium v. Spain)*, 1970 I.C.J. 3, 32 (5 Feb.). The Court further elaborated on the content of these obligations. It held that they "derive, for example, in contemporary international law, from the outlawing of acts of aggression, and of genocide, as also from the principles and rules concerning the basic rights of the human person, including protection from slavery and racial discrimination. *Id. See also East Timor (Portugal v. Australia)*, 1995 I.C.J. 90, 102 (30 June) (stating that "Portugal's assertion that the right of peoples to self-determination, as it evolved from the Charter and from United Nations practice, has an *erga omens* character, is irreproachable"); *Legality of the Threat of Use of Nuclear Weapons*, Advisory Opinion, 1996 I.C.J., 226, 258 (8 July). Similarly, in addressing specifically the crime of genocide, the Court held that "it follows that the rights and obligations enshrined by the Convention [on the Prevention and Punishment of the Crime of Genocide] are rights and obligations *erga omnes.* The Court notes that the obligation each State thus has to prevent and to punish the crime of genocide is not territorially limited by the Convention. *Application of the Convention on the Prevention and Punishment of the Crime of Genocide (Bosnia and Herzegovina v. Yugoslavia)*, Preliminary Objections, 1996 I.C.J. 595, 616 (11 July).

41 A peremptory norm is "accepted and recognised by the international community of States as a whole as a norm from which no derogation is permitted and which can be modified only by a subsequent norm of general international law having the same character." Vienna Convention of the Law of Treaties, Arts. 53, 23 May 1969,1150 U.N.T.S. 331. In reference to the applicability of this definition, James Crawford states "among these prohibitions, it is generally agreed that the prohibition of aggression is to be regarded as peremptory [...] there also seem to widespread agreement with other examples listed in the Commission's commentary to article 53 viz., the prohibitions against slavery and the slave trade, genocide, and racial discrimination and apartheid. There practices have been prohibited in widely ratified international treaties and conventions admitting of no exception. There was general agreement among governments as to the peremptory character of these prohibitions at the Vienna Conference. As to the peremptory character of the prohibition against genocide, this is supported by a number of decisions by national and international courts." JAMES CRAWFORD, ILC'S ARTICLES ON STATE RESPONSIBILITY, INTRODUCTION, TEXT AND COMMENTARIES 283 (2002). The violations of peremptory norms trigger certain rights and duties to subjects to which the obligation is owed. Art. 41 of the Draft Articles on State Responsibility suggests that the international community has a right and a duty to act upon violations of peremptory norms. In the relevant paragraph, the article states "States shall cooperate to bring to an end through lawful means any serious breach within the meaning of article 40 [serious breach by a State of an obligation arising under a peremptory norm of general international law.]" ILC, *Draft Articles on State Responsibility*, Art. 41.

powers of the Security Council, which is an appropriate mechanism to address humanitarian crises. Second, I will analyze unilateral interventions by force by certain members of the United Nations outside Chapter VII of the UN Charter, which is still to be considered a violation of international law.

2.1. *Inclusive Actions to Protect Populations in Need Conducted Under the Delegation of Chapter VII Powers by the Security Council*

Gross violations of human rights in the domestic context are considered a threat to international peace and security only in specific circumstances. Moreover, the principle of non intervention "in matters which are essentially within the domestic jurisdiction" set forth in Art. 2(7) of the UN Charter was considered to be paramount to any humanitarian intervention.

However, it is now impossible to commit gross violations of human rights or crimes against humanity outside the scrutiny of the international community. Further, international law has evolved so that grave human rights violations cannot be considered as matters exclusively within the domestic jurisdiction of a State. Thus, there seems to be an agreement that "if what is going on globally becomes intolerable, humanitarian intervention is morally necessary."[42] This moral imperative is now coupled by a developing legal duty. The specific actions that this legal duty comports, however, are still debatable.

During the Cold War, effective actions by the Security Council in support of the maintenance of international peace and security were often blocked by the use of the veto power of the permanent members of the Council.

With the end of the Cold War, however, a new political consensus arose and the use of the veto substantially declined. At the same time, several countries showed diminished tolerance for human rights abuses and an increased willingness to be involved in upholding the respect for human rights internationally. After the end of the Cold War, the Security Council has authorized the use of force under Chapter VII of the Charter to provide humanitarian relief in a limited number of situations.[43] Because they were taken under Chapter VII, such authorizations allowed Members States to use military force. The goal of such use of force was limited to the delivery of humanitarian assistance and has been allowed only once, in Rwanda, to protect populations at risk of genocide.

---

[42] Francis Kofi Abiew, The Evolution of the Doctrine and Practice of Humanitarian Intervention 137–223 (1999).

[43] *See* Christine Gray, International Law And The Use Of Force 29–59, 195–251 (2d ed. 2004).

The ill-fated mission in Somalia in 1992[44] was the first example of this kind of intervention.[45]

The U.N. Security Council made the necessary determination under Art. 39 of the U.N. Charter[46] that "the continuation of the situation in Somalia constitutes a threat to international peace and security"[47] and decided to deploy a security force – to be called UNOSOM – to "provide urgent humanitarian assistance." The multinational force was given the power to use "all necessary means" (the code-word to use military force) under Security Council Res. 794 (1992), which determined

> that the magnitude of the human tragedy caused by the conflict in Somalia, further exacerbated by the obstacles being created to the distribution of humanitarian assistance, constitutes a threat to international peace and security.

The Security Council, acting under Chapter VII of the Charter of the United Nations, thus authorized the Secretary-General and Member States

> to use all necessary means to establish as soon as possible a secure environment for humanitarian relief operations in Somalia.[48]

The new mission was to be known as Unified Task Force ("UNITAF") and mostly operated under U.S. Command, under a U.N. mandate.

The implementation of the Resolution, however, became increasingly complicated as U.N. forces were attacked and convoys looted.[49] UNITAF was phased out and another U.N.-led mission – UNOSOM II – was put in charge of restoring order with an expanded mandate to:

---

44 Chapter Three describes the situation in Somalia in detail.

45 As Gray states, prior to Somalia "the generally agreed principles that had evolved through state practice required that peacekeeping forces should be impartial, not take sides, lightly armed, not use force except in self-defence, operate with the consent of the host State and should not usually include forces from permanent members of the Security Council or states with a political interest in the host State." Christine Gray, International Law And The Use Of Force 217 (2d ed. 2004).

46 Art. 39 states that " The Security Council shall determine the existence of any threat to the peace, breach of the peace, or act of aggression and shall make recommendations, or decide what measures shall be taken in accordance with Articles 41 and 42, to maintain or restore international peace and security."

47 S.C. Res. 751, U.N. Doc. S/RES/751 (24 Apr. 1992), *available at:* http://www.un.org/documents/sc/res/1992/scres92.htm.

48 S.C. Res. 794, U.N. Doc. S/RES/794 (3 Dec. 1992), *available at*: http://www.un.org/documents/sc/res/1992/scres92.htm.

49 *See* B. Boutros-Ghali, UN Blue Book Series: The United Nations and Somalia: 1992–1996 (1996). *See also* Danesh Sarooshi, The United Nations and the Development of Collective Security 214–217 (1999); Christine Gray, International Law And The Use Of Force, 222–224 (2d ed. 2004).

> Assume responsibility for the consolidation, expansion and maintenance of a secure environment throughout Somalia, taking account of particular circumstances in each locality, on an expedite basis.[50]

The Somalia experiment was not successful, as the United Nations were never able to restore peace and security, but it served as an *imprimatur* for further actions taken for humanitarian relief purposes.[51] It is also estimated that several hundred thousand lives were saved thanks to the delivery of humanitarian assistance. However, the mission was increasingly regarded negatively by Somalis as fighting arose between United Nations and Somali troops, and it was abandoned prior to the achievement of its objectives.

At about the same time, another crisis unfolded with the collapse of the Federal Republic of Yugoslavia collapsed.

Starting in 1991, several Yugoslav Republics declared their independence from the Federation. When Bosnia-Herzegovina also declared its independence, Serb forces attacked to impede secession. A terribly violent conflict ensued, which degenerated into widespread violations of humanitarian law, the commission of genocidal acts and crimes against humanity. By Security Council Res. 713 (1991) the Security Council declared that the situation constituted "a threat to international peace and security" which triggered the intervention of U.N. troops under Chapter VII of the U.N. Charter. On June 8, 1992, the Security Council approved Res. 758 (1992) which allowed for humanitarian intervention. The Resolution, *inter alia*:

> demand[ed] that all parties and others concerned create immediately the necessary conditions for unimpeded delivery of humanitarian supplies to Sarajevo and other destinations in Bosnia and Herzegovina, including the establishment of a security zone encompassing Sarajevo and its airport and respecting the agreements signed in Geneva on 22 May 1992.[52]

The mandate to deliver humanitarian assistance by force, however, was spelled out later. In Res. 770 (1992) the Security Council, reaffirming its previous resolutions and acting under Chapter VII of the UN Charter:

> called upon States to take nationally or through regional agencies or arrangements all measures necessary to facilitate in coordination with the United

---

[50] S.C. Res. 814, U.N. Doc. S/RES/814 (26 Mar. 1993), *available at*: http://www.un.org/Docs/scres/1993/scres93.htm.

[51] *See generally* Sean Murphy, Humanitarian Intervention: The United Nations In An Evolving World Order (1996); Brian D. Lepard, Rethinking Humanitarian Intervention: A Fresh Legal Approach Based on Fundamental Ethical Principles in International Law and World Religions (2002).

[52] S.C. Res. 758, U.N. Doc. S/RES/758 (8 June 1992), *available at*: http://www.un.org/documents/sc/res/1992/scres92.htm.

> Nations the delivery by relevant United Nations humanitarian organizations and others of humanitarian assistance to Sarajevo and wherever needed in other parts of Bosnia and Herzegovina; [and]
>
> demanded that unimpeded and continuous access to all camps, prisons and detention centres be granted immediately to the International Committee of the Red Cross and other relevant humanitarian organizations and that all detainees therein receive humane treatment, including adequate food, shelter and medical care.[53]

U.N. troops stationed in the region were only capable of limited actions, and only achieved limited success. They were incapable of stopping further human rights violations and had to limit their involvement in the mist of the conflict.

In both Somalia and Bosnia, U.N. troops were deployed in circumstances that differed substantially from regular U.N. peacekeeping missions.[54] First, U.N. troops arrived in the midst of conflict. There was no peace-agreement, or cease-fire or any peace to be kept. Troops were involved in everyday fighting, but were not equipped and lacked the mandate to engage in full display of force. Further, the delivery of humanitarian assistance began to be regarded as partial by local populations. This resulted in a perceived loss of neutrality by the United Nations. The two missions have also been criticized for their inefficiency and their lack of results. In effect, these two examples demonstrated that their mandates were not sufficient for the troops to effectively deliver humanitarian assistance to populations in need without the consent of the State in which the action is taken. However, I suggest that a changed, enhanced mandate is necessary, rather than a withdrawal of the mandate: a mandate targeted at protecting domestic populations and reducing international threats.

A third and further example of U.N. intervention to protect human rights was also widely criticized. It came as a *post-hoc* operation after the Rwanda genocide in 1994.

During the terrible Rwanda genocide, which was extensively reported in the news, the Security Council was unable to act. The inability to take action despite such gruesome and public violations of human rights stirred resentment for the organization as well as a strong desire for action.

---

53 S.C. Res. 770, U.N. Doc. S/RES/770 (13 Aug. 1992), *available at*: http://www.un.org/documents/sc/res/1992/scres92.htm.

54 The UN is also involved in several peace-keeping missions, whose mandates normally focus on maintaining peace after the resolution of a conflict and on monitoring cease-fire and peace agreements. *See* United Nations Peacekeeping, *Current Operations*, http://www.un.org/Depts/dpko/dpko/currentops.shtml (last visited 10 Sept. 2009).

In Res. 918 the Security Council decided to expand the mission of the United Nations already present in Rwanda[55] for humanitarian purposes to include additional responsibilities, namely:

1. To contribute to the security and protection of displaced persons, refugees and civilians at risk in Rwanda, including through the establishment and maintenance, where feasible, of secure humanitarian areas;
2. To provide security and support for the distribution of relief supplies and humanitarian relief operations.[56]

However, the number of troops was minimal and thus possible actions few.

In the subsequent Res. 925(1994), the Council strongly condemned the ongoing violence in Rwanda and in particular the systematic killing of civilians decided to extend UNAMIR's mandate, endorsed the deployment of additional troops and reaffirmed that UNAMIR would continue to to act as an intermediary between the parties in an attempt to secure their agreement to a cease-fire.[57] The Security Council further recognized that

> UNAMIR may be required to take action in self-defence against persons or groups who threaten protected sites and populations, United Nations and other humanitarian personnel or the means of delivery and distribution of humanitarian relief.[58]

Finally, acting under Chapter VIII of the U.N. Charter, the Security Council authorized the establishment of a temporary operation under national command and control "aimed at contributing, in an impartial way, to the security and protection of displaced persons, refugees and civilians at risk in Rwanda."[59] The decisions by the Security Council relating to Rwanda were criticized as being too limited and too late.

In sum, these three examples (Somalia, Yugoslavia and Rwanda) show that although the Security Council demonstrated its willingness to become involved in the delivery of humanitarian relief to populations in need and to act to stop gross violations of human rights in the 1990s, the delivery of the assistance and the implementation of the decisions were poor. The obstacles

---

[55] The United Nations Assistance Mission for Rwanda (UNAMIR) was created by S.C. Res. 872, U.N. Doc. S/RES/872 (5 Oct. 1993) to monitor the implementation of the Arusha Peace Agreement, *available at*: http://www.un.org/Docs/scres/1993/scres93.htm.

[56] S.C. Res. 918, ¶ 3, U.N. Doc. S/RES/918 (17 May 1994), *available at*: http://www.un.org/Docs/scres/1994/scres94.htm.

[57] S.C. Res. 925, ¶¶ 2–4, U.N. Doc. S/RES/918 (8 June 1994), *available at*: http://www.un.org/Docs/scres/1994/scres94.htm.

[58] *Id.* ¶ 5.

[59] S.C. Res. 929, ¶¶ 2–3, U.N. Doc. S/RES/929 (22 June 1994) *available at*: http://www.un.org/Docs/scres/1994/scres94.htm.

faced by the United Nations when using force in a territory without the consent of the State, and thus without the support of portions of the local populations, were just too great. Further, mandates were not clear and the missions were not well organized or equipped. The mandates had a political overtone that tainted them as self-serving and partisan.

In the future, these issues must be addressed comprehensively and technically. The use of force must be an *ultima ratio*, but when the decision is made that such action is necessary, a series of principles and guidelines must be developed and strictly followed.

The stakes for the United Nations to show that it had a role to play at times of humanitarian crises and in the maintenance of security and peace have became increasinly high in the aftermath of these high-profile deployment failures.

The 1997 humanitarian intervention in Albania was much less controversial. At the end of the 1990's and after the collapse of the communist regime, Albania entered a period of unrest. In March 1997, Italy offered to lead a multinational force to address the rapidly declining situation.[60]

With Security Council Res. 1101 (1997), the Security Council first determined that the crisis in Albania constituted a threat to international peace and security, and then welcomed the offer by certain Member States to establish "a temporary and limited multinational protection force" to facilitate the safe and prompt delivery of humanitarian assistance and to help create a secure environment for international organizations in Albania.[61]

Further, under Chapter VII of the UN Charter, the Council authorized Member States participating in the multinational protection force "to ensure the security and freedom of movement of the personnel of the [...] multinational protection force."[62]

The Albanian mission was successful, but it was very limited in both time and space, and only provides limited support to future similar actions.

Humanitarian intervention to deliver assistance to populations facing emergencies is an important tool of the international community, which must only be used sparsely and effectively. It could provide a most powerful asset to the international community to act in situation of State failure. However,

---

[60] Dino Kritsiotis, *Security Council Resolution 1101 (1997) and the Multinational Protection Force of Operation Alba in Albania*, 12 Leiden J. Int'l L. 511–547 (1999); *see also* Danesh Sarooshi, The United Nations and the Development of Collective Security (1999).

[61] S.C. Res. 1101, U.N. Doc. S/RES/1101, ¶ 2 (28 Mar. 1997) *available at:* http://www.un.org/Docs/scres/1997/scres97.htm.

[62] *Id.* ¶ 4.

the implementation of this kind of intervention, has, so far, been insufficient and needs to be further analyzed and developed.

The assessment above shows that the United Nations and, particularly, the Security Council must be involved in the decision to use force for humanitarian purposes, as they represent the highest deciding authority of the international community. However, the mandate of these missions must be clearer and empower members of the United Nations to fully tackle emergencies, short of becoming engaged in war, with the goal to restore peace and security for the international community.

2.2. *Unilateral Interventions to Stop Gross Human Rights Abuses*

Since the end of the cold war, certain States have also been willing to rely on the doctrine of humanitarian intervention to secure the respect of human rights in certain limited circumstances.[63] The legality of such actions, however, remains questionable.

The first time that Member States tried to justify the use of force on humanitarian grounds relates to the establishment of safe areas in Iraq after the end of the Gulf War. The U.N.-authorized intervention in Iraq and Kuwait to liberate Kuwait in 1992, after Iraq's invasion had strengthened the Kurds and Shi'ites minorities. When the U.N. forces left the region, Iraq began a campaign of repression of these minorities to punish them for their support of foreign troops. The Security Council was at first slow to react. In Res. 668 (1991) the Security Council

> Condemn[ed] the repression of the Iraqi civilian population in many parts of Iraq, including most recently in Kurdish populated areas, the consequences of which threaten international peace and security in the region; [...]
>
> Deman[ed] that Iraq, as a contribution to removing the threat to international peace and security in the region, immediately end this repression;

[63] Christine Gray clarifies "[u]ntil recently, unilateral humanitarian intervention was not put forward as a legal doctrine by States. The Indian action in Bangladesh (1971) which helped the people to secure independence from Pakistan and to end repression, the Tanzanian action in Uganda (1979) which led to the overthrow of Idi Amin, and the Vietnamese invasion of Cambodia (1978) which let to the overthrow of Pol Pot were not in fact justified by India, Tanzania and Vietnam on the basis of humanitarian action; rather, the States using force focused mainly on self-defense. [...] During the Cold War it was writers rather than states that argued in favour of the doctrine of humanitarian intervention as a justification for the use of force by States." CHRISTINE GRAY, INTERNATIONAL LAW AND THE USE OF FORCE 31–32 (2d ed. 2004) (internal citations omitted).

> Insist[ed] that Iraq allow immediate access by international humanitarian organizations to all those in need of assistance in all parts of Iraq and to make available all necessary facilities for their operations.[64]

Despite the lack of express authority, the U.S., the UK and France intervened to protect the minorities and established safe havens at the border of Iraq and later created no-fly zones ("*Operation Haven*").

The British Foreign and Commonwealth Office justified these actions declaring that

> We believe that international intervention without the invitation of the country concerned can be justified in cases of extreme humanitarian need. This is why we were prepared to commit British forces to *Operation Haven*, mounted by the coalition in response to the refugee crisis involving the Iraqi Kurds. The deployment of these forces was entirely consistent with the objectives of SCR 688.[65]

Similarly, U.S. President Bush declared that it was a "'humanitarian effort under the auspices of U.N. Security Council Resolution 688' that needed no further authorization."[66]

Patrolling and enforcement activities continued for several years and indeed until 2003, when the Coalition invaded Iraq, although France had withdrawn its troops and its support earlier. The operation never received formal approval by the United Nations, at the same time protests by Iraq did not lead to condemnation by either the Security Council or the General Assembly, hence providing at least a tacit support.[67]

The intervention in Iraq was widely criticized as a violation of State sovereignty. Moreover, the ultimate motives of the American and British governments were disputed.[68] The invasion of Iraq in 2003 by coalition forces led by the U.S. and the UK that toppled Saddam Hussein has further undermined the case in support to the first Iraqi mission. In effect, the example of Iraq cannot be considered an endorsement of unilateral action by the international community.

---

[64] S.C. Res. 688, ¶¶ 1–3, U.N. Doc. S/RES/688 (5 Apr. 1991), *available at*: http://www.un.org/Docs/scres/1991/scres91.htm.

[65] *UK Materials on International Law, reprinted in* Christine Gray, International Law And The Use Of Force 35 (2d ed. 2004).

[66] Danesh Sarooshi, The United Nations and the Development of Collective Security 228 (1999).

[67] *See* Christine Gray, International Law And The Use Of Force 31–37, 204–205 (2d ed. 2004); Danesh Sarooshi, The United Nations and the Development of Collective Security 226–232 (1999).

[68] Lea Brilmayer, *What's the Matter With Selective Intervention?* 37 Ariz. L. Rev. 955 (1995) (analyzing interventions by the United States).

A second unilateral intervention occurred in 1999 with the violent repression of the Albanian ethnic minority in Kosovo by the Federal government of Yugoslavia headed by Slobodan Milosevic.[69] Seized of the matter, the Security Council had already affirmed in September 1998 that

> deterioration of the situation in Kosovo, Federal Republic of Yugoslavia, constitute[d] a threat to peace and security in the region.[70]

However, it also reaffirmed, in a Res. 1203 of 24 October 1998 that

> under the Charter of the United Nations, primary responsibility for the maintenance of international peace and security is conferred on the Security Council.[71]

Thus, the Security Council made clear that it saw itself as the primary body responsible for approving any use of force. However, Russia and China clearly opposed any action within the territory of Yugoslavia, and it was clear that no military action could be approved by the Security Council without their support.

At the same time, the Resolution appeared to give a possible leeway for action to NATO, as the Council stated that it had primary responsibility, not sole responsibility. NATO's *Operation Allied Force* began its bombing campaign on 23 March, 1999 and ended it by 10 June, 1999. The intervention in Kosovo sparkled lively debate about the legality of humanitarian interventions without U.N. mandate.[72] Bruno Simma, now Judge of the International Court of Justice, held that the intervention and the use of force in such cir-

[69] For a comprehensive analysis of the Kosovo crisis, *see* Larry Minear, Ted van Baarda, & Marc Sommers, *NATO And Humanitarian Action In The Kosovo Crisis* (Institute for International Studies, Brown University, Occasional Paper 36, 2000).

[70] S.C. Res. 1199, U.N. Doc. S/RES/1199 (23 Sept. 1998), *available at*: http://www.un.org/Docs/scres/1991/scres91.htm.

[71] S.C. Res. 1203, U.N. Doc. S/RES/1203 (24 Oct. 1998), *available at*: http://www.un.org/Docs/scres/1998/scres98.htm.

[72] *See*, for example, the debate between Bruno Simma, now Judge of the International Court of Justice, and Judge Cassese, then Presiding Judge of the Tribunal for the Former Yugoslavia. Both jurists support the intervention, though only Cassese supports its legality. *See* Bruno Simma, *NATO, the UN and the Use of Force: Legal Aspects*, 10 Eur. J. Int'l L. 1 (1999); Antonio Cassese, *Ex iniuria ius oritur: Are We Moving Towards International Legitimation of Forcible Humanitarian Countermeasures in the World Community?*, 10 Eur. J. Int'l L. 23 (1999). For harsh views against intervention, *see* I. Brownlie, Principles of International Public Law 712 (6th ed. 2003) ("The 'practice', such as it is [of humanitarian intervention] involves a small number of adherent States, and the contemporary debates in the Security Council reveal marked divisions of opinion. Finally, the partisans of humanitarian intervention either ignore the conditions for the formation of new principles of customary law or, on occasion, propose that the requirement of *opinion juris* be relaxed.").

cumstances, and without the approval of the United Nations, was not legal. He elaborated that

> Contemporary international law establishes beyond any doubt that serious violations of human rights are matters of international concern. Impressive networks of rules and institutions, both at the universal and regional levels, have come into being as a result of this international concern. In the event of human rights violations which reach the magnitude of the Kosovo crisis, these developments in international law allow States, acting individually, collectively or through international organizations, to make use of a broad range of peaceful responses. According to the dominant doctrine in the law of State responsibility (developed by the United Nations International Law Commission), the obligation on States to respect and protect the basic rights of all human persons is the concern of all States, that is, they are owed *erga omnes*. Consequently, in the event of material breaches of such obligations, every other State may lawfully consider itself legally "injured" and is thus entitled to resort to countermeasures (formerly referred to as reprisals) against the perpetrator. Under international law in force since 1945, confirmed in the General Assembly's Declaration on "Friendly Relations" of 1970, countermeasures must not involve the threat or use of armed force.[73]

In a reply to Simma's article, Antonio Cassese, then the Presiding Judge of the International Tribunal for the Former Yugoslavia, also concluded that legal actions fell short of the unilateral use of force, but argued that a new principle may be forming. Judge Cassese affirmed that

> First, it is a truism that today human rights are no longer of exclusive concern to the particular State where they may be infringed. Human rights are increasingly becoming the main concern of the world community as a whole. There is a widespread sense that they cannot and should not be trampled upon with impunity in any part of the world.
>
> Second, the concept is now commonly accepted that obligations to respect human rights are *erga omnes* and, correlatively, any State, individually or collectively, has the right to take steps (admittedly, short of force) to attain such respect.
>
> Third, the idea is emerging in the international community that large-scale and systematic atrocities may give rise to an aggravated form of State responsibility, to which other States or international organizations may be entitled to respond by resorting to countermeasures other than those contemplated for delictual responsibility.

[73] Bruno Simma, *NATO, the UN and the Use of Force: Legal Aspects*, 10 Eur. J. Int'l L. 1, 1–2 (1999) (internal citation omitted). *See also* M. Ragazzi, The Concept of International Obligations Erga Omnes (1997); I. Brownlie, Principles Of Public International Law 488–490 (6th ed. 2003).

> Fourth, and consistent with this trend, the international community is increasingly intervening, through international bodies, in internal conflicts where human rights are in serious jeopardy.[74]

In sum, unilateral use of force to stop gross violations of human rights does not seem to be considered legal at this time. However, States can take more actions to defend fundamental human rights, which are undoubtedly considered peremptory and *jus cogens* norms.

Moreover, the Security Council did not condemn NATO's actions in Kosovo. A draft resolution condemning the intervention was rejected by the Council, and received only three votes in favor (China, Russia and Namibia) and twelve against. The inability and unwillingness of the Security Council to condemn the act gives further support to humanitarian interventions of this kind and could be seen as an *ex post* approval.[75]

The unilateral use of force in support of domestic population is a highly unbalanced instrument. At this stage, unilateral actions without the approval of the UN remain illegal. Historically, unilateral interventions have indeed occurred too selectively and have been based on political considerations rather than populations' needs. However, the fact that these interventions were selective does not mean that they should not be allowed in the future, but rather that they should be better regulated and more generally enforced. In any case, they must always be approved by the United Nations.

3. *Conclusion*

In this chapter, I focused on the mechanisms developed and available to the international community to address humanitarian crises as threats to the peace and security of the international community in failed States.

In the first section of this chapter, I studied the activities of U.N. agencies to provide assistance to needy domestic populations in crises countries, including the delivery of food, sanitation and health services. These activities are fundamental actions in support of humanitarian emergencies, and are thus also required.

These kinds of activities originate from different rules of engagement for different agencies, which are clearly spelled out in the instruments creating the agencies. Thus, OCHA can only act with the consent and in prin-

---

[74] Antonio Cassese, *Ex iniuria ius oritur: Are We Moving Towards International Legitimation of Forcible Humanitarian Countermeasures in the World Community?*, 10 Eur. J. Int'l L. 23, 33 (1999).

[75] Christine Gray, International Law And The Use Of Force 40 (2d ed. 2004).

ciple with the appeal by the country where it operates. UNICEF's mandate requires the consultation and consent of the country. In the case of WFP, the Secretary General can request assistance and intervention on behalf of certain populations.

These different mandates are important to the development of a coherent intervention approach in failed States.

In the second section of this chapter, I explored the collective and unilateral use of force to redress humanitarian crises. I argued that gross violations of human rights and humanitarian disasters constitute a threat to the stability of the international community, and are violations of obligations owed to the international community, and thus entail a right and an obligation of the international community to act. Two kinds of interventions using force are appraised. First, collective interventions using the delegated powers of the Security Council under Chapter VII of the U.N. Charter, which allow for a limited use of force in certain circumstances. These include humanitarian interventions to provide humanitarian assistance and humanitarian interventions to stop gross violations of human rights. Collective use of force has demonstrated several short-comings of these kinds of interventions. However, they are necessary, especially in situations of State failure.

As Sir Robert Jennings and Arthur Watts remarked

> If humanitarian intervention is ever to be justified, it will only be in extreme and very particular circumstances. Crucial consideration are likely to include whether there is a compelling and urgent situation of extreme and large-scale humanitarian distress demanding immediate relief; whether the territorial State is itself incapable of meeting the need of the situation or unwilling to do so (or is perhaps itself the cause of it); whether competent organs of the international community are unable to reason effectively or quickly enough to meet the demands of the situation; whether there is any practicable alternative to the action to be taken; and whether the action taken is limited both in time and scope to the needs of the emergency. In short, it would have to be a peaceful action (which need exclude it being carried out by military personnel) in a compelling emergency, where the transgression upon a State's territory is demonstrably outweighed by overwhelming and immediate considerations of humanity and has the general support of the international community.[76]

Humanitarian emergencies are security threats for the international community, and actions to assist populations in emergencies must be available in situations of State failure.

The use of force is an important, ultimate mechanism which ensures that humanitarian emergencies are properly addressed by the international

[76] Oppenheim's International Law 443, n. 18 (Sir Arthur Watts & Sir Robert Jennings eds., 9th ed. 1992).

community, including in failing and failed States where the State is unable to provide relief to their populations. If interventions are allowed, however, they must be only in extreme and specific circumstances. The urgency and scale of the crisis and the ability of the State to act by itself are all elements that have to be assessed and taken into consideration before any action by the international community is performed.

The use of force must be an *ultima ratio*, and when the decision is taken that such action is necessary, a series of principles and guidelines must be developed and strictly followed.

Strict rules for engagement must be developed for an intervention to be lawful. However, when these requirements are met, protection in case of humanitarian emergencies must follow. Principled rules for interventions should be developed to ensure an efficient, neutral and certain action by the international community, with a mandate by the United Nations, in situations of grave human rights violations.[77]

[77] *See generally* HUMANITARIAN INTERVENTION: ETHICAL, LEGAL AND POLITICAL DILEMMAS (J.L. Holzgrefe and Robert O. Keohane eds., 2003) (regarding humanitarian interventions).

Chapter Eight

Conclusion: A Set of Principles to Approach State Failure

State failure is a common phenomenon of contemporary international society.

In this book, I define it as a prolonged implosion of governmental structures and the ensuing incapacity of the government to provide political goods to its internal and external constituencies. At the same time, State failure is better described as a phenomenon in evolution, which, in a graphical representation, can be visualized as a line, not a point. Thus, while complete State collapse is the final stage of the phenomenon, there are several stages that link complete failure to a fully functioning State, depending on the residual capacity of a State to fulfill its obligations. Any approach to address crisis situations in State failure must take these differences into consideration.

Further, State failure is not fully understood by the international legal system, which considers failing States as fully sovereign. This lack of recognition of a situation of crisis undermines and qualifies possible actions taken by international actors.

The main challenge to international action in support of State failure is that it generally requires the consent of the State or the territory of which or on behalf of which action needs to be taken. The example of Somalia, which I studied in some detail in Chapter Three, demonstrates that no single approach is available, and reactions by the international community have been *ad hoc*. In Chapter Four, I also identify some larger theoretical questions, for example the fiction that, regardless of the reasons for its collapse, a State may exist without a government and without being capable of performing international obligations. Further, the Montevideo Convention requires four concurrent elements to award statehood, failed States do not possess the minimum requirements set out by this principle, but are nonetheless considered States: a failed State is considered sovereign regardless of its ability to perform sovereign actions.

My study aims to provide a practical solution to the problems arising from the non-performance of certain obligations that have an impact on the international public order. Thus, in the main section of this book, I have also explored the mechanisms available to the international community to address crisis situations in certain domains. Although there is an assumption that international obligations are a quintessential symbol of sovereignty, the implementation of international obligations by alternative parties has historical precedents. In several instances, third parties have fulfilled international obligations of other States, while recognizing the sovereignty of their counterparts. States consented to this arrangement either by treaty or because they were defeated by war or because of other conditions. This historical analysis (Chapter Two) demonstrates that the performance of certain obligations by a substitute actor is not a novelty.

In Chapters Five and Six, I assess international mechanisms available to confront health and environmental emergencies. Both sectors relate to threats to external actors, and the discriminating factor for intervention in these domains is the risk faced by the international community if no action is taken.

Several instruments are available to address health emergencies that have been proven to be effective in certain circumstances. I explore those in Chapter Five. These do not relate to State failure specifically, but can easily be adapted to situations of State failure. First, the New International Health Regulations provide coordinated guidance for actions in situations of health emergencies. WHO Members States that have agreed to be bound by NIHR have a duty to notify the WHO Secretariat within 24 hours from the discovery of a health emergency, and undertake certain actions in response to the event. Because they rely upon a general definition of public health emergency, based also on its potential impact in other States, NIHR can also be useful to address unknown pathologies with potential international risks in failing States. Further, the WHO and other actors in the health sector have also developed GOARN, as an instrument to monitor and report the occurrence and spreading of disease. GOARN is interesting because it is founded on operational premises and groups together several actors of the international community, including NGOs and international organizations, who are medical experts and work mostly 'on the ground.' GOARN may be used as an example of an instrument that can be used in failing States to report and provide first relief in health emergencies, as it is based on an alternative set of actors.

Chapter Six focuses on environmental emergencies. The environment is a heavily regulated field. However, there are no comprehensive treaties that address environmental emergencies in general. Moreover, existing treaties and conventions are mostly regional in scope and address specific elements of the environment. Further, they all require certain actions by the State in which an emergency occurred before any action can be taken. Nonetheless, the environmental regime offers interesting elements for the development of a principled approach to State failure. First, it is based on general principles of international law which can also provide a framework for action in situations of State failure. Namely, all actions are based upon the principle of cooperation and upon a duty not to cause transboundary harm. Second, treaties rely on several specific obligations that can also be used to ensure tackling emergencies in failing States. Specifically, the relevant obligations are: the duty of notification of an emergency, the obligation to be prepared to confront emergencies, the obligation of the international community to provide assistance on demand and the possibility of unilateral intervention in the event of an accident in specific circumstances.

International law can create obligations toward domestic populations and toward the international community. In Chapter Seven, I focus on how the international community reacts when humanitarian emergencies occur in failed States. In the case of failed States, the international community can, and has a duty to, intervene to assist internal populations in emergencies. Humanitarian crises are threats to the peace and security of the international community and must be appraised by the international community comprehensively. In the first part of Chapter Seven, I focus on actions taken by the United Nations to deliver assistance to civilians in conflict. Specifically, I assess the role of OCHA, WFP and UNICEF. These programs perform fundamental functions to assist populations in crisis countries. However, their mandates rely mostly on the consent or request of a State. It is important to develop a mechanism that may be used when requests and consent are not available because State failure has reached such a level as to result in the inability of a State to perform such actions.[1] Depoliticization of aid, however, is also needed. In the context of the lack of request, the statute of WFP provides a useful instrument which allows, in Art. IX, the U.N. Secretary-General to request emergency food and associated aid directly to WFP. This is only possible in exceptional circumstances and with full coordination of the United Nations and other members of the international community.

[1] A related question is, of course, whether intervention to address gross violations of human rights is contrary to a State's will. This problem was recently highlighted by the refusal of the military government in Burma to allow delivery of assistance to victims of Cyclone Nargis. The question of external fulfillment of domestic international obligations needs to be addressed together with the issue of consent of the State whose obligations needed to be fulfilled, and to the duty of non-intervention in internal affairs. *See* CHRISTINE CHINKIN, THIRD PARTIES IN INTERNATIONAL LAW (1993). In fact, when fulfilling international obligations of other states, the actor is substituting a national authority. In many cases, as I have pointed out, the action is taken to fulfill the inability of a national authority to do so. However, the national authority can also be unwilling to take action. To explore the issue of consent, one has to take into consideration two variables of the same equation: ability and willingness to perform an action. This is a different and substantial question not directly addressed in this study.

In certain exceptional circumstances, Member States, acting under the mandate of the Security Council, may be mandated to deliver humanitarian assistance or end gross violations of human rights by the use of force. Such interventions must remain an *ultima ratio*, only available in extreme emergencies where a State is completely unable to act and the humanitarian emergencies constitute a threat to the entire international community. Past interventions have been rightly criticized as self-serving and partial. I argue, however, that the possibility of mandating the international community or its members to act in humanitarian emergencies is necessary to protect and ensure the respect of international obligations related to human rights of populations living in failing States. Such interventions, however, need to be depoliticized and generalized. A series of general principles for interventions must guide actions by U.N. Member States, and ensure a consistent approach.

In the next few paragraphs, I will translate the conclusions reached in my study in a series of principles that I believe should guide the actions of the international community in situations of State failure.

1. *Principles for Action in Failed States*

I support the adoption of a set of principles that should guide actions in situations of State failure. These principles would ensure the lawfulness of planned assistance to help or replace State actions. The principles should be based on the assessment of the risks that the international community would suffer in case of inaction. Risks should be valued in terms of lower and higher threats to the security of the international community, urgency to act in terms of immediacy of the threat, availability of alternative responses and in terms of the consequences at home and abroad for action and inaction.

I highlighted above that State failure is a continuum, better pictured as a line, which starts with sovereignty and ends with State collapse. Intermediate stages are situations of crisis, fragility, State failing and State failure. In a graph, this will be the X axis. Risk and danger to the international community would be represented in the Y axis of the graph.

Competent agencies of the United Nations or NGOs in the field may be mandated with routine and low-impact actions, such as monitoring and reporting. For example, and following the examples set out in East Timor, Somalia and Kosovo, specific international actors *in loco* could be mandated to perform specific actions. In these cases, the mandate should be limited to administrative acts. For example, in the case of Somalia, a U.N. agency, like FAO or WHO, could be given the power to certify public health requirements for export. Issues of monitoring and reporting could be generally mandated to organizations similar to GOARN and, for reporting, NIHR. More long-term and high-impact reactions would require a higher level of threat. Thus, more complex actions, including the maintenance of air space and boundary security, would also require a higher level of consent and decision-making ability.

Understanding and interpreting State failure in terms of risks and threats to the international community means that the legal authority to act on these kinds of governance issues can derive from Chapter VII of the U.N. Charter. In Chapter VII, Article 39 of the Charter allows the Security Council to determine whether a "threat to the peace, breach of the peace, or act of aggression" exists. Further, Article 41 of the U.N. Charter does not limit the kind of decisions that the Security Council can take in cases of threat to the peace and security. The Article states that the Council may decide what actions to take to delimit the threat, some of the possible actions are listed, but the list is exemplary and not exclusive.[2] Franck affirms that it is for the Security Council to determine the existence of threats to the peace and security. He concludes that

> substantively, 'enforcement measures' may be taken whenever the requisite [Security] Council majority is convinced that there exists "any threat to the peace, breach of the peace, or act of aggression," for which such remedies are appropriate. It is apparent that the Council has broad discretion, but that it is to be exercised *bona fide* and *intra vires*, in accordance with [the] specific procedural and substantive standards spelled out in the Charter. The substantive standard is particularly important because it legitimates what would otherwise be an open-ended, indeed wholly arbitrary, vitiation of the central purpose of Article 2(7), namely the protection of members states' sovereignty from interference in essentially internal matters at the whim of the Organization's majority.[3]

[2] Art. 41 states that " the Security council may decide what measures not involving the use of armed forces are to employed to give effect to its decisions, and it may call upon the Members of the United Nations to apply such measures. These *may include* complete or partial interruption of economic relations and of rail, sea, air, postal, telegraphic, radio, and other means of communication, and the severance of diplomatic relations" (emphasis added). For example, the establishment of judicial bodies – like the International Criminal Tribunal for the Former Yugoslavia ("ICTY") and the International Criminal Tribunal for Rwanda ("ICTR") – are not specifically listed in Art. 41, but the Security Council created them under Article 41. Their legality have been recently confirmed by the ICTY Appeal Chambers, which claimed that even if "the establishment of an international criminal tribunal is not expressly mentioned among the enforcement measures provided for in Chapter VII, and more particularly in Articles 41 and 42 [...]. It is evident that the measures set out in Article 41 are merely illustrative *examples* which obviously do not exclude other measures." *Prosecutor v. Tadic*, Appeal on Jurisdiction, No. IT – 94 – AR72, ¶¶ 32–38 (2 Oct. 1995), 35 I.L.M. 32 (1996).

[3] Thomas M. Franck, Fairness in International Law and Institutions 220 (1995).

For example, in a rare application of this principle, the Security Council recently used Chapter VII to permit certain States in specific circumstances to enter Somali waters to repress acts of piracy.[4] The Security Council also used its Chapter VII function for conflict or humanitarian crises, and could apply it for interventions that are directed at fulfilling the general interests of the international community. Importantly, Articles 25 and 48 further ensure that once the Security Council has determined the existence of a threat or a breach of the peace, Member States are compelled to comply with this decision.

Following the explanations above, the guiding principles for action to maintain international public order in situations of State failure should read:

Principle 1: States have a duty to cooperate and protect one another in the various spheres of international relations in order to maintain international peace and security.

Principle 2: Every State has a duty to notify other States of any emergency occurring in its territory which could have transboundary effects. Notification must be done as soon as possible, and no later than twenty four hours after the discovery of the emergency, and should indicate the location of the threat, the nature of the threat and its possible transboudary effects.

Principle 3: International organizations and other organizations present on the ground may bring to the attention of the international community any emergency situation that threatens peace and security and may have a transboundary effect, in the absence of State's notice.

Principle 4: Every State has the duty to provide assistance on demand to States that request such assistance to address emergency situations which may have a transboundary impact posing a risk to international peace and security. All States involved in the provision of assistance must cooperate in the management of the operations. The United Nations may provide assistance and guidance as required.

Principle 5: The Secretary-General and other competent actors may request assistance to deal with an international threat to peace and security in the absence of a State request for assistance. In such a case, every effort should be made to consult with national authorities before any action is taken.

Principle 6: As a last resort, and if the risk is imminent, the authority to address the emergency situation in a State that is incapable of action may be given by the Security Council – or by an *ad hoc* Commission – directly to specific international organizations and State Members.

[4] S/RES/1816(2008), analyzed in details in Chapter 3.

Principles 7: Any action taken without the express request of a Member State must be limited, as much as possible, to addressing the international consequences of the emergency as threats to its security. Every effort should be made to consult local authorities.

Principle 8: Whether a State is incapable of taking action in an emergency may be assessed by the Secretary-General of the United Nations (or by and *ad hoc* Commission) in consultation with the Security Council and General Assembly. Such assessment shall be limited to the specific emergency and shall bear no consequence for the sovereignty and existence of the State.

2. *These Principles Do Not Violate the Sovereignty of Failing States and They Do not Represent Intervention in the Internal Affairs of a State*

Some critics may find that some of these principles could amount to intervention in internal affairs of a State, and thus violate national sovereignty. However, stating that taking care of international obligations of failed States is a form of illegal intervention that violates sovereignty is based on a wrong understanding of the meaning of sovereignty.[5]

The tension between the duty of non-intervention identified in Article 2 of the U.N. Charter[6] and the necessity to fulfill international obligations is only potential. It does not need to surface if the meaning of intervention is rightly considered.

The prohibition of intervention in internal affairs of a State in the letter of Article 2 of the Charter is a corollary to the principle of sovereignty and of the independence of nations. Article 3 of the Draft Declaration on Rights and Duties of States of the International Law Commission restated this principle and provides that "every State has the duty to refrain from intervention in the internal or external affairs of any other State."[7] This obligation, however, needs to be qualified: as stated by Jennings and Watts

---

[5] W.M. Reisman, *Sovereignty and Human Rights in Contemporary International Law*, 84 Am J. Int'l L. 866, 869 (1990) (stating that "although the venerable term 'sovereignty' continues to be used in international legal practice, its referent in modern international law is quite different. International law still protects sovereignty, but – not surprisingly – it is the people's sovereignty rather than the sovereign's sovereignty.").

[6] Which states that "nothing in the present Charter shall authorize the United Nations to intervene in matters which are essentially within the domestic jurisdiction of any state."

[7] Oppenheim's International Law 429 (Sir Arthur Watts & Sir Robert Jennings eds., 9th ed. 1992).

> (a)lthough states often use the term 'intervention' loosely to concern such matters as criticism of another's state's conduct, in international law it has a stricter meaning, according to which intervention is forcible or dictatorial interference by a state in the affairs of another state, calculated to impose certain conduct or consequences on that other state.[8]

They further argue that unlawful interventions can take several forms, and can include the use of armed forces or other forms of support from an external actor to oppose activities in a another State. The key distinguishing factor of unlawful intervention "is its coercive character, thus some other economic and political actions could also be deemed to be interference in internal affairs if perpetuated contrary to the will of a national government."[9]

Moreover, a distinction should be drawn for collective intervention in the general interest of the international community. In fact,

> the notion and the prohibition of intervention cannot accurately extend to collective action undertaken in the general interest of states or for the collective enforcement of international law. This means that while prohibition of intervention is a limitation upon states acting in their individual capacity, it does not properly apply to remedial or preventive action undertaken by or on behalf of the organs of international society.[10]

Interventions to fulfill international obligations of other States must be included in this exception. As a matter of fact, when States fail, people suffer and actions to address the situations must be performed following agreed principles. The tension with possible interventions in internal affairs of States is not there.

Traditionally, States have consented to varying degrees of interference by other States and the international community in general.[11] International community actors participated in fulfillment of obligations relating to internal affairs of States in several different ways. For example, as discussed in Chapter Two, in many cases where a State is not fully capable of providing for the essential rights and needs of its people, many States have established development assistance programs. In these situations, international organizations and foreign States often provide substantial budgetary and technical support to essential governmental activities.

---

[8] *Id.* at 430.

[9] *Id.* at 434. The ICJ analyzed this distinction in *Military and Paramilitary Activities Case (Nicaragua v. U.S.)*, in which it held that the U.S. was violating the principle of non-intervention by supporting opposition groups in Nicaragua.

[10] *Id.* at 447.

[11] *See* M. Reisman, *Sovereignty and Human Rights in Contemporary International Law*, 84 Am J. Int'l L. 866, 869 (1990).

In fact, the definition of matters that are essentially domestic has changed so that interventions in support of certain serious conditions of the internal population have become accepted practice.[12]

As I have demonstrated, this has resulted in a developing practice of intervention of external actors to defend and uphold human rights.[13] As Kirgs acknowledges

> Unquestionably, a great many governmental policies and courses of conduct that were widely thought to be within the 'domestic jurisdiction' of states in 1945 are no longer so regarded. The primary examples are found in the category of human rights.[14]

Other examples include other actions taken by States in situations of emergencies to the international community.

The question of consent should also be qualified by the general rights of interaction and duty of cooperation among States. This requirement was initially described in Article 23 of the Covenant of the League of Nations as entrusting the League to generally supervise the execution of several kinds of international agreements.[15] The U.N. Charter does not contain similar

---

[12] *See, inter alia*, A. Tanca, Foreign Armed Intervention in Internal Conflict (1993). *See* Chapter VII *supra*.

[13] Professor Reisman notes that "[t]he United Nations Charter, replicated the "domestic jurisdiction-international concern" dichotomy, but no serious scholar still supports the contention that internal human rights are "essentially within the domestic jurisdiction of any state" and hence insulated from international law." *See* M. Reisman, *Sovereignty and Human Rights in Contemporary International Law*, 84 Am. J. Int'l L. 866, 869 (1990).

[14] Frederic L. Kirgis, *Editorial Comment, Security Council Governance of Post-conflict societies: a Plea for Good Faith and Informed Decision Making*, 95 Am. J. In't L. 579, 579 (2001).

[15] Which stated that "[s]ubject to and in accordance with the provisions of international conventions existing or hereafter to be agreed upon, the Members of the League: (a) will endeavor to secure and maintain fair and humane conditions of labour for men, women, and children, both in their own countries and in all countries to which their commercial and industrial relations extend, and for that purpose will establish and maintain the necessary international organisations; (b) undertake to secure just treatment of the native inhabitants of territories under their control; (c) will entrust the League with the general supervision over the execution of agreements with regard to the traffic in women and children, and the traffic in opium and other dangerous drugs; (d) will entrust the League with the general supervision of the trade in arms and ammunition with the countries in which the control of this traffic is necessary in the common interest; (e) will make provision to secure and maintain freedom of communications and of transit and equitable treatment for the commerce of all Members of the League. In this connection, the special necessities of the regions devastated during the war of 1914–1918 shall be borne in mind. (f) will endeavor to take steps in matters of international concern for the prevention and control of disease." League of Nations Covenant, Art. 23.

provisions. However, the Declaration on Principles of International Law concerning Friendly Relations and Cooperation among States in accordance with the Charter of the United Nations requires a State to observe a less stringent principle of cooperation "in the maintenance of international peace and security."[16]

The issue of illegal intervention in a territory of a State that is unable to perform international obligation must be assessed against the interests of other States in reducing threats to security. The principle of non-intervention in internal affairs is of limited applicability in this context because it needs to be balanced with the general interest of States in upholding peace and security and enforcing international law. Moreover, it also needs to be qualified by the existing duty of cooperation and right of interaction that exists in the international community.

3. *The International Responsibility of Failing and Failed States Should not be Engaged*

A further issue to be addressed is whether failed and failing States are legally responsible for their inability to fulfill their international obligations.

The inability of a failed or failing State to perform certain international obligations should separate and distinguishable from their international responsibility. Thus, the question of performing an obligation of a failed State by the international community needs to be addressed irrespectively of any potential international responsibility of failing and failed States. Formally, however, failing States that are unable to perform certain obligations still remain responsible for their fulfillment, as their inability may trigger international responsibility.

Article 1 of the Draft Articles on Responsibility of States for Internationally Wrongful Act ("Draft Articles") adopted by the International Law Commission and submitted to the General Assembly of the United Nations in 2001 states that "every internationally wrongful act of a State entails the international responsibility of that State." The two elements of an internationally wrongful act of State, attribution and breach of an international obligation, are detailed in Art. 2 of the Draft Articles.[17] In general, only the conduct of

---

[16] G.A. Res. 2625 (XXV), U.N. Doc. A/2625 (24 Oct. 1970).

[17] International Law Commission, *Draft Articles on Responsibility of States for Internationally Wrongful Act With Commentaries, text adopted by the International Law Commission at its fifty-third session*, U.N. Doc. A/56/10 (9 June 2001), *available at*: http://untreaty.un.org/ilc/texts/instruments/english/commentaries/9_6_2001.pdf.

organs of government, or other actors that have acted under the direction or control of governmental organs is attributable to the State. Articles 4 to 11 further define the circumstances in which an act is attributable to a State. Both acts of omission and commission may be attributable. The Articles are very comprehensive and include most conduct by government or its legitimate or apparent agents.[18]

[18] Thus, Art. 4 includes conduct of any State organ, whether the organ is exercising legislative, executive, judicial or any other functions, regardless of the position the organ holds in the organization of the State and the character as an organ of the central government or of a territorial unit of the State. Because both acts of omission and commission are included in this Article, even the absence of action by an absent (failed) State may generate responsibility. Article 5 attributes to the State the conduct of a person or an entity which is not an organ of the State as such, but which is empowered by the law of the State to exercise elements of governmental authority, provided that such person or entity acts in that governmental capacity in the particular instance at issue. Art. 6 includes as attributable to the State the conduct of organs placed at the disposal of a State by another State. Further, Art. 8 provides that the conduct of a person or a group of persons acting under the direction or control of the State is also attributable to the State. Art. 10 deals with the conduct of insurrectional or other movements and Art. 11 with conduct acknowledged and adopted by a State as its own. Two further provisions are particularly relevant in the case of failing and failed States and would cover most of their actions not included in the provisions above. First, Art. 7 provides that even the conduct of an organ of a State or of a person or entity empowered to exercise elements of the governmental authority is considered attributable to the State even if the organ, person or entity exceeds its authority or goes against its instructions. Second, Art. 9 is particularly relevant in situations of failing and failed States because it attributes to the State the conduct of a person or group of persons exercising elements of the governmental authority in the absence or default of the official authorities and in circumstances such as to call for the exercise of those elements of authority. Thus, the focus is on the actions taken, which must be governmental, regardless of the presence of an effective governmental authority. The application of this principle to failing and failed States, i.e. in States where governmental authority is absent or in default, would mean that any persons or entity exercising some form of governmental authority would be deemed as acting for the State and therefore engaging its international responsibility. As the ILC Special Rapporteur and leading drafter of the Articles and Commentaries, James Crawford, explains, this situation is exceptional, and cases include "revolution, armed conflict or foreign occupation, where the regular authorities dissolve, are disintegrating, have been suppressed or are for the time being inoperative." (*Id.* at 109) Crawford also comments that "the second condition [for the application of this Article] "in the absence or default of" is intended to cover both the situation of total collapse of the State apparatus as well as cases where the official authorities are not exercising their functions in some specific respects, for instance, in the case of a partial collapse of the State or its loss of control over a certain locality. The phrase "absence or default" seeks to capture both situations (*Id.* at 111) This article may be relevant to some situations of State failure, where governmental actions on behalf of the government are taken by a person or a group of persons in the absence of official authority.

In most cases, the elements required to attribute the conduct to the States are also met in failing and failed States, which could incur international responsibility like any other State member of the international community.

Chapter V of the Draft Articles sets out six circumstances precluding the wrongfulness of the conduct that otherwise would have entailed international responsibility. Importantly, these circumstances protect the State from incurring international responsibility while maintaining that the conduct was illegal.[19] Of these, the circumstances described in Articles 23 and 25, recognizing *force majeure* and state of necessity respectively, are particularly relevant.

Art. 23 deals with situations of *force majeure*, and provides that wrongfulness of an act of a State not in conformity with an international obligation is precluded if the act is due to *force majeure*, defined as "irresistible force or of an unforeseen event, beyond the control of the State, making it materially impossible in the circumstances to perform the obligation." However, this circumstance is only applicable if the situation of *force majeure* is not due to the conduct of the State invoking it, either alone or in combination with other factors.[20] So, for example, *force majeure* does not cover situations "in which performance of an obligation has become more difficult, for example due to some political or economic crisis. Nor does it cover situations brought about by the neglect or default of the State concerned, even if the resulting injury itself was accidental and unintended."[21] Thus, this circumstance will have only limited application in situation of State failure.

An analysis of state of necessity would yield a similar conclusion. Art. 25 provides that acts taken under necessity may preclude the wrongfulness of

[19] *Id.* at 169–209. The other circumstances are described in Arts. 20, 21, 22 and 24. Article 20 provides that valid consent of a State to the commission of a given act by another State precludes the wrongfulness of that act in relation to the former State. Art. 21 states that the wrongfulness of an act of State is precluded if the act constitutes a lawful measure of self-defense taken in conformity with the U.N. Charter. Further, Article 22 precludes the wrongfulness of an act of State not in conformity with an international obligation towards another State if and to the extent that the act constitutes a countermeasure taken against the latter State in accordance with the Draft Articles. These conditions have only limited application in situations of State failure. Article 24 precludes the wrongfulness of acts of States taken in situations of distress when the author of the act had no other reasonable way of saving his life or the lives of others entrusted to him. The applicability of this Article is limited to situations in which the distress is not due to the conduct of the State invoking it or if the act is likely to create a comparable or greater peril. Historically, cases of distress have involved, for the most part, aircrafts or ships. The applicability of this circumstance to State failure will probably be limited.

[20] *Id.* at 183–189.

[21] *Id.* at 184.

an act. The provision includes strict criteria that restrict its applicability. The Article, drafted in the negative, provides that

1. Necessity may not be invoked by a State as a ground for precluding the wrongfulness of an act not in conformity with an international obligation of that State unless the act:
   (a) Is the only way for the State to safeguard an essential interest against a grave and imminent peril; and
   (b) Does not seriously impair an essential interest of the State or States towards which the obligation exists, or of the international community as a whole.
2. In any case, necessity may not be invoked by a State as a ground for precluding wrongfulness if:
   (a) The international obligation in question excludes the possibility of invoking necessity; or
   (b) The State has contributed to the situation of necessity.

A strict application of the norm would probably find that a failing of failed State has contributed to the situation of necessity.[22]

In sum, failing States may remain responsible for their inability to perform certain obligations, possibly triggering their international responsibility. This results from the wrong assumption that they remain fully sovereign. However, even if the requirements for the preclusion of wrongfulness are not met and, thus, the international responsibility of a State is engaged, this responsibility has no bearing on the necessity for the international community to respond to and address State failure. In fact, actions by the international community may be seen as a fulfillment of the obligation.

The correct characterization is to look at the urgency of the execution of the actions for the international community. In fact, the performance of some national obligations is more urgent and necessary in certain situations than others, and the differentiating character should be the threat and danger that the international community would suffer in the absence of the specific performance by a national authority of a particular act. For example, cases of imminent and concrete danger like the spreading of a highly contagious

[22] The provision has recently been tested repeatedly in investment tribunals examining the actions of Argentina during the 2001 economic crisis. Most Tribunals have found that the situation did not warrant the application of the necessity plea, however in *LG&E v. Argentina*, the Tribunal excused the non-performance of certain international obligations by Argentina in a period between 2001 and 2003 because of a state of necessity. The Tribunal, however, found that "Emergency periods should be only strictly exceptional and should be applied exclusively when faced with extraordinary circumstances." *LG&E Energy Corp., LG&E Capital Corp. and LG&E International Inc. v. Argentine Republic*, ICSID Case No. ARB/02/1, Decision on Liability, ¶ 228 (3 Oct. 2006).

disease like Ebola, should require a lower threshold for international action than cases that have a more remote possibility of danger, like commercial transactions or financial obligations. Within this framework, the issue of international responsibility of the State becomes irrelevant.

* * *

In sum, it is possible to develop a number of principles that would allow the international community to address situations of emergencies that threaten international security in failed, failing and fragile States. This requires a balanced approach framed within the cooperation principle, which provides reassurance to all actors involved.

It is my hope that my research will be the source of meaningful discussion and will result in the development of a coherent approach to fragile, failing and failed States. This discussion is needed and it is, in fact, long overdue.

Index